A FEMINIST PERSPECTIVE ON

Renaissan

B

For Mum, Barbara and Yo

and

Dad, David and Robert

— an inspiring combination of pioneering women
and older and newer men

A FEMINIST PERSPECTIVE ON

Renaissance Drama

ALISON FINDLAY

First published 1999

2   4   6   8   10   9   7   5   3   1

Blackwell Publishers Ltd
108 Cowley Road
Oxford OX4 1JF
UK

Blackwell Publishers Inc.
350 Main Street
Malden, Massachusetts 02148
USA

British Library Cataloguing in Publication Data

A CIP catalogue record for this book is available from the British Library

Library of Congress Cataloging-in-Publication Data

Findlay, Alison, 1963–
    A feminist perspective on Renaissance drama / Alison Findlay.
        p.   cm.
    Includes bibliographical references (p.   ) and index.
    ISBN 0-631-20508-X (alk. paper). – ISBN 0-631-20509-8 (alk. paper)
    1. English drama – Early modern and Elizabethan, 1500–1600 – History and criticism.   2. Feminism and literature – England – History – 16th century.   3. Feminism and literature – England – History – 17th century.   4. Women and literature – England – History – 16th century. 5. Women and literature – England – History – 17th century.   6. English drama – 17th century – History and criticism.   7. Renaissance – England.   I. Title.
PR658.F45F56   1999
822'.309–dc21
                                                                          98-30069
                                                                          CIP

Typeset in 10 on 12pt Garamond
by York House Typographic Ltd, London
Printed in Great Britain by MPG Books Ltd, Bodmin, Cornwall

This book is printed on acid-free paper

Contents

Acknowledgements

I wish to thank the staff at Lancaster University Library and the Brotherton Library, Leeds, and Marie Rowlands, University of Wolverhampton, for their help while I have been researching material for this book. Members of the Northern Renaissance Seminar and staff and students at Dundee University made helpful comments when I presented early versions of my ideas at seminars, and I appreciate their input. I also thank Stephanie Hodgson-Wright and Scott Wilson, who read two of the chapters and offered good suggestions for improvements. I am grateful for the support of my colleagues, who make Lancaster a stimulating environment in which to work and think. I owe special thanks to Richard Dutton, who read drafts of nearly all the chapters and who helped me a great deal with encouragement and judicious advice. My gratitude also goes to Andrew McNeillie at Blackwell and Brigitte Lee, my copy-editor, for the enthusiasm and efficiency with which they worked to get the book into print. My husband David was wonderful, especially in the last frantic stages. Without his help there wouldn't have been a book so, of course, my biggest debts are to him, and to our son Robert, who sacrificed a lot of playing time while I was writing.

Alison Findlay
Lancaster University

Note

All references to plays by Shakespeare are to the *Norton Shakespeare*, based on the Oxford edition, ed. Stephen Greenblatt, Walter Cohen, Jean E. Howard and Katherine Eisaman Maus (W. W. Norton, New York and London, 1997). All biblical references are to the King James Bible (1611).

Introduction

'Feminism's impulse is often, not surprisingly, to make a celebratory identification with a rush of women onto the historical stage,' writes Denise Riley.[1] Like other feminist critics working on the Renaissance, I am aware of the dangers of eliminating cultural differences between women of the sixteenth and seventeenth centuries and ourselves, yet the desire to uncover a 'rush of women onto the historical stage' is still a pressing one. The histories we write of the Renaissance shape the way we think now, what is possible, what is important to know, and how knowledge about the past is constructed. In the case of English Renaissance drama, though, identification with that 'rush of women' onto the commercial stage is not possible. In professional theatre companies the actors were all male, not by law but by a custom which was peculiar to the British Isles.[2] Playwrights for these companies were also male: Shakespeare, Jonson, Middleton, Marlowe, Webster, Ford, to name the most famous. Women dramatists and performers did find other arenas in which to stage themselves; some even inherited shares in commercial theatres.[3] Nevertheless, the names of professional companies like the Admiral's Men or the Lord Chamberlain's Men indicate all too clearly that drama was written and presented by men, or by boys in the case of the children's companies.

The absence of women from these companies does not mean that professional Renaissance drama is an all-male activity. The meanings of plays presented on the commercial stages were not produced solely by the writers and actors. Spectators were an integral element in Renaissance drama, as in any performance text. There may not have been a rush of women onto the stage of the Globe or Whitefriars Theatres, but we do know that women made up a significant part of Renaissance theatre audiences. That historical female audience is the starting point for my feminist perspective on the drama.

1

Andrew Gurr's *Playgoing in Shakespeare's London* concludes from records in diaries, correspondence, official documents and playtext references that women from across the social spectrum attended the theatres between 1567 and 1642.[4] It seems likely that different classes of women, as well as men, were attracted to different venues. Susan Zimmerman has argued that there is insubstantial evidence to prove a large attendance of aristocratic women at public theatres, though we do have evidence that Lady Smith requested an escort to the Globe in 1624, and we must remember that a lack of evidence is not, in itself, proof that they did not attend.[5] Noblewomen certainly saw plays in private theatres and plays which transferred to the court. For example, Lady Jane Mildmay accompanied her husband to the private playhouses on several occasions in the 1630s, while Lady Anne Clifford's diary records that in 1617 she saw Fletcher's *The Mad Lover* presented at court.[6] The biography of Lady Elizabeth Cary, written by one of her daughters, tells that after her husband's death 'she never went to Maskes, nor Playes not so much as all the Court, though she loved them very much especially the last extreamly.'[7] These words suggest that playgoing, as distinct from participation in masques, was a courtly activity.

For women who could not go to the theatre, reading plays offered an alternative perspective on the drama, though one that was obviously unlike seeing a production. In 1639 Anne Merricke wrote to her friend Mistress Lydall:

> I cu'd wish my selfe with you . . . to see the Alchymist, which I heare this tearme is revis'd, and the newe playe . . . but for want of these gentile recreationes, I must content my selfe here, with the studie of Shackspeare, and the historie of woemen, All my countrie librarie.[8]

It is interesting that Merricke lists the works of Shakespeare alongside the 'historie of woemen' as substitutes for going to see Ben Jonson's *The Alchemist* or a new play. Her words imply that theatregoing and playreading offer 'recreationes', opportunities to re-create oneself as a woman through entertainment and 'studie'.

In addition to specific records of attendance, women are mentioned in prologues and epilogues to plays and in anti-theatrical pamphlets. Taken together, these three types of evidence build up a picture of women's tangible presence in the theatres of Renaissance England. Some examples will show how that female constituency, regardless of the numbers of spectators involved, was significant: that it excited the discomfort of men and seemed to unsettle the hierarchy of gender relations.[9]

Stephen Gosson's anti-theatrical pamphlet, *The Schoole of Abuse* (1579), concluded with an epistle addressed to 'the Gentlewomen, Citizens of

London' recommending that they should stay at home rather than risk their reputations by entering the public arena of the playhouse. He warned them 'they which shew themselves openly desyre to be seene', and that once they became the objects of men's lustful gazes by 'entring to places of suspition', their chastity would be severely compromised: 'though you go to Theaters to see sport, Cupid may cache you ere you departe'.[10] The belief that theatres were hothouses of illicit amours, and that by going there a woman implicitly made her sexuality 'public' like a prostitute, was typical of anti-theatrical writings. Women who wished to 'go to Theaters to see sport' in the form of plays had to defend themselves against such prejudice.

A Letter Sent by Maydens of London (1567) mounts such a defence. In this pamphlet, the maidens or maidservants of the title deftly answer the objections of a male writer who 'wold not have us resort to Playes'. The opening of the Red Lion playhouse in Whitechapel in 1567 suggests the currency of theatregoing in this year.[11] The maidservants address the *Letter* to their matrons and mistresses, and co-opt the support of these women with the words 'your wisdomes know well, that in a godly play or enterlude . . . may be much learning had: for so lively in them are set forth the vices and vertues before our eyes, in gestures and speach, that we can bothe take learning and pleasure in them.'[12] The matrons and mistresses cannot help but defend plays since it is implied that they are theatregoers themselves. The maidens' appeal creates a defensive bond between women on the grounds of gender, in spite of status differences. Their argument in favour of the morally educative nature of theatre was a common tactic in defences of the stage. Even while arguing for its instructive power, though, these female voices assert their rights to pleasure. '[W]e can bothe take learning and pleasure' in plays, they claim, as though theatregoing gives them rights, as individuals, to exercise their tastes and please themselves.

In her impressive analysis of the social significance of playgoing, Jean Howard has argued that, as paying customers, women were granted access to 'the pleasure and privilege of gazing, certainly at the stage and probably at the audience as well'. This was the case no matter who paid for the tickets. As spectators, women were empowered to exercise judgement on what they saw, so enjoying an autonomy that inevitably 'problematizes women's status as objects within patriarchy'.[13] Theatregoing can be seen as a feminist act since the monetary nature of admission eliminated gender inequalities, albeit on a temporary basis. The tastes of female spectators had to be acknowledged and catered for by the companies whose productions they paid to see.

Richard Levin's survey of prologues and epilogues to plays demonstrates that women spectators were thought of as a distinct constituency by those who worked in the theatre.[14] The epilogue to Shakespeare's *As You Like It*, for example, addresses women as a gendered group, no matter what class differences existed between them, while the epilogue to *Henry IV Part 2* appeals to the audience as his 'gentle creditors' (Epilogue.11), as though the price of a ticket has bought them gentle status and put him in their debt. He salutes 'all the gentlewomen' as the leaders of taste, saying that because they have excused his repayment, the gentlemen will follow (Epilogue.18–21). Sometimes women's tastes are prioritized above those of men. As Levin points out, plays which presented a battle between the sexes were often angled in favour of the woman's part.[15] This is certainly the case in the prologue to *Swetnam the Woman Hater Arraigned by Women*, an anonymous play of 1620 which dramatized a literary battle between the misogynist Joseph Swetnam and three feminist defenders of the sex. Loretta opens the play with the words

> *The Women are all welcome; for the men,*
> *They will be welcome: our care's not for them.*
> *'Tis we, poore women, that must stand the brunt*
> *Of this dayes tryall: we are all accused.*
> . . .
> *Lend but your kind assistance; you shall see*
> *We will not be ore-come with Infamie,*
> *And slanders that we never merited.*
> *Be but you patient, I dare boldly say,*
> *(If ever women pleased) weele please to day.*[16]

Women's satisfaction is the company's first concern; men are dismissed as insignificant appendages. Loretta interpellates female spectators as participants in the drama by including them in the phrase 'we are all accused'. As we have observed from anti-theatrical writing, the very act of coming to the theatre makes women part of 'this dayes tryall' since it exposes them to 'Infamie' and 'slanders that we never merited' from men. The play's refutation of unjust slanders against the sex is the spectators' project as much as the characters'. The arraignment of Swetnam is also a defence of women's rights to come to the theatre and pass judgement.

Loretta's prologue demonstrates the undeniable importance of women in Renaissance theatre audiences and their active critical engagement with the drama. Writing women into the historical record like this is important from a feminist point of view but does not yet provide a perspective on the plays themselves. How might women have responded to the drama they saw presented? The prologues and epilogues which Levin analyses in his article offer general indications of women's emotional reactions, especially their capacity to weep at moving scenes like Hieronimo's passion in *The Spanish Tragedy*, or pathetic plots and situations in Beaumont and Fletcher's plays.[17] The epilogue of Shakespeare and Fletcher's *Henry VIII* is even more tantalizing since it suggests that women would respond warmly to the play because of its positive characterization of 'such a one we showed 'em' (Epilogue.11), presumably Katherine but also possibly Anne or even the baby Elizabeth – the epilogue leaves them free to insert their favourite female character.

As Levin rightly points out though, these reactions are all written by men. They are a form of ventriloquism no less than the Renaissance stage itself. We do not know how women read the plays in Renaissance theatres because their own words about the performances they saw have not come down to us in written form (or have not yet been discovered). For most lower-class spectators lack of literacy would prevent them from writing about a play, though not from enjoying it or holding a critical opinion. For literate women, the dominant culture's disapproval of their speaking or writing in public may have discouraged the expression of strongly held views about the plays, especially if these were unconventional. Women spectators, however powerful a starting point for a feminist recovery of the drama, are hidden from history, it seems.

I believe there is a way to negotiate this problem or apparent dead end. My book uses women's writing to create a doorway through which a historicist feminist perspective on the drama can be constructed. We may not have any direct critical commentary from Renaissance women on the plays they saw, but we do have a remarkable wealth of their writing in published forms and in manuscript. Uncovering and analysing these texts has been, and continues to be, an exciting project for feminist scholars. The range of diaries, letters, religious meditations, poems, plays and prose fiction represents 'a rush of women onto the historical stage', though it is important to remember that the voices are mostly those of middle- or upper-class women. Once discussed and valued in their own right, these texts must be integrated into the literary culture of the period. As Maureen Quilligan remarks, it is important to 'deghettoize them', since their presence serves to counterbalance the canon. Including writing by women on Renaissance literature courses, in bibliographies or in literary histories, accords them value and obliges us to rethink our definitions of what constitutes Renaissance literature. Setting women's texts alongside those by men 'completes the conversation', as Quilligan puts it, adds something that has been missing from our perception of the dominant authors: 'the other side of the conversation, the women to whom, in fact, they were speaking and to whom they might quite well have been listening'.[18]

Women's writing allows us to recreate an imagined female audience for Renaissance drama, an audience of customers whose situations, opinions and tastes male dramatists probably responded to. This book uses texts by sixteenth- and seventeenth-century women to construct a critical perspective on male-authored Renaissance drama and to suggest possibilities for reading the plays available to female spectators of the time. I must stress that my primary interest is in producing new readings of plays, so these inevitably dominate my discussions with the effect of relegating women's writings to the position of 'secondary' texts in most cases. This feels uncomfortable from a feminist point of view, yet I would remind the reader that my project here is to write women into Renaissance drama as consumers rather than producers. Creating a canon of female-authored drama and examining the many other 'stages' on which they performed or for which they wrote is a huge task, beyond the scope of the present book.[19] What I do here, with drama by men, is to appropriate extracts from women's texts in order to place the analysis of gender politics centre stage. For example, in the first chapter, I use women's religious compositions to open up readings of *Doctor Faustus*, *Measure for Measure* and *'Tis Pity She's A Whore* as texts which interrogate conventional beliefs that underpinned relations between men and women. I believe that even the use of short extracts can unsettle the canon by opening a dialogue that highlights its exclusions.

Such a dialogue is essentially artificial, as the picture on the cover of my book signals. The contemporary prints of women superimposed onto Vissher's 1616 image of the Globe Theatre (itself a copy taken from another map), serves as a reminder that none of these readings is 'authentic'.[20] Nor could they ever be, since even if we could go back in time to the reality of Renaissance London to ask women what they thought, we would understand what we saw and heard with modern sensibilities. Like any historicist reading, mine are constructed according to the values, interests and biases of the critic and the particular historical moment in which she is writing. I have selected and juxtaposed the texts, like the pictures, to produce particular feminist analyses from a range of possibilities.

The book's chapters are arranged thematically and my selection of topic for each has been guided by what I feel are key issues in Renaissance culture for women, and by the dominant genres of Renaissance drama. Plays are deeply implicated in producing and changing the power relations of the cultures in which they are themselves produced, so it is not surprising that popular dramatic genres such as revenge tragedy, city comedy or the history play mirror the critical zones in which ideas were being contested. As Hamlet tells the players, the purpose of playing 'both at the first and now, was and is to hold the mirror up to nature, to show virtue her own feature, scorn her own image, and the very age and body of the time his form and pressure' (3.2.19). The England of the Renaissance was an arena of change – religious change; economic change (the decline of feudalism and the beginnings of a capitalist economy); the growth of print culture; and, intertwined with these, changes in gender relations. Such a climate opens a range of possibilities, and dramatic texts are alive to the conflicts between these.

Renaissance England was dominated by an oppressive patriarchal culture, yet pressure points – at which contradictions in the positioning of women occurred – created opportunities for resistance. Each of the chapters focuses on an area in which traditional definitions of woman and her position in Renaissance culture are being challenged in literary texts. Since biblical authority was the foundation of woman's subjection, the first chapter examines dramatizations of religious belief. Chapter 2 explores how revenge tragedy taps into deep fears and longings about women's agency and maternal power. Sexual desire and female pleasure are the focus of chapter 3, which examines woman's position in romance in comedy and tragedy, and the liberties offered by the city. Chapter 4 focuses on the household space as a specifically female form of imprisonment, analysing domestic tragedies in the light of Renaissance women's experiences. The final chapter discusses women's interventions into masculine history and the contradictions between the positions of queen and female subject which inevitably troubled Renaissance patriarchy.

To explore these areas, my selection of dramatic texts has deliberately concentrated on the work of mainstream writers like Shakespeare, Jonson and Middleton, and classics of their genre such as *The Spanish Tragedy*, *The Revenger's Tragedy* and *A Woman Killed With Kindness*. These are the texts and major authors that we are most likely to encounter as students or teachers, and a project dedicated to re-reading Renaissance drama from a historicized feminist perspective must claim the cultural 'high ground' of these wonderful plays. At the same time, I have also included some less well-known drama by men such as Shirley's *The Maid's Revenge*, Thomas Drue's *The Duchess of Suffolk* or Greene's *James The Fourth*, which offer interesting angles on the construction of woman.

The Renaissance women's writings used to read the plays offer women's own constructions of their sex, although it is vital to remember that these too are produced from within the dominant patriarchal discourse. Poems and prose are discussed as they relate to issues in the plays rather than examined in their entirety, as I mentioned above, though I hope that readers who are not familiar with these writings will be encouraged to follow up references to the most accessible texts in anthologies or editions. I have given fuller discussions of Elizabeth Cary's play *The Tragedy of*

Mariam in chapters 2 and 4 and, to a lesser extent, Lady Mary Wroth's tragi-comedy *Love's Victorie* in chapter 3. In spite of the non-commercial performance arenas for which they were written, these plays can be readily integrated into the canon of Renaissance drama with interesting results.

Texts by Renaissance women give us indirect access to individual voices, although the relationship between the written word and the author's own voice can often be complex, as Betty Travitsky has pointed out.[21] Literary conventions and styles are other influential factors which must be taken into account. Most importantly, it is vital to remember that the ideas expressed in, say, a poem or a letter are those of a woman of a particular class, cultural background and personal experience. It would be foolish to suggest, for example, that Aemelia Lanyer's ideas on religion or Isabella Whitney's on London are representative of 'Renaissance Woman'. This is also true of any woman's response to a Renaissance play, of course. Each spectator would read what she saw according to her own cultural positioning. Nevertheless, whatever differences existed between them, women were often grouped together once they entered the theatre, in prologues, epilogues or anti-theatrical pamphlets. In the *Letter Sent by Maydens of London*, or the prologue to *Swetnam the Woman Hater* quoted above, theatregoing seems to form a defensive alliance between women, even between maidservants and mistresses. That collective gendered consciousness holds the seeds of feminist demands for equality. In the chapters that follow then, I offer some tentative suggestions about how 'women' could have read moments or aspects of the plays, while always conscious that such a category is problematic. Denise Riley astutely reminds us

> 'Women' is a volatile collectivity in which female persons can be very differently positioned, so that the apparent continuity of the subject of 'women' isn't to be relied on; 'women' is both synchronically and diachronically erratic as a collectivity, while for the individual, 'being a woman' is also inconstant.[22]

That very inconstancy in what it meant to be a woman in Renaissance England is what allowed women to reformulate identities in a time of both patriarchal oppression and ideological change. The struggle to reinvent the gendered self lies at the heart of feminist politics. Writing was one way in which a new self could be created. Going to the theatre to see a play was another. Steven Mullaney has shown that the 'Liberties' or districts in which theatres were located were liminal spaces, both geographically and culturally speaking. Like Renaissance women under patriarchy, they were officially under the control of the City Fathers, and yet they had a disturbingly semi-autonomous existence. 'Entering a Liberty, whatever its location, meant crossing over into an ambiguous territory.'[23] The theatres and the plays themselves were even more ambiguous territories which offered women opportunities to redefine themselves. The dialogue between women's writing and male-authored drama thus allows us to create a 'rush of women onto the historical stage' and to explore the emergence of feminist perspectives in Renaissance England.

Notes

1 Denise Riley, *'Am I That Name?': Feminism and the Category of 'Woman' in History* (Macmillan, Basingstoke, 1988), p. 8.

2 See Stephen Orgel, *Impersonations: The Performance of Gender in Shakespeare's England* (Cambridge University Press, Cambridge, 1996), p. 2.

3 See *Renaissance Drama By Women: Texts and Documents*, ed. S. p. Cerasano and Marion Wynne-Davies (Routledge, London, 1996). Susan Greene inherited shares in the Red Bull playhouse and Marie Bryan inherited a one-twelfth share in the Fortune (p. 174).

4 Andrew Gurr, *Playgoing in Shakespeare's London* (Cambridge University Press, Cambridge, 1987), pp. 55–63.

5 Susan Zimmerman, 'Disruptive Desire: Artifice and Indeterminacy in Jacobean Comedy', in *Erotic Politics: Desire on the Renaissance Stage* (Routledge, London, 1992), pp. 39–63; p. 58, n. 15.

6 Gurr, *Playgoing in Shakespeare's London*, pp. 199, 193.

7 Lille MS A. D. N. xx (Archives départementales du Nord, Lille), fol. 24.

8 Cited in Heidi Brayman Hackel, '"Rowme of Its Own": Printed Drama in Early Libraries', in John Cox and David Scott Kastan (eds), *A New History of Early English Drama* (Columbia University Press, New York, 1997), pp. 113–30; p. 118.

9 The following argument is indebted to the work of Jean E. Howard in her book *The Stage and Social Struggle in Early Modern England* (Routledge, London, 1994), pp. 73–92.

10 Stephen Gosson, *The School of Abuse*, reprinted for The Shakespeare Society (The Shakespeare Society, London, 1841), pp. 48–9.

11 John Orrell, 'The Theaters', in Cox and Kastan (eds), *A New History of Early English Drama*, pp. 93–112; p. 102.

12 F. J. Fehrenbach, 'A Letter Sent by Maydens of London (1567)', *English Literary Renaissance* 14 (1984), 285–304; pp. 299, 301. For further discussion of this pamphlet see chapter 3.

13 Howard, *The Stage and Social Struggle*, p. 79.

14 Richard Levin, 'Women in the Renaissance Theatre Audience', *Shakespeare Quarterly* 40 (1989), 165–74.

15 Ibid., p. 171.

16 *Swetnam the Woman-hater: The Controversy and the Play*, ed. Coryl Crandall (Purdue University Studies, Lafayette, IN, 1969), p. 54.

17 Levin, 'Women in the Renaissance Theatre Audience', pp. 170–1.

18 Maureen Quilligan, 'Completing the Conversation', *Shakespeare Studies* 15 (1997), 42–9.

19 Alison Findlay, Stephanie Hodgson-Wright and Gweno Williams are currently writing a volume, *Women and Dramatic Production 1550–1700*, to be published by Longman. S. P. Cerasano and Marion Wynne-Davies's important book, *Renaissance Drama by Women*, cited above (n. 3), has already made an important start on the recovery of a female dramatic tradition. The final aim should be to integrate it into the canon to create a broader picture of Renaissance drama.

20 See R. A. Foakes, *Illustrations of the English Stage 1580–1642* (Stanford University Press, Stanford, 1985), pp. 18–19.

21 Betty S. Travitsky, 'Reconstructing the Still, Small Voice: The Occasional Journal of Elizabeth Egerton', *Women's Studies* 19 (1991), 193–200.

22 Riley, *'Am I That Name?'*, p. 1.

23 Steven Mullaney, *The Place of the Stage* (University of Chicago Press, Chicago, 1988), p. 21.

CHAPTER 1

'Heavenly matters of theology'

Religion was at the centre of life in the Renaissance. Biblical authority formed the backbone of the laws governing behaviour in the family and in society at large. Church attendance was compulsory, so God and a knowledge of scripture was part of everyone's consciousness. The Reformation had opened up rival interpretations of the Bible, though. Differences between Catholic and Protestant doctrine led to a variety of different types of religious belief and worship; the Church of England was something of a misnomer, since the appearance of unity it conveyed was contradicted by recusancy on the part of Catholics and members of nonconformist sects. Because religion was so central and at the same time so controversial a topic, it is not surprising that plays often engaged in the debates over 'heavenly matters of theology' (*Doctor Faustus*, Prologue.18).

What position did women occupy in the current of religious belief and debate? Even though they could not preach in churches, religion was one of the few areas in which they were licensed to read, to hold an opinion and even to write. Religious textbooks were prescribed reading for women; prefaces and dedications show they are addressed primarily to a female audience. Vives's highly influential *Instruction of a Christian Woman*, translated by Richard Hyrde and printed in eight editions by 1592, proposed that 'on holy days continually and some time on working days let her read or hear such as shall lift up the mind to God'.[1] It is not surprising that women should want to debate matters themselves: discussing or, less often, writing about religious topics. Meditations or prayers were a form in which they could enter the literary world and publish with minimum danger to their reputations. However, their authority to pronounce on religious matters was strictly limited. Anne Wheathill is typical in excusing her lack of skill in *A handfull of holesome (though homelie) hearbs* (1584). Her preface to 'all Ladies, gentlewomen, and others which love true religion and virtue'

11

introduces her writings as 'a small handfull of grose hearbs; which I have presumed to gather out of the garden of Gods most holie word':

> Whereupon of the learned I may be judged grose and unwise; in presuming, without the counsell or helpe of anie, to take such an enterprise in hand; nevertheless, as GOD doth know, I have doone it with a good zeale, according to the weaknes of my knowledge and capacitie.[2]

Wheathill's caution about offering her ideas in public, and attempts to belittle her own expertise, are bound up in the metaphor of God's garden. Eve's sin in gathering the fruit of the Tree of Knowledge cast a long shadow over women in the Renaissance. Wheathill's admission that she gathered herbs from the garden of God's holy word already conjures up images of that trespass, so it is not surprising that she stresses the 'weaknes' of her 'knowledge'. For a woman to write as a learned authority on scripture would have been to repeat Eve's earlier folly, to presume beyond her station, to aspire to the god-like position of father or husband; in short, to enter the province of men.

The Bible stated that Eve's sin was seeking after knowledge in response to the serpent's promise that 'your eyes shall be opened and you shall be as gods knowing good and evil':

> And when the woman saw that the tree was good for food, and that it was pleasant to the eyes, and a tree to be desired to make one wise, she took of the fruit thereof, and did eat, and gave also unto her husband with her, and he did eat. (Genesis 3.6)

Sex, sin and death were the result of Eve's trespass. St Augustine reasoned that the taint of original sin was transmitted in intercourse, not through the sexual act itself, but through the desire or concupiscence which accompanied it.[3] From the death of innocence came the birth of desire, an involuntary impulse that could never be extinguished, a lack that could never be fulfilled. By tasting the fruit of knowledge, Eve combined desire with death in the act of eating, consuming to satisfy a lack.

Eve was a key figure in the formal controversy over the nature of women in the Renaissance.[4] Anti-feminist writers drew on the idea, frequently repeated in sermons, that she was ultimately responsible for all human misery. John Calvin was unequivocal on this point:

> There is no other shift but women must needs stoop and understand that the ruin and confusion of mankind came in on their side, and that through them we be all forlorn and accursed and banished the kingdom of heaven: when women (say I) do understand that all this came of Eve and of womankind ... there is

none other way but for them to stoop and to bear patiently the subjection that God hath laid upon them, which is nothing else but a warning to them to keep themselves lowly and mild.[5]

These judgements on women refer back to God's punishments for Eve, detailed in Genesis 3.16, where he tells her 'I will greatly multiply thy sorrow and thy conception; in sorrow thou shalt bring forth children; and thy desire shall be to thy husband, and he shall rule over thee'. The pain of childbirth, with all its dangers, once again brought together birth, desire and the possibility of death for both mother and child. In addition, Eve was forced to submit to the rule of her husband.

Defences of women often tackled the difficult problem of Eve by emphasizing her innocence. In the pamphlet *Ester hath hang'd Haman* (1617), an answer to Joseph Swetnam's *Araignment of Lewde, idle, froward, and unconstant women* (1615), the author says that although people may think she is biased because she is female, she is determined to assert woman's essential goodness: 'In that which I write, Eve was a good woman before she met with the serpent; her daughters are good virgins if they meet with good tutors'.[6] Sin is located with the serpent rather than with Eve and it is not knowledge that is damned, but the abuse of knowledge by the serpent or teacher. In defence of herself as a mistress of exegesis, the author asserts the value of learning and implicitly sets herself up as the 'good tutor' able to counter Swetnam's evil accusations against the sex. As we have seen from Anne Wheathill's book, however, this was an unusual tactic since female claims to learning drew them dangerously close to the fatal Tree of Knowledge.

More often, Eve's innocence was associated with ignorance. Those anxious to excuse her argued that, in spite of what she repeats to the serpent in Genesis 3.3, she did not know about the prohibition on the Tree of Knowledge, because God told Adam before she was created (Genesis 2.16). Aemelia Lanyer's defence of Eve in her poem *Salve Deus Rex Judaeorum* (1611) implicitly uses this line of argument:

> Our mother Eve, who tasted of the tree,
> Giving to Adam what she held most dear,
> Was simply good, and had no power to see;
> The after-coming harm did not appear; . . .
> For had she known of what we were bereaved,
> To his request she had not condescended . . .
>
> (l. 763)[7]

In addition to defences of Eve, other biblical figures such as Sarah, Rebecca, Judith, Deborah, Hester, Ruth, Martha and Mary Magdalene were held up as exempla demonstrating the virtue of women. The most powerful of these was the Virgin Mary, a 'second Eve' whose love, humility and virginity redeemed the fault of the first. The idea of Mary's Immaculate Conception allowed her to escape the inheritance of original sin which was transmitted through conventional conception and birth 'in pain and sorrow'. Mary's virginity, a symbol of intact purity, was a counter-image to the Garden of Eden, whose walls had been penetrated by the serpent. The miracle of the Virgin Birth perpetuated this reversal of the Fall in the person of Christ. Christ's Passion redeemed the sin of Eve by setting up a repetition of her transgression through the Eucharist. The consumption of bread and wine, the flesh and blood of Christ, is a feast to redeem humanity which parallels Eve's feasting on the fruit of knowledge. In Luke's gospel, this too is associated with desire: 'With desire I have desired to eat this passover with you before I suffer: For I say unto you I will not eat any more thereof until it be fulfilled in the kingdom of God' (Luke 22.15).

Because of the opposition between Eve and Mary, women's relationship to sex, desire, death and knowledge is critical to all plays dealing with religious topics. Looking at three different plays allows us to see how the tropes of chastity and passion, in both its negative and positive senses, can contribute to the construction of women inside the theatre and beyond.

The Tragicall History of Doctor Faustus by Christopher Marlowe does not offer much to the feminist reader at first glance.[8] Female characters play only small roles in contrast to that of the male protagonist, whose spiritual struggle is at the centre of the morality pattern. Faustus's quest for infinite knowledge and bargain with the devil is modelled on the Fall. In Marlowe's rewriting of the story and in his source, *The English Faust Book*, female characters are depicted after the legacy of Eve, personifying the combination of sin, desire and death. *The English Faust Book* tells that whenever Faustus thinks of turning to God, 'straightways the devil would thrust him a fair lady into his chamber, which fell to kissing and dalliance with him through which means he threw his godly motions in the wind, going forward still in his wicked practices to the utter ruin both of his body and soul'.[9] Marlowe's play follows the same pattern. Indeed, Kay Stockholder sees Faustus driven by a simultaneous desire for and fear of women.[10] Both Lucifer and Mephistopheles use women to tempt Faustus into hell. Mephistopheles promises Faustus 'the fairest courtesans' to satisfy his 'wanton and lascivious' desires (2.1.144–57) and Lucifer's pageant of the seven deadly sins comes to a climax with Lechery, a 'Mistress Minx' (2.3.157). The most important female character, Helen of Troy, appears at a key moment in Faustus's damnation: first, before the Old Man tries to persuade Faustus to 'leave this damned art' and return to God (5.1.35–51), and again when Faustus rejects his advice. Marlowe seems to confirm misogynist gender oppositions, presenting Helen as a demonic counterpart to the godly patriarch who is Faustus's only chance of salvation. It is her embraces which will 'extinguish clear' any thoughts of repentance (5.6.89). Helen seals Faustus's damnation with a kiss:

> Sweet Helen, make me immortal with a kiss.
> [They kiss]
> Her lips suck forth my soul. See where it flies!
> Come, Helen, come, give me my soul again.
> [They kiss again]
>
> (5.2.96)

By tasting the fruit of Helen's lips, Faustus repeats Adam's sin, trying to become immortal and all-knowing. W. W. Greg argues that Helen is a spirit from the demonic world, and that by choosing to commit intercourse with her, Faustus cuts himself off from any possible redemption.[11] Helen of Troy was often included alongside Eve in lists of 'wicked' women in the formal controversy, so her use as a figure of final temptation and damnation is not surprising.

Even the Duchess of Vanholt, an apparently innocent female character, is depicted after the legacy of Eve. In Act 4, Scene 6, the Duchess is significantly pregnant, embodying the punishment inflicted on women to bring forth children in sorrow. When Faustus promises her what she most desires, the grapes he offers hold the same mysterious danger as the apple. The Duchess's greedy consumption of the fruit is part of a wider pattern of eating and drinking in the play. Filling the body with food is an attempt to compensate for lack: the lost paradise of Eden and, especially for female spectators, the unsatisfied appetite for knowledge. She perhaps speaks for that audience when she says 'we are much beholding to this learned man' (4.6.122).

In encouraging spectators to identify with Faustus as an everyman figure, the play appears to gender its audience (or readers) as male. Indeed, the prologue to the 1604 text addresses them as 'Gentlemen'. It seems that to empathize with Faustus's experience, women spectators must become transvestite readers who condemn their own sex as the cause of his downfall. The misogynist bias of the text inclines them to regard themselves as responsible, according to Calvin, for 'the ruin and confusion of mankind'. More interestingly, though, the play also allows female spectators to see their own situations represented in the protagonist. Read alongside the Eden story, *Doctor Faustus* can be seen as a tragedy of knowledge which debates women's relationship to learning as much as men's. The prologue to the second quarto (1616) modifies its mode of address from 'Gentlemen' to 'gentles', as if in recognition of the fact that its daring ideas were addressed as much to female spectators as to male. In terms of the quest for knowledge, it is Eve rather than Adam who is the progenitor for Marlowe's central character, so although he is male, female experience is encoded into the play's structure. Faustus repeats Eve's sin in seeking knowledge which God deems is beyond his scope. He says 'A sound magician is a demigod. Here, tire my brains to get a deity' (1.1.61). The play shows that such an enterprise is damned. The epilogue moralizes

> Faustus is gone. Regard his hellish fall.
> Whose fiendful fortune may exhort the wise
> Only to wonder at unlawful things,
> Whose deepness doth entice such forward wits
> To practise more than heavenly power permits.
> (Epilogue.4)

True wisdom consists in keeping strictly within the limits of the law, defining oneself according to its strictures, and not seeking to know more than one's allotted place.

The 'evil' of knowledge is highlighted by the use of books as demonic props in *Doctor Faustus*. Mephistopheles offers Faustus a book to contemplate (2.1.158), as does Lucifer after the pageant of the seven deadly sins (2.3.168). Learning and sexual pleasure are equated in the verb 'ravished', used to describe the exciting effect of knowledge. For women, reading forbidden texts and 'ravishment' were connected in an even more literal way, since it was believed that from secular literature, especially romances, they would learn promiscuity. The growth in published fiction and plays from the 1580s suggests that such recreational reading by women was on the increase.[12] Through repeated reference to books as 'damned', the play cautions female spectators that contact with such literature is dangerous. Even the most liberal books on women's education recognized this. Vives's *Instruction of a Christian Woman* warned that secular fiction was sure to corrupt, and that 'a woman should beware of all these books, likewise as of serpents or snakes'.[13] Reading supposedly destroyed innocence, taught wives and daughters how to cuckold their husbands, arrange assignations with their lovers, and subvert paternal authority. When Lady Arbella Stuart secretly married William Seymour, for example, King James purportedly said that she had 'etne of the forbidden trie'.[14]

Doctor Faustus picks up on male insecurity about women's 'knowledge' in the cuckoldry jokes Faustus plays on Frederick, Martino and Benvolio (4.1), and in the scene where Robin boasts that his master's wife has become his mistress in both senses of the word (2.1.19–25).[15] In a speech unique to the first quarto text (1604), her infidelity is linked explicitly to learning. Robin boasts 'my master and mistress shall find that I can read – he for his forehead, she for her private study' (A Text, 2.3.17–18). Robin's ability to read and conjure allows him to cuckold his master, but it is the mistress's addiction to learning which makes her vulnerable to Robin's advances. Her private study is both a physical place in which they can meet secretly to have sex, and the reading which teaches her how to transgress.

Writing was even more condemnable than reading for women. Vives was opposed to all forms of original composition, recommending that when a girl learned handwriting she should restrict herself to copying 'some sad sentence, prudent and chaste, taken out of the holy scripture' which would remind her of her subordinate position.[16] Any writing which moved beyond the passive repetition of conventional spiritual wisdom invited an autonomous expression of self. The play implicitly reminds women that this is damnable through the use of writing at pivotal moments of Faustus's history. To confirm his pact with the devil, Faustus has to 'bequeath' his soul by writing a deed of gift. It is a legal document whose importance would strike all spectators, but the act of writing, as that which seals his fate, would have had special significance for women. Marlowe increases the dramatic tension in Act 2, Scene 1 by showing how Faustus experiences difficulty in writing as his blood congeals:

> What might the staying of my blood portend?
> Is it unwilling I should write this bill?
> Why streams it not, that I may write afresh?
> 'Faustus gives to thee his soul' – O, there it stayed!
> Why should'st thou not? Is not thy soul thine own?
> Then write again: 'Faustus gives to thee his soul'
>
> (2.1.65)

The anxiety of authorship which Faustus experiences is akin to that felt by any woman in the Renaissance who ever considered putting pen to paper. The opportunities which this deed opens up, the self-possession it represents, would have excited spectators who entertained ideas of moving beyond their allotted positions as wives or daughters, and thinking as authors of themselves. 'Why should'st thou not? Is not thy soul thine own?' voices their own emergent desire for autonomy, their claim, by rights, to determine their own futures rather than simply be guided by the men in their families. The congealing of the ink-blood graphically dramatizes the agonizing process of self-expression, difficult enough for any author, but for women whom convention relegated to silence and chastity, even more traumatic.

17

Faustus's writing of his death warrant would find an echo in the minds of female spectators with regard to their own reputations. Women could not even speak or write publicly in their own defence, since to do so would be rather to confirm a slander than to discredit it. Constantia Munda neatly summarizes the impossible position they were placed in:

> Nay, you'll put gags in our mouths and conjure us all to silence; you will first abuse us, and then bind us to the peace. We must be tongue-tied, lest in starting up to find fault, we prove guilty of those horrible accusations.[17]

Through the fate of its author-scholar protagonist, *Doctor Faustus* seems to warn women again of the dangers of writing, learning, self-possession. Faustus's damnation gives a vivid picture of the fate that awaits them if they dare to follow their desires and trespass into the forbidden world of knowledge. Seen as a moralistic play, *Doctor Faustus* conjures women to silence for fear of losing their souls, or at least their reputations. It persuades them to accept their inheritance from Eve and their subsequent role as the weaker vessel. Only by complete subjugation to male authority and instruction (which would, of course, confirm these ideas of guilt and inferiority) could they mitigate their position as daughters of the woman who had plucked the forbidden fruit.

The possibility of sympathy for Faustus and for Mephistopheles opens up another, less conservative way of reading the play with more appeal for feminist sympathizers. The upward trajectory of Faustus's progress and the simultaneous sense of loss represented by Mephistopheles lead back to a radical reinterpretation of the Eden narrative and Eve's role. In this sense, as much as in the charges of atheism raised against Marlowe, the text constitutes a rebellion against conventional church wisdom. Female spectators in the Renaissance, and even now, could see their own situations represented in Mephistopheles and Faustus.

Mephistopheles is a feminized figure in that he represents lack. In Freudian and Lacanian theory, and in culture more generally, woman has been read in negative terms: lacking a penis rather than having a womb. Female identification with nothingness (the symbol 0) serves to guarantee male superiority in the Symbolic Order, the language system governing social exchanges which privileges the phallus as a primary signifier. Lack is accompanied by desire, in Freudian terms 'penis envy', on the woman's part. The story of the Fall defines Eve in similar terms. God tells her 'thy desire shall be to thy husband, and he shall rule over thee' (Genesis 3.16). Eve's inferior role, her lack, brings with it a desire for (to be like) her husband. Although Mephistopheles is a male character, all that we learn about him places him in the 'female' position of lack and its concomitant presence of desire. Since Faustus cannot understand that Mephistopheles can be in hell and still be talking to him, Mephistopheles explains:

> Why, this is hell nor am I out of it.
> Think'st thou that I, that saw the face of God
> And tasted the eternal joys of heaven,
> Am not tormented with ten thousand hells
> In being deprived of everlasting bliss?
>
> (1.3.78)

Mephistopheles speaks like one who has had a taste of the Tree of Knowledge, become like a god and seen the bliss, but who is then deprived of access to such blessings, having to watch in silence while men like Faustus enjoy the pursuit of learning. As Mephistopheles explains, hell is not a physical space; it is a state of lack:

> Hell hath no limits, nor is circumscribed
> In one self place, for where we are is hell,
> And where hell is must we ever be.
>
> (2.1.124)

The experience of hell that Mephistopheles describes was shared, consciously or subconsciously, by women spectators. Hell is the loss or lack of autonomy experienced in the family, under the control of one's father or husband. At least one character in Renaissance drama, Jessica in *The Merchant of Venice*, feels 'our house is hell' (2.3.2), and although she is escaping from a Jewish father, her words may well have struck a chord with Christian daughters or wives in the playhouse. Mephistopheles, like women spectators, is subject to the commands of men. The contract he makes with Faustus mirrors the unequal relationship between the sexes after the Fall. Faustus tastes the 'fruit' offered by Mephistopheles, the temptations of power, and sells his soul in return for twenty-four years of all-encompassing mastery: the ability to command at home and abroad and a virtual monopoly on learning. Mephistopheles, like Eve, is relegated to a subordinate position by the terms of the contract:

> First, that Faustus may be a spirit in form and substance.
> Secondly, that Mephistopheles shall be his servant, and be by him commanded.
> Thirdly, that Mephistopheles shall do for him and bring him whatsoever.
> Fourthly, that he shall be in his chamber or house invisible.
> Lastly, that he shall appear to the said John Faustus at all times in what shape and form soever he please.
>
> (2.1.95)

19

The roles assigned to Mephistopheles would have been immediately recognizable to women as the duties prescribed for them in household conduct books. William Gouge's popular guide, *Of Domesticall Duties* (1622), pointed out that a wife should always be willing to yield to her husband's command and '*performe what businesse he requireth of her*'. To show reverence for him, she should follow the pattern set by Rebecca in the Bible, who covered her face with a veil (Genesis 24.65). The wife's gesture and speech, such as it was, was a metaphorical veil to obscure her and glorify her husband; like Mephistopheles, she was to be practically invisible in her lord's chamber or house.[18] An earlier conduct book, Dod and Cleaver's *A godly form of household government* (1598), pointed out that 'a certain discretion and desire [was] required of women to please the nature, inclinations and manners of their husbands, so long as the same importeth no wickedness'.[19] By echoing this in the last term of the demonic contract, *Doctor Faustus* implies that such domination does import wickedness, that it is necessarily evil. Identifying with Mephistopheles as a victim is undoubtedly difficult for an audience whose spiritual framework is Christian, but the lines which Marlowe gives the character are moving, and do allow women readers or spectators to read against the grain of the play's morality structure.

While Mephistopheles is a devil, and therefore immediately suspect, Faustus is an 'everyman' with whom the audience are encouraged to identify. Those women who felt trapped by the conventions laid down in conduct books must have had some sympathy with his frustration at the beginning of the play, when he complains that the sphere in which he is confined makes his work 'too servile and illiberal' (1.1.34). Because his study of books is a space normally forbidden to them, they recognize his quest for forbidden knowledge. Faustus's ability to transcend boundaries enacts a basic human fantasy, but one which must have seemed all the more wonderful to those whose gender necessarily put them in thrall. His pact with the devil opens up a wealth of wisdom which appears dangerously attractive in the play. Faustus's magnificent verse embodies the pleasures of secular learning and literature even as it describes them, threatening to 'ravish' the audience just as much as the protagonist (2.3.24–30). As Faustus's fellow scholar realizes, 'wondrous knowledge' (5.5.16) exerts its own magnetic pull on the hearts of those who witness the tragical history, making simple moral judgements inadequate. Even in the epilogue passing sentence on Faustus, the value of learning shines stubbornly through:

> Cut is the branch that might have grown full straight
> And burned is Apollo's laurel bough
> That sometime grew within this learned man.
>
> (Epilogue.1)

We are tempted to celebrate the 'learned man', to lament an overwhelming sense of loss, a waste of potential and intellectual riches. In spite of the play's condemnation of Faustus, we sense the possibility of reading his thirst for knowledge as laudable rather than damnable.

Hermetic philosophy offered Renaissance audiences a way of interpreting Faustus's quest in positive terms. Taken up by occult thinkers such as Bruno, Agrippa and Ficino, it claimed that a scholar could expand the mind to become like God and, through learning, actually unite with him:

> unless you make yourself equal to God, you cannot understand God; for the like is not intelligible save to the like. Make yourself grow to a greatness beyond measure, by a bound free yourself from the body; raise yourself above all time, become Eternity; then you will understand God. Believe that nothing is impossible for you, think yourself immortal and capable of understanding all, all arts, all sciences, the nature of every living being.[20]

Marlowe would have been familiar with these ideas from the occult tradition through his links with Walter Ralegh's circle, as John Mebane points out, so it is not surprising that he should draw on them in *Doctor Faustus*.[21] Much of the protagonist's thinking is based on the hermetic idea of transcendence through mental self-improvement. For women it has special significance.

Reading the acquisition of knowledge as a step towards God reverses patriarchal interpretations of the Eden story. Femininity, as represented by Eve, symbolizes openness to experience and growth, whereas paternal law is prohibition and confinement. A feminist re-reading produces a fable about maturation instead of fall, with Eve as a leading figure in human progress. Lyn M. Bechtel argues that Genesis 2.4–3.24 can be better understood as a story of growth from childhood to adulthood, where knowledge of sex, desire and death is a natural progression through adolescence rather than the result of sin.[22] Given the fact that girls usually mature more quickly than boys, Eve is naturally the first to taste the apple. According to this view, she is not the weaker vessel or the second sex but the primary one: she opens the gateway to maturation and, through her knowledge of desire and death, begins the process of renewing life. Feminist readings of Genesis which regard Eve and women's relationship to knowledge positively were to be found in the Renaissance. Rachel Speght's *Moralities Memorandum, with a Dreame Prefixed* (1621) confidently asked 'wherefore shall / A woman have her intellect in vaine, / Or not endeavor *Knowledge* to attaine'.[23] By focusing on the most radical example, Aemelia Lanyer's poem *Salve Deus Rex Judaeorum*, we can see how women watching *Doctor Faustus* might have

21

identified with the protagonist's quest in opposition to the play's morality pattern.

Lanyer's defence of Eve is the centrepiece of her poem's project to promote the interests of learned women, herself included. She tells Queen Anne of Denmark that it is a serious piece of exegesis 'which I have writ in honour of your sex'.[24] Lanyer, like Bechtel and like Faustus, sees knowledge as a means of development. In a cheeky reversal of the usual gendered associations, she says that Adam fell for the sensual beauty of the fruit, whereas 'If Eve did err, it was for knowledge sake' (l. 797). Eve is the more mature character. Rather than offering an apple to her teacher, she gives it like a teacher to her pupil, anxious to educate him and raise him to her level of understanding. Generosity is the only fault she can be charged with:

> ... Eve, whose only fault was too much love
> Which made her give this present to her dear,
> That what she tasted he likewise might prove,
> Whereby his knowledge might become more clear.
> He never sought her weakness to reprove,
> With those sharp words which he of God did hear;
> Yet men will boast of knowledge, which he took
> From Eve's fair hand, as from a learned book.
>
> (l. 801)

The conventional labels of 'fault' and 'weakness' are brought into question by Lanyer's account. There is nothing intellectually weak about an Eve whose hand offers lessons like a 'learned book'. Her only 'fault', or mistake, is in trusting Adam. Her unselfish act is rewarded by Adam's selfish one: snatching knowledge and power for himself while condemning her to a life without learning or autonomy. Since Eve was obviously the intellectual pioneer, her subsequent deprivation is both unjust and tragic. In a passionate outburst which reminds us of the pain of loss expressed by both Mephistopheles and Faustus, Lanyer proclaims 'Then let us have our liberty again / And challenge to yourselves no sov'reignty' (l. 825). In *Doctor Faustus* Marlowe re-presents Eve's tragedy; from a male perspective, it is true, but one in which female spectators could see themselves. Faustus's growth and self-determination, cut off so brutally, offers an image of the way in which their potential for development is repressed and their power is demonized by a society which took its ultimate authority from patriarchal interpretations of the Bible.

Aemelia Lanyer extends her feminist reading of the Eden narrative in the final section of her poem, 'The Description of Cookeham', where she describes an all-female 'paradise' (l. 21) of scholarly activity. Cookeham was the family home of Margaret Clifford, Countess of Cumberland, for whom *Salve Deus Rex Judaeorum* was written. Its garden is a place where women's reading and writing are blessed with grace. At the centre of the garden, as in Eden, is a 'stately tree' (l. 53), which is associated with the beneficial powers of knowledge. It allows Margaret 'goodly prospects' (l. 54), not unlike the vast horizons that are opened up to Faustus; it welcomes and elevates her so that all the surrounding countryside seems to kneel in salute. As well as giving her command over the material world, the tree enables the Countess to understand the Creator's majesty, and here, Lanyer's view of knowledge is very close to the hermetic idea. Lanyer recounts how she, Margaret and her daughter Anne are forced to leave Cookeham and take up their positions in the wilderness of patriarchal society. In another line that recalls Mephistopheles's sense of loss, Aemelia Lanyer laments being robbed of Anne Clifford's company: 'Whereof deprived, I evermore must grieve' (l. 125). Anne, who leaves to get married, chooses to say goodbye at the tree. The poem's feminist ideas on female learning, sisterhood and loss all come together here:

Where many a learned book was read and scanned;
To this fair tree, taking me by the hand,
You did repeat the pleasures which had passed,
Seeming to grieve they could no longer last.

(l. 161)

The feminist interpretation of Genesis put forward by Lanyer suggests that alternative views about knowledge were in circulation when *Doctor Faustus* was being performed, and may have had a special appeal to women. Like Marlowe, Lanyer uses a conventional Christian tale, the form of writing most acceptable for women, as a vehicle for the promotion of radical ideas. Her passionate celebration of female learning and literacy points to the possibility of an unorthodox response to *Doctor Faustus* on the part of some women.

Approaching the play via these ideas about Eve and knowledge produces very different readings of Faustus's journey and Helen's role. The audience can understand that the access to wisdom, beauty and pleasure which Faustus has been given is too valuable to lose, so he cannot repent. Faustus asks 'Why should I die, then, or basely despair?' (2.3.29). While the audience recognize that he is deceiving himself, they are tempted to share his belief that immersion in the classics will allow him to transcend the Christian heaven and hell. Helen represents the climax of this alternative existence:

Here will I dwell for heaven is in these lips,

23

And all is dross that is not Helena.
I will be Paris, and for love of thee
Instead of Troy shall Wittenburg be sacked ...
O, thou art fairer than the evening's air,
Clad in the beauty of a thousand stars.
Brighter art thou than flaming Jupiter
When he appeared to hapless Semele,
More lovely than the monarch of the sky
In wanton Arethusa's azured arms;
And none but thou shalt be my paramour.

(5.2.99)

Helen embodies knowledge, sexuality and pleasure. Read using the feminist interpretation of Eve, she is not the demon who causes Faustus's downfall but the summit of his intellectual and sensual experience; his coming of age or maturity. (Interestingly, the B text omits the Old Man's damning commentary on the couple, leaving this speech more open to positive responses from the audience.) Faustus's knowledge stretches across time and space, from the ancient world of Trojan history to the Wittenberg of the present, from classical myth to nature and astronomy. That Faustus is moving closer to heaven through this vast panorama of experience, as in the hermetic tradition, does not seem ridiculous. It is possible to share, or at least understand his view that he does not need anything beyond the wealth that is Helen, since the 'heaven' of knowledge 'dwells in these lips'. Heaven is no longer a patriarchal space since Helen outshines Jupiter, and Arethusa cradles the 'monarch of the sky' in her arms like a mother. 'Feminine' knowledge is an overwhelming force which envelops the human subject in pleasure rather than fear.

The hermetic idea of human development collapses the moral framework of *Doctor Faustus*, as Nicholas Brooke demonstrates in one of the most powerful anti-orthodox readings. He argues that Christian doctrine's insistence on subjection to the will of a superior god is anathema to the individual wishing to grow and explore independently, and that in Marlowe's play the human desire to create an autonomous self is inimical to divine will because the order of God is 'an order of servitude'. From this perspective 'Heaven is the subjection of self, Hell in this sense is the assertion of the self'.[25] The play's preoccupation with a quest for selfhood is an intrinsic part of its appeal to audiences of women struggling to establish identities in the face of paternal laws which demanded servitude. Women like Aemelia Lanyer, seeking to move beyond the roles assigned to them, can sympathize with Faustus's goal to 'be admired through the furthest land' (3.1.63). His tragic loss and downfall mirrors their own story as

24

daughters of Eve, but his very daring in transgressing the heavenly Father's law so confidently, so absolutely, offers a beacon of possibility to those women anxious to strike out and pursue their own 'bright fame' (3.1.62), against all the rules.

John Ford's play 'Tis Pity She's A Whore (1632) takes up many of the religious ideas found in Doctor Faustus.[26] It is a much more social play; characters are moulded and judged by the institutions within the city – the family and the church – rather than by supernatural figures. Nevertheless, religious motifs occupy a central place. The passion of Giovanni and Annabella dramatizes how desire and death are inextricably entwined in the post-lapsarian world. The difference between men's and women's experiences is made explicit as Ford sets up a parallel between the Faustus-like male protagonist and his sister. The title 'Tis Pity She's A Whore puts Annabella rather than Giovanni centre stage, and indicates that the play's primary concern is with woman's position in religious discourse. Giovanni is the character who drives the plot to its tragic conclusion but his active role serves primarily to demonstrate how, by contrast, Annabella is constructed as a figure of desire and of sacrifice by the men around her. Unlike him, she does not have the power to fashion herself. All she can do is to negotiate a pathway between the various roles laid out for her by the male characters.

Giovanni and Annabella are united by birth and by the incestuous love that leads to their deaths. In the first scene Giovanni tries to justify their passion with reference back to their creation:

> Say that we had one father, say one womb
> (Curse to my joys) gave both us life and birth;
> Are we not therefore each to other bound
> So much the more by nature? by the links
> Of blood, of reason? nay, if you will have't,
> Even of religion, to be ever one,
> One soul, one flesh, one love, one heart, one all?
>
> (1.1.29)

Giovanni's self-justification uncovers the incestuous subtext of the creation myth. If Adam and Eve were both made by God the father, then by bringing his children together he authorizes what is, in effect, an incestuous union. (If Eve is created from Adam then we have an example of father–daughter incest.) The relationship Giovanni describes is apparently one of equality, where Eve is of the same flesh as Adam, not subject to him. At first, the love of brother and sister maintains this sense of equality. It is Annabella who takes the lead in kneeling and contracting herself to

25

Giovanni. She is as passionate as he and takes as much active pleasure in consummating their love. She tells Putana 'what a paradise of joy / Have I passed over' (2.1.40).

Their paradise of sexual pleasure is very fragile, however. It can only exist in the absence of paternal law. Giovanni deliberately lies to Annabella, telling her that the holy church allows their love, whereas the opposite is true. The Friar, addressed as 'father' by both brother and sister, represents the law which intervenes to judge and condemn them. They seem conscious of its destructive presence even as they make their vows to each other and declare 'Love me, or kill me' (1.2.252). The law of the father kills pleasure even as it is born. There is no world elsewhere to which they can retreat.

Giovanni tries to step outside conventional morality, abandoning his faith in heaven and hell in favour of Annabella. He believes he can 'wipe away that rigour / Which would in other incests be abhorred' (5.1.72). His sin is wilful, like that of Faustus. He is a 'miracle of wit' (1.1.47), tutored by the Friar in 'the schools / Of knowledge' (1.1.57) at Bologna University, yet he chooses 'to converse with lust and death' (1.1.67). The arguments Giovanni constructs to justify his passion are 'ignorance in knowledge' (2.5.27), deliberately ignoring or excluding the Christian law which he knows condemns incest. Like Faustus, he has the freedom to make choices, to move about the city and to make his own grotesque contribution to the banquet at the end.

Annabella, by contrast, has no such autonomy. She sins in ignorance and her 'tut'ress' (1.2.67) is the antithesis of Giovanni's Friar. Putana is an expert in matters of the flesh who assesses all Annabella's suitors according to their physical attributes: Grimaldi may be impotent because he is a soldier, Bergetto is but a 'dearth of flesh' (1.2.124). Soranzo is to be preferred because he has a good track record at pleasing women, proved by his affair with Hippolita, and is probably free from sexual diseases. Putana prioritizes pleasure; she has no respect for paternal law. She places little value on chastity and is not in the least disturbed to find that the 'paradise' of Annabella's joy is incestuous. Her bawdy comment again reveals the incestuous subtext of the creation myth:

> Nay, what a paradise of joy have you passed under! ... Your brother's a man, I hope, and I say still, if a young wench feel the fit upon her, let her take anybody, father or brother, all is one.

> (2.1.41)

Putana's tutelage bolsters the arguments put forward by Giovanni and keeps Annabella in a fool's paradise, a blissful darkness of ignorance, until her pregnancy and the arranged marriage with Soranzo transform her into a tragic sacrifice. Putana's 'feminine' knowledge of the body and Giovanni's academic learning are starkly juxtaposed in Act 3, Scene 3. While his university education cannot help him interpret Annabella's physical symptoms, Putana immediately knows what they mean. Her gynaecological expertise makes her threatening and, like many midwives or wise women, she is persecuted as a witch. Vasques calls Putana a 'damnable hag' (4.3.224) and has her imprisoned in a coal house where she is gagged and her eyes put out. She may be the woman whom the Cardinal sentences to be burned to ashes (5.6.133–6), though his lines could also refer to Annabella's body.

Annabella, unlike Giovanni, has no freedom of movement. It is true that her father says that his care 'is how to match her to her liking' (1.3.10), but he already seems to have resolved to marry her to Soranzo. She is forced to go through with the match when her pregnancy is discovered. By the beginning of Act 5 she is trapped in a web of female roles dictated by the men around her, none of which satisfy her own desires:

Here like a turtle (mewed up in a cage)
Unmated, I converse with air and walls,
And descant on my vile unhappiness.

(5.1.14)

Her physical confinement mirrors the cultural and spiritual oppression she suffers. She is moulded by a religious discourse which casts her in the role of either Eve or Mary. Giovanni sees her as Eve: an extension of himself formed from the same flesh and blood, and (when he discovers his love is reciprocated), a mirror of his own passion. She is able to play this role successfully for a while. Nevertheless, the appearance of equality is deceptive. He tells Annabella, 'Wise nature first in your creation meant / To make you mine' (1.2.232), and the possessive pronoun defines her as the object of his love rather than a desiring subject.

The suitor Bergetto presents no real threat to Annabella and Giovanni's affair because his desires are infantile in nature. There is a certain charm in his outspoken honesty which allows Annabella to answer him with a direct refusal when she is forced to speak. Even Bergetto's attraction to Philotis is modelled on childish pleasures, so his brutal murder is genuinely shocking. Like Annabella, he falls victim to the machinations of more powerful men and after his death receives no justice from the church. The Cardinal's decision to take the murderer, Grimaldi, into the protection of the Pope rightly horrifies Donado. His outraged questions 'Is this a churchman's voice? Dwells justice here?' (3.9.61) sound again in the minds of the audience when the Cardinal comes to pronounce judgement on Annabella.

Soranzo's desire for Annabella is what unhinges the private paradise she has built for herself with Giovanni. Soranzo idolizes her as a pattern of virgin purity; to him she represents the opposite of the sinful lust he has enjoyed with Hippolita. When Soranzo presents his suit, overheard by Giovanni from above, Annabella's awkward positioning between the passions of two men is physicalized on stage. She tries escape from being the object of Soranzo's fantasies by mocking his formal postures of courtly love and assuring him that she speaks for nobody but herself in refusing his love (3.1.49–50). In spite of her attempt to assert her independence, both men interpret her role of 'chaste disdain' (3.1.34) in accordance with their own desires. Giovanni sees her refusal as proof of her constancy to him, but Soranzo reads it as evidence of her determination to 'live and die a maid' (3.2.21). Her promise that she will never marry perpetuates his fantasy of virgin purity, inflaming rather than decreasing his passion. Her fainting, which could be the result of a votary's fasting as much as a symptom of pregnancy, adds fuel to the fire. Of course the virginity that Soranzo finds so attractive is only a sham, and its lack of substance is figured in the performance of the wedding masque. The dancers appear to be 'lovely virgins' (4.1.36), costumed in white robes and bearing willow garlands, but behind the mask, Hippolita brings lust, sin and death into the marriage. The curse she gives Soranzo before she dies proves chillingly accurate: Annabella's womb already holds Giovanni's bastard child. Richardetto feels that divine justice is now beginning to work (4.1.87), but for Annabella the situation becomes impossible.

Annabella is much less able to resist the power of religious condemnation than Giovanni. The Friar's lecture on hell (3.6.1–32) is designed to terrify her. It envelops her in the familiar legacy of Eve, making her see herself as nothing more than a guilty, wretched creature in need of paternal guidance. The graphic picture of damned souls follows in the tradition of hell-visions like that presented to Faustus (5.2.120–32), sombre enough to strike fear into the stoutest hearts, especially for an audience who readily believed in the physical existence of such a place. Elizabeth Melvill's poem *A Godlie Dreame*, first published in an anglicized version in 1606 and then reprinted in 1620, demonstrates how potent the vision of hell could be as a means to subjugate women. The spiritual journey Melvill depicts forms an illuminating parallel to Annabella's own.

Melvill, the dreamer in the poem, is taken by Christ on a quest towards personal salvation, travelling an arduous path through deep waters, wild woodlands, and fire. Like Annabella, she attempts to take a short cut to Paradise, trying to climb a steep stairway directly to the heavenly palace on her own. Christ, the intervening voice of paternal law, tells her she must go through the torments of hell and leads her, as the Friar metaphorically leads

Annabella. When she looks into the pit of hell, her fear nearly overcomes
her faith:

> I looked down, and saw a pit most black,
> Most full of smoke, and flaming fire most fell.
> That uglie sight made me to flee aback:
> I feared to heare so many shout and yell.[27]

Melvill loses all confidence in her own abilities and entreats Christ 'Oh,
help me now, I have no force nor might' (2A3). She awakens assured of her
salvation, but the struggle to keep faith, to cling onto the holy life rather
than falling into the pit of sin, is very tangible. She counsels her readers to
be prepared for suffering:

> The thornie cares of this deceitfull life
> Will rent your hearts and make your souls to bleed:
> Your flesh and spirit will be at deadly strife,
> Your cruell foe will hold you still in dread.
>
> (2A4v)

The conflict Melvill describes is experienced directly by Annabella, whose
heart will literally be torn at the end of the play, and whose emotions are
torn between her love for Giovanni, the flesh, and the spiritual awareness
awoken by the Friar.

After her interview with the Friar, Annabella no longer tries to live
outside religious discourse, but rather than accepting its doctrines and her
own guilt, she moulds it to her own purposes. When her pregnancy is
discovered by Soranzo, the only way she can reconcile the conflicting roles
required of her by the two men is through identification with the Virgin
Mary, the second Eve whose sexual experience is God-given and for whom
motherhood is a source of redemption, not the result of damnation. Soranzo
immediately assumes that because she is not a virgin, she must be a whore,
taking out his anger by insulting her and dragging her about the room. Her
response to such savage treatment is spirited. She makes no denial of the
pregnancy but models herself on the most powerful religious icon available
to women, casting Giovanni in the role of God:

> This noble creature was in every part
> So angel-like, so glorious, that a woman
> Who had not been but human, as was I,
> Would have kneeled to him, and have begged for love.

29

You! Why, you are not worthy once to name
His name without true worship, or, indeed,
Unless you kneeled, to hear another name him.

(4.3.36)

Annabella is truly daring in comparing herself to the Virgin Mary and
relegating her angry husband to the part of a doubtful Joseph. Since
religious discourse frames her in a number of fixed roles, she makes active
use of them. Her appropriation of scripture preserves the mystery of her
affair with Giovanni and simultaneously mocks the official church which
condemns their union. The power of the Virgin icon allows her to transcend
all social norms for a brief time, and continue her incestuous affair. She
responds to Soranzo's threats with mocking indifference, laughing, singing
and triumphant, while he says 'I carry all hell about me' (4.3.149).

Annabella's triumph is only temporary. Before long, the power of the
Friar's judgement is back with her; her conscience, she says, 'now stands up
against my lust' (5.1.9) and fills her with dread. She dismisses her pleasures
as an illusion of 'false joys' (5.1.2), and reconfigures herself as the guilty
protagonist in 'a wretched, woeful woman's tragedy' (5.1.8). The same
pattern of recognition and repentance is found in Elizabeth Melvill's *A
Godlie Dreame*. The spiritual journey continues after the end of the main
poem in a song about renouncing the pleasures of the world. The protagonist realizes that the vain world, 'bewitcher of mine heart' (B3), has offered
a false love that can only deceive or beguile, but one which is hard to
surrender: 'Loath I am to forgoe / That sweet alluring foe' (B3v). Annabella's difficulty in divorcing herself from the bliss she feels with Giovanni,
even though she knows it is damned, is of the same kind. The speaker in the
song appeals to Christ for help to avoid being devoured by the sins of the
flesh. Having renounced earthly passion, she feels strangely empty:

What shall I doe? Are all my pleasures past?
Shall worldlie lustes now take their leave at last?
Yea, Christ, these earthly toys, Shal turn to heavenly joys.

(B3v)

The journey from worldly lust to heavenly salvation concludes with an
image of sacrifice which is disturbingly close to the one dramatized in *'Tis
Pity She's A Whore*. The 1620 edition of *A Godlie Dreame* ends with an
emblem depicting a bleeding heart impaled on a dagger and surrounded by
a crown of thorns. The text which accompanies the image, taken from
Psalm 51, verse 17, reads 'The sacrifices of God are a contrite spirit: a
contrite and broken heart, O God, thou wilt not despise' (B4). The

30

pilgrim's heart is offered as a symbol of repentance, suffering and sacrifice akin to that of Christ.

Annabella embraces the same fate in *'Tis Pity She's A Whore*. Once she fully accepts heavenly judgement, the only role left to her is that of tragic sacrifice. She longs to take the burden of Giovanni's sins upon her and feel 'the torment of an uncontrolled flame' alone, to redeem him (5.1.23). In the final scenes their outlawed passion is transformed into a Christ-like passion, culminating at the banquet. Annabella is prepared for the last supper, warning Giovanni 'there's but a dining-time / 'Twixt us and our confusion' (5.5.17). Giovanni's decision to kill her and take her heart into the banquet is unexpected, and as she says, 'unkind' (5.5.93). It seems to be an act of madness, evidence that his reasoning has shattered under the pressure of trying to maintain faith in a world where incest is not sinful. The bringing of Annabella's heart into the play's last supper completes her progress through the key icons in the biblical story of creation, fall, virgin birth and sacrifice. The perversion of the Christian Eucharist is emphasized by the presence of the Cardinal, whose virtue has already been brought into question. Without realizing the black comedy of his words, Soranzo invites the Cardinal to 'taste these coarse confections' (5.6.3) and Giovanni enters with the bleeding heart. Annabella is the feast on which they have all fed to satisfy their desires, but only in that sense is she a whore. It is they who have constructed her, consumed her, sacrificed her independence by offering her only a narrow choice of parts to play.

The other female roles in *'Tis Pity She's A Whore* reinforce the lack of choice which Annabella faces. Hippolita's freedom to move from place to place as a widow is unreal since her husband is spying on her. Her readiness to plot against Richardetto and her former lover means that she is demonized for her 'lust and pride' (4.1.101). Vasques's label 'Mistress She-Devil' (4.1.68) seems to be borne out when the poison takes effect and she dies feeling 'heat above hell fire' (4.1.91). The other characters merely see a 'wonderful justice' (4.1.87) in her failure. It seems that in Parma there is no escape from the uncompromising demands on women to accept guilt and subjection. The only woman who survives is Philotis, sent by her uncle to become a nun in an all-female community where her virginity can redeem her:

> Your home your cloister, your best friends your beads.
> Your chaste and single life shall crown your birth;
> Who dies a virgin lives a saint on earth.
>
> (4.2.26)

By withdrawing into nunneries, women were able to escape the penalties of the Fall. Their choice of virginity freed them from subjection to men in marriage and the pain and sorrow of childbirth. Conventual life drew them closer to the Virgin Mary, the most powerful symbol of the pure virgin body. The custom of fasting enhanced the likeness because fasting induces amenorrhoea (the absence of menstruation), thus removing their bodily connection with Eve, the first mother.[28] Theseus in Shakespeare's *A Midsummer Night's Dream* (1595) gives a telling picture of the nun's life of denial:

> For aye in shady cloister to be mewed,
> To live a barren sister all your life,
> Chanting faint hymns to the cold fruitless moon.
> Thrice blessèd they that master so their blood
> To undergo such maiden pilgrimage.
>
> (1.1.71)

The lines outline problems with conventual life. In addition to the way in which it usually involves submission to the anti-feminist ideology of the Roman Catholic church, it also constitutes a complete denial of the natural functions of the female body. The moon, symbol of menstruation, is turned into a symbol of chastity, rendered 'fruitless'; the woman effectively transforms herself into a man by 'mastering' her blood. Theseus implies that such self-denial is only possible for a remarkable few, the 'thrice blessèd', who can transcend the limits of their own bodies and dehumanize themselves. 'Maiden pilgrimage' is also dependent on withdrawal to an all-female community. The sisterhood is 'mewed' or enclosed from the world by the walls of the convent, which physically recreate the impenetrable body of the Virgin, separating nuns from the world of men like an architectural hymen. For the maiden pilgrimage to survive, the hymen must remain intact. In *Measure for Measure* (1604) Shakespeare shows how fragile the boundaries are, how difficult such a withdrawal is for women.

At the beginning of the play, two opposite spaces are clearly defined: the city and the convent. Vienna is a world of flesh, a wilderness of unlicensed sexuality, the province of Eve. Mistress Overdone, who has already exhausted nine husbands, is the queen, or quean, of this realm. Her influence and that of her bawd, Pompey, has infected the whole population with a desire whose excess contains the seeds of its own destruction. Sin, pregnancy and death exist cheek by jowl, the presence of each implied in the others. Not even the city authorities and their families can escape. Mistress Elbow, heavily pregnant, is drawn into Mistress Overdone's house by a longing for stewed prunes, and throughout the comic examination of Pompey, her reputation suffers at the hands of her own husband. In Elbow's malapropisms sexual looseness and the slipperiness of language are brought together to illustrate the uncontrollable disease. He claims that his wife has never been a respected woman (2.1.157–9); on the contrary, he proudly asserts that he detests both himself and her (2.1.63–8). The unintentional sense of disgust at her pregnant body is present even as he tries to defend her. Similarly, Claudio feels that his desire for Juliet, which has made her pregnant, is sinful appetite and the wages of sin is death:

> So every scope by the immoderate use,
> Turns to restraint. Our natures do pursue,
> Like rats that raven down their proper bane,
> A thirsty evil; and when we drink, we die.
>
> (1.2.107)

Juliet personifies the position of women within the fallen world of Vienna. Her brief speaking role shows how she is defined by misogynist religious discourse as a daughter of Eve. The Duke (disguised as Friar) tells her that since she committed fornication willingly with Claudio, her sin is of 'heavier kind' (2.3.30). In literal terms, her heavier sin is the baby she is carrying and metaphorically, it is the weight of blame which, Calvin reminds us, makes women 'stoop and bear patiently the subjection God hath laid upon them'. Juliet is both a transgressor and a dutiful believer who recognizes and repents her sin. She accepts, with the role, the paradoxical status of Eve as bringer of life and death. For Juliet, imminent motherhood is the source of life, and her own respite from execution, but also causes Claudio's imminent death:

> ... O injurious law,
> That respites me a life, whose very comfort
> Is still a dying horror.
>
> (2.3.42)

The convent of St Clare stands apart from Vienna, a space of chastity and withdrawal. In Renaissance England all monasteries had been dissolved after the Reformation, although it is possible that a convent of Minoresses (a branch of the Poor Clares), which stood outside Aldgate until 1539, could have provided one source for the play.[29] For women watching *Measure for Measure* in Shakespeare's day, retiring to a local nunnery was not a viable possibility but alternative conventual lifestyles did exist at home and abroad. The closeted Catholicism of recusant households took over the role of the official convent, especially in the remoter parts of the kingdom, where women played an important role by leading religious worship behind closed doors. In addition, English monasticism survived by moving abroad. In 1596 Lady Mary Percy established a Benedictine community for women in Brussels, and the early years of the seventeenth century saw the foundation of several English houses of Discalced Carmelites. The popularity of 'maiden pilgrimage' and the limited autonomy it could offer seemed to be on the increase during the seventeenth century, when the number of English nuns on the continent (over three hundred) exceeded that of monks for the first time.[30] The rapid growth of English convents was due partly to the work of Mary Ward. After joining the St Clares in 1606, she founded a new convent for English women, and in 1609 established her own missionary order, the Institute of Mary. This was like the Jesuits' order but founded on principles of female leadership. The nuns were well educated, with some knowledge of the classics and even the new sciences. They often worked in the community, teaching Latin, Greek, modern languages, mathematics, geography, astronomy, needlework and music, and even encouraging their female pupils to give public performances of Latin plays. The Institute of Mary was so successful that it expanded rapidly in spite of opposition from English Jesuits and the male-dominated hierarchy of the Roman church. It attracted young women from many Catholic families in England and by 1629 Ward had set up new houses in Liège, Cologne, Trier, Rome, Naples, Munich, Prague and Vienna.[31]

In *Measure for Measure*, Isabella's desire to become a member of the Order of St Clare can therefore be seen in relation to a wider pattern of women's behaviour in the Counter-Reformation of the early seventeenth century. Reading Isabella's role alongside the writings of Mary Ward allows us to suggest how female spectators, then and now, might identify with Isabella in ways which resist the masculine bias of the text and its ways of categorizing women. Even if the conventual life holds no specific appeal for spectators or readers, the integrity and autonomy which Isabella and Mary Ward represent, their refusal to be positioned easily by men, makes them attractive to feminists. To regard *Measure for Measure* as an anti-monastic satire, where Isabella's ideas 'are meant to differ sharply from those of a largely Protestant audience', fails to take account of the ways in which women might share her point of view because of their religious or feminist sympathies.[32] It also fails to acknowledge that Shakespeare's own attitude to Catholicism may have been ambivalent, particularly if he had spent the so-called 'lost years' of his youth as a schoolteacher in a Catholic household in Lancashire, as has been suggested.[33]

Both Isabella and Mary Ward welcome the life of self-denial offered by the convent. Isabella, not quite secure in the sanctuary it offers, wishes for 'a more strict restraint' on the sisterhood. When Mary Ward joined the Poor Clares, the austere life of fasting, silence and vigil pleased her. She says that nothing could have disturbed her 'except to hear that there was some

Order in the Church of God more austere and more secluded'.[34] The Order of St Clare, unlike male Franciscans who went out preaching, were 'mewed up' from contact with men. In *Measure for Measure* the restrictions on speech and on showing one's face in the presence of a man are outlined by Francesca (1.4.10–13). Both the face and the mouth represent possible gateways to corruption. Francesca cannot talk to Lucio because she is already sworn to the sisterhood, an insider.

Isabella occupies a liminal position. She stands on the threshold between the city and the convent, and even though Lucio calls her 'a thing enskied and sainted' (1.4.33), she still has access to both worlds. Her move into the city mirrors Mary Ward's decision to leave the Poor Clares and found an order which would not be mewed up in the cloister. In both cases, relocating the Cult of Virginity in the public realm brought with it particular dangers. Because it posed a threat to patriarchal power, it simultaneously became very vulnerable. Once Isabella leaves the convent, her virgin identity is under threat. She recognizes that, in pleading to Angelo to pardon the vice 'that most I do abhor' (2.2.29), she has fractured herself from virgin whole into a double creature, speaking partly against herself in defence of the sins of the flesh. In Vienna, mercantile sexuality and holy chastity exist in each other's sinews; desire and transcendence turn out to be causally related rather than diametrically opposed. Here, Isabella's quest for absolute perfection will always be frustrated because that very perfection contains the seeds of its own undoing. Once she moves outside the convent, her wish to transcend desire actually provokes desire.

Isabella's vulnerability is obvious the first time we see her. Lucio brings into the walls of the nunnery the very concept of woman she is trying to escape, by telling her about the 'fallen' Juliet, whose fertile body he describes in much more detail than is necessary (1.4.39–43). His initial greeting raises doubts about her chastity: 'Hail virgin, if you be – as those cheek-roses / Proclaim you are no less' (1.4.16). The virgin's blush, as Danielle Clark has argued, was widely used in texts depicting the Virgin Mary but had its origins in the secular tradition of love poetry and romance.[35] It could signify either modesty or guiltiness. To a lover's eye the blush is an erotic invitation on the part of the mistress, betraying knowledge of his intents even as it shows her shock at being approached. To the religious devotee, it is a sign of the Virgin's perfect modesty. The two kinds of gaze cannot easily be separated though, as the author of *The Paradise of Delights* (1620) recognized in his description of Mary:

Neither was her virginal comelynes such as usually doth stir up wanton lustes, or inflame bad desires; but altogeather so far contrary that who so should behold

the beautifull blush of her modest and virginall countenance, could not choose,
but be inflamed with most chast desires and fervent love towardes this vertuous
Queene.[36]

The gentleman doth protest too much. His zealous project to differentiate
the religious appeal from the sensuous one is confounded by their proximity. Virginal comeliness and 'bad desires' merge into one another by the
end of his sentence, where the devotee is paradoxically 'inflamed' with a
passion or 'fervent love' for chastity. This is exactly the situation Angelo
finds himself in when he meets Isabella. In fact, when she blushes at his
proposal that she yield her virginity to him, he points out that those very
marks of modesty provoke his 'sharp appetite' (2.4.161–3).

Angelo is the most fatal opposite that Isabella could meet because he is
so like her. His name and the Duke's language establish him as a divinely
chosen creature and Angelo sees himself in pre-lapsarian terms. Like
Isabella, he believes that an austere life redeems him from the penalty of
Adam and separates him from normal humankind. This is why he resents
both Escalus's and Isabella's attempts to compare him with Claudio. The
'precise' Angelo strives to distance himself from fallen humanity and 'scarce
confesses / That his blood flows' (1.3.50–2). He too behaves like a 'thing
enskied', cutting himself off from the natural functions of the body in the
pursuit of saintly perfection. According to Lucio the Lord Angelo is:

> . . . a man whose blood
> Is very snow broth; one who never feels
> The wanton stings and motions of the sense,
> But doth rebate and blunt his natural edge
> With profits of the mind, study, and fast.
>
> (1.4.56)

Like the nuns, Angelo masters his blood until it is frozen with the
purifying chill of chastity. His self-denial is so complete that he is
mythicized in the same terms as the Virgin Mary, as the product of an
immaculate conception. Lucio says that Angelo 'was not made by man and
woman after this downright way of creation' (3.1.350), isolating him from
the intercourse that follows the Fall, and translating him into an ethereal,
desexualized, yet ultimately sterile form, 'a motion ungenerative'
(3.1.356).

When Angelo meets Isabella he sees a mirror image of himself. She is as
dangerous to him as he is to her. As a 'very virtuous maid' (2.2.20) she
presents a different female figure from Juliet, 'the fornicatress' (2.2.23),
whom Angelo has just had removed. Paradoxically, Angelo rejects Isabella's pleas because he is attracted to her. Her references to Christ's

example (2.2.75–9) and her reminders about man's essential weakness and pride (2.2.120–6) are powerful arguments for mercy, but Angelo cannot accept them because they refer to the fallen image of humanity which he is trying to escape. Although she pleads on behalf of sin, Isabella is costumed in the habit of chaste perfection which Angelo so much wants to assume, metaphorically if not literally. She 'bribes' him with the saintly image he most desires:

> . . . true prayers,
> That shall be up at heaven and enter there
> Ere sunrise, prayers from preservèd souls,
> From fasting maids whose minds are delicate
> To nothing temporal.
>
> (2.2.155)

Angelo's soliloquy confirms what we have suspected all through the interview: it is Isabella's chastity that has tempted him to sin, he desires her 'foully' precisely for the things which 'make her good' (2.2.178–9). His speech, with its insistent, bewildered questions, its tone of repulsion and fascination, describes his own fall but, interestingly, it does not follow the usual misogynist interpretation of Genesis and cast Isabella as the seductive temptress:

> . . . Is this her fault or mine?
> The tempter or the tempted, who sins most, ha?
> Not she, nor doth she tempt . . .
> O cunning enemy, that, to catch a saint,
> With saints dost bait thy hook! Most dangerous
> Is that temptation that doth goad us on
> To sin in loving virtue.
>
> (2.2.167)

Isabella is not grouped with the serpent and Eve because Angelo's temptation is far from ordinary. On one level it is a sin of pride – he already sees himself as a saint, but more frighteningly, the soliloquy plays out the temptation facing religious devotees: to perversely eroticize the Virgin through praise of her chastity. He imagines his fall from saintly innocence into the knowledge of desire as a corruption of the Virgin body (2.4.4–7). 'The strong and swelling evil / Of my conception' (2.4.6) describes both his fantasy of seducing and impregnating Isabella, and his own sinful conception as a morally imperfect member of the post-lapsarian world.

Isabella's reaction to his outrageous proposal is to retreat further into her religious role. She constructs herself as a virgin martyr, a model which

37

intensified the sacrificial life of the convent. Renaissance England had its own tradition of martyrs; recusant women such as Margaret Clitherow who had been tied up half-naked in the form of a cross and crushed to death between two doors for refusing to confess to the charge of harbouring priests, in 1586.[37] Since many women had direct experience of persecution, in more or less extreme forms, in their families, Isabella's image of martyrdom could have been a collective experience, shared by female spectators. Virgin martyrdom was the fulfilment of an ideal, but the tortures suffered were often sexual in nature, revealing the sadomasochistic appeal of the assaulted female body.[38] Isabella imagines her own martyr-dom in just these terms:

> Th' impression of keen whips I'd wear as rubies,
> And strip myself to death as to a bed
> That longing have been sick for, ere I'd yield
> My body up to shame.

> (2.4.101)

Isabella is fired with a passion which comes close to Angelo's eroticization of religious icons. Mary Ward's fervent longing for martyrdom contains nothing explicitly sexual, but for her too it represents a passionate kind of pleasure: 'I had during these years burning desires to be a martyr and my mind for a long time together fixed upon that happy event; the sufferings of the martyrs appeared to me delightful for attaining to so great a good and my favourite thoughts were how? And when?' (p. 11). While Angelo's fantasies are anchored on the chaste Isabella, those of the women wishing to enter the nunnery are for a death which, because it is non-sexual and designed to preserve chastity, is often paradoxically charged with erotic overtones.

Angelo and Isabella are engaged in a struggle over her identity in Act 2, Scene 4. He attempts to bring her down from a 'thing enskied' with reminders of human frailty: 'Be that you are, / That is a woman; if you be more you're none', and urges her to put on the 'destined livery' of woman as a sexualized, conceiving mother (2.4.134–8). She talks about her sex firstly from the outside, as though she had succeeded in separating herself completely, and then, as her pronouns move from 'them' to 'us', admitting kinship with the weaker vessel:

> Women? – Help, heaven! Men their creation mar
> In profiting by them. Nay, call us ten times frail,
> For we are soft as our complexions are,
> And credulous to false prints.

> (2.4.126)

This is not simply an anti-feminist speech. It marks Isabella's own futile attempt to transcend the role of Eve in a community where women's self-created roles are always re-created, or rather marred, by men.

Isabella's soliloquy of resolution (2.4.171–87), and her famous line 'More than our brother is our chastity', must be understood in terms of this struggle to escape from male misconstructions and to fashion herself. Her response to Angelo and later to Claudio in the prison may appear cold and uncharitable, particularly to our modern ears, but as an expression of free will, virginity is a powerful feminist symbol. Chastity and the life of the convent represent an escape from the 'destined livery' of Eve as a desired and desiring subject. It is a form of desexualization which leads back to pre-lapsarian autonomy and equality. Again the writings of Mary Ward help us to appreciate the positive value of denial. She sees chastity as a means of redemption, believing that life as a nun will allow her to recover an innocence where sense and reason obey divine will, to return to the beginning because 'those in Paradise before the first fall were in this estate' (p. 40). Mary told the nuns who joined her Institute that they were to ignore the scoffs of a Holy Father who claimed that their fervour would soon decay because they were 'but women':

> There is no such difference between men and women . . . . Heretofore we have been told by men what we must believe. It is true, we must, but let us be wise and know what we are to believe and what not, and not to be made [to] think we can do nothing . . . . I confess wives are to be subject to their husbands, men are head of the Church, women may not administer sacraments nor preach in public churches, but in all other things, wherein are we so inferior to other creatures that they should term us 'but women'? As if we were in all things inferior to some other creation, which I suppose to be men! Which, I dare be bold to say, is a lie and, with respect to the good Father, may say it is an error. I would to God that all men understood this verity, that women, if they will, may be perfect, and if they would not make us believe we can do nothing and that we are 'but women', we might do great matters. (p. 57)

The feminist claims of Mary's speeches were translated directly into the way her Institute was governed. She was determined that her sisters were to take their authority from nobody but the Pope. Her proposals included the radical clause 'this Institute for just causes is subject to no Religious Order of men, but the sisters decided to live wholly as disciples of Christ, who is the Master and Lord of all Christians and in the School of the Blessed Mary (special patron of all Christians)' (p. 36). Such determination to be self-governing and to live a mixed life, working as scholars and teachers in the public domain, aroused inexorable opposition from the male ecclesiastical hierarchy.

The power of Mary's convictions about female independence and equality is matched by Isabella's impassioned defence of her chastity in *Measure for Measure*. There is, however, an important difference between their views. For Isabella chastity is like a possession, to be protected or bestowed as she chooses. For Mary Ward, it is something over which the individual has no control:

> I saw suddenly and very clearly that the gift of chastity . . . was always *a peculiar gift of God* and not . . . in the power of man, thus corrupted, either to bring forth or conserve in himself . . . . Then I acknowledged what I had of this to be wholly his gift. I thanked him for it and asked pardon for thinking it in any part my own, or in my ability to get or keep. (p. 43)

The fundamental difference between Mary Ward and Isabella's views marks their different places in the convent. Mary, the insider, has taken the imitation of the Virgin to its complete fulfilment: her chastity is the special gift of God, to be disposed of according to his will. Isabella, not yet sworn to the sisterhood, still owns her chastity. It endows her with secular power as well as the potential to enter the religious life. In purely practical terms, Isabella's refusal to yield to Angelo stops a chain of potential exploitation (as he claims that Claudio's execution will put a stop to fornication), by protecting other women whose virginity might be traded to buy justice.

Talking to Claudio in the prison, Isabella recognizes the social significance of chastity as well as its religious dimension. His request that she agree to Angelo's plan begets a breakdown of the patriarchal family structure: her potential loss of chastity makes her doubt her mother's fidelity and Claudio's legitimacy. The perfect nuclear family is ruptured by vicious desires, adultery and even incest, and its offspring are the children of a wilderness:

> Wilt thou be made a man out of my vice?
> Is 't not a kind of incest to take life
> From thine own sister's shame? What should I think?
> Heaven shield my mother play'd my father fair,
> For such a warpèd slip of wilderness
> Ne'er issued from his blood.
>
> (3.1.139)

Barbara Baines has argued that Isabella's chastity is not dependent on her religious convictions but is 'psychically and socially determined' by the 'economy of secular power' which surrounds her and subjugates her. Certainly the above speech shows awareness of the importance of chastity as the foundation of genealogical inheritance and identity, but to say that her religious beliefs do not 'adequately account for her choice' is to ignore the whole conventual discourse which promoted the idea that chastity was the one way in which women could separate themselves from women's subjection after the Fall.[39] Isabella's use of religious imagery is not just a mask for the 'real' power of her chastity; it has its own weight. To lose her virginity would be to stoop to spiritual pollution, not just to Angelo's lust. Sexual 'death', or orgasm, would 'fetter [her] till death' (3.1.64) and translate her from a virgin votary to a daughter of Eve. Her horror at this alternative betrays her adolescent fear of sex itself, the jump from innocence to knowledge, but it is also a fear of spiritual loss which makes Isabella resolve 'Then Isabel live chaste, and brother, die' (2.4.184). For the sake of her soul she is prepared to sacrifice the brother she loves, in imitation of the Virgin's own maternal sacrifice.

Isabella is not as unbending as this declaration seems to indicate. She is willing to compromise and participate in the Friar's plot in a way that brings her closer to the Virgin pattern of sacrifice, even as it seems to take away her absolute chastity. Like Mary, who is nearly rejected by Joseph because she is with child (Matthew 1.19), Isabella undergoes the shame of being deemed unchaste. At the gates of the city, another important threshold, she declares that she has been violated by Angelo. It is Mariana's cooperation in the bed trick which allows Isabella to remain chaste, a true copy of the Virgin pattern, unlike Annabella in 'Tis Pity She's A Whore. There is no reason why she should not still be wearing the habit which declares her dedication to maiden pilgrimage when she appears to accuse Angelo.

Mariana is another marginal figure, living on the outskirts of St Luke's, presumably some kind of monastic order, but wishing to move in the opposite direction to Isabella, towards marriage. The moated grange, surrounded by water like that which killed her brother, isolates her from the city whose women are caught up in a cycle of abundant fertility and reproduction. Mariana is marooned by her brother's death, stranded between betrothal and marriage. Her sexual status is also rendered marginal by the 'discoveries of dishonour' which Angelo invents to 'rupture' the match (3.1.221–8). The bed trick intensifies these, of course. When she appears before the Duke, she identifies herself as neither maid, widow nor wife, and Lucio's fourth alternative, 'a punk', alludes correctly, albeit crudely, to her sexual experience (5.1.170–8). It is Mariana who completes Isabella's translation of Angelo from saint to mortal, modifying it from a fall to the completion of a worldly contract. His virginity is suggested by the venue for their meeting: Angelo's version of the nunnery is 'a garden circummured with brick' (4.1.25). In another microcosm of the Eden story, Mariana enters to bring temptation and sexual knowledge into the garden.

41

In contrast to Isabella, whose costume proclaims her likeness to the Virgin, Mariana comes before the Duke veiled, symbolizing her subjection to her husband. She pleads for Angelo's life as a fallen woman, like Juliet who willingly committed fornication with Claudio. She acknowledges and excuses Angelo's faults as a natural part of his humanity, proof of his conception the 'downright way of creation':

> They say the best men are moulded out of faults,
> And, for the most, become much more the better
> For being a little bad. So may my husband.
>   (5.1.431)

Isabella's intercession in the suit brings her still closer to the Virgin ideal, Mary being the key mediating figure between humanity and divinity according to Mariological teaching. The Duke's curious and apparently cruel behaviour in perpetuating the fiction of Claudio's death is designed to enhance the Marian imitation. Isabella's apparently willing sacrifice of her beloved brother for the common good is followed by her pleas for Angelo, the very sinner who was responsible for his death. It mirrors the Virgin's willingness to intercede even for those sinners whose redemption was bought at such a cruel price.

Having promoted Isabella's saintly image, the Duke strives to dismantle it because it poses too great a threat. Angelo's life is to be redeemed not by a programme of sacrifice and selfless intercession, but by a retributive justice based more on Old Testament law (Leviticus 24.17–20) and the lesson in Matthew 'with what measure ye mete, it shall be measured to you again' (Matthew 7.2). The Duke rules 'An Angelo for Claudio; death for death' (5.1.406). This system allows him to appear 'like power divine' (5.1.366), saving Angelo's life by apparently resurrecting Claudio and presenting him to an amazed Isabella. Isabella is reduced from a powerful, self-determining mediator to a passive instrument of his 'divine' will. The Duke's proposal of marriage, one of the most surprising elements of the play's denouement, is designed to complete the containment process and reveals his essentially manipulative nature.

Although the Duke adopts a religious costume he is constantly shadowed by sin, in particular the sins of the city. Lucio's report that the Duke 'had some feeling of the sport' (3.1.362) of lechery is hard for the 'fantastical Duke of dark corners' (4.3.147) to shake off. He may wish to model himself on virtue as Isabella and Angelo strive to, but because he is a man that aims 'especially to know himself' (3.1.456), he realizes that human nature makes such perfection almost impossible to attain. The only absolute he trusts is mortality. He counsels Claudio to be 'absolute for

42

death', advising him to accept human lack, desire and frailty as the inevitable legacy of the Fall (3.1.5–25), reminding him 'thou art not certain / For thy complexion shifts to strange effects / After the moon' (3.1.23). Based on his own experience, the Duke believes that no human being can be 'certain', fixed in their determination to transcend the mortality of the flesh, let alone achieve such perfection. Presumably it is his own certainty of this that leads him to believe Isabella would be better placed as his wife than as a nun. Angelo's behaviour does confirm his view that desire destroys such absolute perfection, but is he therefore just in assuming that Isabella is moulded out of the same faults?

The Duke's attraction to Isabella is like the priest's idealization of the Virgin as a passive model of female goodness. As Mary Daly observes, 'safely relegated to her pedestal, she serves his purpose, his psychological need, without having any purpose of her own. For the celibate who prefers not to be tied down to a wife, or whose canonical situation forbids marriage, the "Mary" of his imagination could appear to be the ideal spouse'.[40] In the priest's hands the Cult of Virginity is disempowered, Mary becomes a silent subject with no independent will. The Duke tries to shape Isabella in the same way. He loves her not from a respect for her person, or even with sexual passion like Angelo, but from a need to appropriate the power of her chastity in the service of the patriarchal church and state. In ecclesiastical terms, his wish to marry Isabella represents the Church's need to subjugate women's religious orders. The power of virginity could not be allowed to exist independently of male control. Mary, the model of all good women, must be subservient to her male superiors, enclosed in the cloister where sisters could not exercise authority or undertake work supposedly unsuitable for women. Isabella, who moves about the city, figures the threat posed by Mary Ward, who struggled to free women's religious communities from male control and to bring them into the public domain.[41] In England, recusant households provided numerous models of female independence, as it was the women who were generally responsible for maintaining Catholicism in the absence of structures of clerical authority.[42] Spectators who were striving to carve out a religious identity for themselves in opposition to dominant patriarchal influences, whether Roman Catholic or not, would have readily understood Isabella's position at the end of the play.

The Duke's proposal to Isabella has as much to do with secular politics as religious ones. In spite of his diffidence about public display, he is fascinated by the power of government, and by going underground he increases that power rather than decreasing it. Richard Wilson has argued that *Measure for Measure* engages directly with contemporary ideas about the polity because it measures the power of the state by the birth rate of its population. The Duke, who sees the importance of producing new subjects (those who willingly subject themselves to Vienna's laws), is therefore a 'modern' ruler, an 'enlightened despot who breaks the stocks to discharge offenders into fertile procreation'.[43] While the Duke's attitude may meet with approval from Lucio, Claudio and Juliet, he hardly seems to be very 'enlightened' as far as Isabella is concerned. He does not command her to marry him; in fact for his plan to work, she must incline to his offer with 'a willing ear' and choose to transpose her chastity from the convent to the family. The proposals come amidst other orders and thanks, making it easy to see how he puts gentle pressure on Isabella to subject herself to him apparently of her own volition. By even asking the question in public, the Duke blatantly ignores everything she has been striving for.

Does marriage to the Duke represent justice for Isabella? As a potential sister of St Clare, and of Mary Ward, her concept of justice is probably very different from his. Mary Ward discussed it in these terms:

> The word Justice, and those in former times that were called just persons, works of justice, done in innocence, and that we be such as we appear, and appear such as we are: these things often since occurred to my mind with liking for them. (p. 40)

Self-integrity, 'that we be such as we appear', is central to Mary Ward's idea of justice. It is also the basis of the Duke's project to find out 'what our seemers be', to split the appearance of virtue from virtue itself, and it works with devastating effect on Angelo. If the Duke were judged by the same doctrine, according to his own prescription of 'Measure still for Measure', his behaviour would not stand up to scrutiny. Throughout the play he has deceived Isabella by pretending to be the Holy Friar, and by assuming the role of divine justice, a figure who can resurrect the dead. Is Isabella likely to respect or accept such a man?

Isabella never replies to either of the Duke's two proposals. She remains silent and that silence can be read as an act of resistance rather than consent. Barbara Baines reminds us that Isabella's response implicitly allies her with the sisters of St Clare because she follows their rules, showing her face but holding her tongue, 'perhaps with the key to the convent still in her pocket'.[44] Isabella is not likely to cooperate with the Duke's plan for a self-subjecting population because for her, as for other women, subjection took a very specific, immediate form. To go back to Calvin: 'There is no other shift but women must needs stoop and understand the ruin and confusion of mankind came in on their side . . . there is none other way but for them to stoop and to bear patiently the subjection God laid upon them.' Isabella knows that there is another way. This is what makes her so threatening, what makes the Duke so anxious to recontain her in the patriarchal family rather than releasing her to the sisterhood. Isabella's choice of the convent over the Duke would constitute a refusal to submit to male government, just as Mary Ward turned down four proposals of marriage to pursue her vocation and resisted attempts to suppress her Order and bring it under male control.[45] The convent was a dangerous other, a community where an all-female paradise, like that celebrated by Aemelia Lanyer, could exist independently of men. Mary Ward's Institute of Mary, with its emphasis on equality, learning, self-knowledge and a public life outside the cloister, gives a glimpse into such an environment:

> Women may be perfect as well as men, if they love verity and seek true knowledge. I mean not learning, though learning is a great help and how much I esteem it may hereafter be seen.... You are spectacles to God, angels and men ... all look upon you as new beginners of a course never thought of before, marvelling at what you intend, and what will be the end of you. (p. 58)

This is the temptation which faces Isabella at the end of *Measure for Measure*: the chance to escape from a world where the nexus of power/knowledge relations is centred round men. The ways in which that world constricted and sacrificed women is demonstrated in *'Tis Pity She's A Whore*, the dangers of trying to escape from it and pursue forbidden knowledge are played out in *Doctor Faustus*. At the end of *Measure for Measure*, however, Shakespeare shows that 'heavenly matters of theology' might have represented one way in which women could exercise some limited form of self-determination.

Notes

1 Kate Aughterson (ed.), *Renaissance Woman: Constructions of Femininity in England, A Sourcebook* (Routledge, London and New York, 1995), p. 171.
2 Anne Wheathill, *A handfull of holesome (though homelie) hearbs* (1584), in Betty Travitsky (ed.), *The Paradise of Women: Writings by Englishwomen of the Renaissance*, Morningside edition (Columbia University Press, New York, 1989), p. 146.
3 St Augustine, *The City of God*, quoted in Marina Warner, *Alone of All Her Sex: The Myth and Cult of the Virgin Mary* (Alfred Knopf, New York, 1976), p. 54.
4 See Linda Woodbridge, *Literature and the Nature of Womankind 1540–1620* (Harvester, Brighton, 1984), pp. 11–136.
5 John Calvin, *The Sermons of M. John Calvin upon the Epistle of S. Paul to the Ephesians*, trans. Arthur Golding (London, 1577), in Aughterson (ed.), *Renaissance Woman*, p. 17.
6 Ester Sowernam (pseud.), *Ester hath hang'd Haman: or An anser to a lewd Pamphlet entituled The Arraignment of Women* (London, 1617), in Simon Shepherd (ed.), *The Women's Sharp Revenge* (Fourth Estate, London, 1985), p. 89.

7 Aemelia Lanyer, *Salve Deus Rex Judaeorum* [Hail Christ, King of the Jews] (London, 1611), in Diane Purkiss (ed.), *Renaissance Women: The Plays of Elizabeth Cary and the Poems of Aemelia Lanyer*, Pickering Women's Classics (Pickering and Chatto, London, 1994), p. 295, l. 801. All subsequent line references to the poem are to this edition.

8 Christopher Marlowe, *Doctor Faustus: A and B Texts (1604, 1616)*, ed. David Bevington and Eric Ramussen, Revels Plays (Manchester University Press, Manchester, 1993). All quotations are taken from the B text.

9 *The English Faust Book: A Critical Edition Based on the Text of 1592*, ed. John Henry Jones (Cambridge University Press, Cambridge, 1994), p. 112.

10 Kay Stockholder, '"Within the massy entrailes of the earth": Faustus's Relation to Women', in Kenneth Friedenreich, Roma Gill and Constance B. Kuriyama (eds), *A Poet and a Filthy Playmaker* (AMS Press, New York, 1988), pp. 203–20.

11 W. W. Greg, 'The Damnation of Faustus', in John Jump (ed.), *Marlowe, Doctor Faustus: A Casebook* (Basingstoke, Macmillan, 1969), pp. 71–88; pp. 86–7.

12 Anne Laurence, *Women in England 1500–1760: A Social History* (Weidenfeld and Nicolson, London, 1994), p. 174.

13 Aughterson (ed.), *Renaissance Woman*, pp. 170–1.

14 *The Letters of Lady Arbella Stuart*, ed. Sara Jayne Steen (Oxford University Press, New York, 1994), p. 292.

15 On the cuckoldry jokes, see Stockholder, '"Within the massy entrailes of the earth"', pp. 210–11.

16 Aughterson (ed.), *Renaissance Woman*, p.169. See also Valerie Wayne, 'Some Sad Sentence: Vives' *Instruction of a Christian Woman*', in Margaret p. Hannay (ed.), *Silent But for the Word: Tudor Women as Patrons, Translators and Writers of Religious Works* (Kent State University Press, Kent, 1985), pp. 15–29.

17 Shepherd (ed.), *The Women's Sharp Revenge*, p. 137.

18 William Gouge, *Of Domesticall Duties* (London, 1622), The English Experience (Walter Johnson Inc., Theatrum Orbis Terrarum, Amsterdam, 1976), pp. 319 and 277.

19 Aughterson (ed.), *Renaissance Woman*, p. 81.

20 Quoted in John S. Mebane's lively discussion of the play in *Renaissance Magic and the Return of the Golden Age* (University of Nebraska Press, Lincoln, NB, and London, 1992), p. 123.

21 Ibid., pp. 113–14.

22 Lyn M. Bechtel, 'Rethinking the Interpretation of Genesis 2.4b–3.24', in Athalya Brenner (ed.), *A Feminist Companion to Genesis* (Sheffield Academic Press, Sheffield, 1993), pp. 77–118; p. 103.

23 Rachel Speght, *Moralities Memorandum, with a Dreame Prefixed* (1621), in Germaine Greer, Jeslyn Medoff, Melinda Sansone and Susan Hastings (eds), *Kissing the Rod: An Anthology of Seventeenth-century Women's Verse* (Virago, London, 1988), pp. 68–78; p. 71.

24 'To The Queen's Most Excellent Majesty', in Purkiss (ed.), *Renaissance Women*, p. 243.

25 Nicholas Brooke, 'The Moral Tragedy of Doctor Faustus' (1952), in Jump (ed.), *Marlowe, Doctor Faustus: A Casebook*, pp. 101–33; pp. 118–19.

26 John Ford, *'Tis Pity She's A Whore*, ed. Brian Morris, New Mermaids (A & C Black, London, 1968).

27 Elizabeth Melvill, *A Godlie Dreame compiled by Elizabeth Melvill, Ladie Culros the younger at the request of a Friend* (Edinburgh, Andro Hart, 1620), 2A1v. Extracts from the 1603 Scottish version are reprinted in Greer et al. (eds), *Kissing the Rod*, pp. 34–8, and extracts from the 1606 anglicized one can be found in Travitsky (ed.), *The Paradise of Women*, pp. 25–8.

28 Warner, *Alone of All Her Sex*, pp. 73–4.

29 Daryll Gless, *Measure for Measure, the Law and the Convent* (Princeton University Press, Princeton, 1979), pp. 262–4 informs us that a manuscript containing details of the 'Isabella Rule', the constitution of this order, passed into the library of Charles Howard (patron of the Admiral's Company), so it may have been known to Shakespeare and prompted the name of his heroine.

30 See Laurence, *Women in England 1500–1760*, pp. 181–92 and Marie B. Rowlands, 'Recusant Women 1560–1640', in Mary Prior (ed.), *Women in English Society 1500–1800* (Methuen, London and New York, 1985), pp. 149–80.

31 Rowlands, 'Recusant Women', pp. 169–70; Henriette Peters, *Mary Ward: A World in Contemplation*, trans. Helen Butterworth (Gracewing, Leominster, 1994).

32 Gless, *Measure for Measure, the Law and the Convent*, p. 104.

33 See E. A. J. Honigmann, *Shakespeare: The 'Lost Years'* (Manchester University Press, Manchester, 1985).

34 Mary Ward, *Till God Will: Mary Ward Through Her Writings*, ed. M. Emmanuel Orchard (Darton Longman and Todd, London, 1985), pp. 9, 23. All subsequent quotations from Ward's writings are from this edition.

35 Danielle Clarke, 'The Iconography of the Blush: Marian Literature of the 1630s', in *Voicing Women: Gender and Sexuality in Early Modern Writing*, Renaissance Texts and Studies (Keele University Press, Keele, 1996), pp. 111–28.

36 I. Sweetnam, *The Paradise of Delights Or the B. Virgins Garden of Loreto* (London, 1620), quoted in Clarke, 'The Iconography of the Blush', pp. 119–20.

37 Ward, *Till God Will*, p. xi. A report of Margaret Clitherow's martyrdom was circulated amongst Catholic families in Yorkshire like that of Mary Ward. See Rowlands, 'Recusant Women', pp. 158–9.

38 See Warner, *Alone of All Her Sex*, pp. 70–1.

39 Barbara Baines, 'Assaying the Power of Chastity in *Measure for Measure*', *Studies in English Literature* 30 (1991), 283–301; p. 284.

40 Mary Daly, *The Church and the Second Sex* (Beacon Press, Boston, 1985), p.161.

41 Ibid., pp. 102–3.

42 Rowlands, 'Recusant Women', pp. 160–2.

43 Richard Wilson, 'Prince of Darkness: Foucault's Shakespeare', in Nigel Wood

(ed.), *Measure for Measure: Theory in Practice* (Buckingham, Philadelphia, Open University Press, 1996), pp. 133–78; p. 161.
44 Baines, 'Assaying the Power of Chastity,' p. 299.
45 See Peters, *Mary Ward*, pp. 41–4.

CHAPTER 2

Revenge Tragedy

Revenge tragedy is a carnival escape from everyday norms: gaudily spectacular, repulsive and yet fascinating. The audience who paid to see Kyd's *The Spanish Tragedy* (1587), Shakespeare's *Titus Andronicus* (1591), or *The Revenger's Tragedy* (1606) were admitted to a hall of mirrors in which appearances, gender identities and forms of behaviour could be grotesquely distorted. Religious truths or conventional values could be bent, even inverted. Revenge often launches characters and spectators onto a roller-coaster of fanatic action where daring and fear as well as nauseous pleasure grip the participants. As Muriel Bradbrook noted, revenge tragedy 'allowed the projection of deep fears, the exorcism of guilt which the actors and audience shared'.[1] For Bradbrook, such anxieties were caused by religious condemnations of performing and playgoing. As I shall argue, revenge tragedies also tap into fundamental fears about women, relating to maternal power and to female agency.

I

Revenge tragedy is a feminine genre in spite of the fact that the revenge protagonists are usually male and female characters appear to play more passive roles. Perhaps the most striking example of female passivity is Gloriana's skull in *The Revenger's Tragedy*, probably by Middleton. At the opening of the play, she is reduced to an object of desire: the Duke's desire in the past and now Vindice's desire for revenge:

> Thou sallow picture of my poisoned love,
> My study's ornament, thou shell of Death,
> Once the bright face of my betrothed lady, ...

> ... then 'twas a face
> So far beyond the artificial shine
> Of any woman's bought complexion
> That the uprightest man – if such there be,
> That sin but seven times a day – broke custom
> And made up eight with looking after her.
>   (1.1.14)[2]

The living Gloriana and the dead skull are both objects of the male gaze. They provoke a burning lust for satisfaction in sexual terms or in the form of retribution. The other women are treated as objects too. Antonio's wife appears only as a dead body; her act of suicide, prompted by the rape, is self-destructive in more than the immediate sense, since it redefines her as Antonio's possession, a 'fair comely building' (1.4.2). Castiza describes herself using similar imagery: 'A virgin honour is a crystal tower' (4.4.152), and Vindice's behaviour towards his mother and sister tests his ownership of her sexuality. Prostitution, which would allow them to make money for themselves, would deprive him of his right as head of the family to arrange a match for Castiza and use her in property negotiations. In the opening scene of *The Revenger's Tragedy*, Gloriana's skull seems to typify women's roles as objects rather than actors in that drama.

However, revenge itself is a feminine impulse which lurks within the empty skull. Vindice appeals to a female 'Vengeance' to 'keep thy day, hour, minute, I beseech, / For those thou hast determined' (1.1.39–42). He is confident that she will pay back Gloriana's murder by stripping the courtiers' flesh until they too look like the 'shell of Death' (1.1.44–9). The levelling spirit of revenge quickens Gloriana's skull to 'bear a part / E'en in its own revenge' (3.5.100). In Vindice's artful plot it is attired and perfumed to seduce and poison the Duke, just as he abused Gloriana. Vindice's grim humour with the 'bony lady' in Act 3, Scene 5 has an edge of nervousness caused by the disturbing feminine power she represents. As Katherine Rowe has argued with reference to *Titus Andronicus*, the female victim or object can acquire a mysterious sense of agency as an icon advocating revenge. Gloriana's skull, like Lavinia's dismembered body, is animated so as to 'blur the boundaries between instrument and principal, actor and prop in disturbing yet compelling ways'.[3] In *The Revenger's Tragedy*, Gloriana's participation in the quest for retribution is echoed by the Duchess, who vows 'my vengeance shall reach high' (1.2.174) and cuckolds the Duke for failing to release her son. Even Castiza takes a form of revenge on her mother by accepting the role of whore and preparing to give herself to Lussurioso. All these revenges remind us that female sexuality is much less easy to control than the men in the play would wish.

The spectre of Gloriana stands for the possibility of female agency, always ready to be awoken by the call to revenge.

The power of vengeance to deconstruct male authority, independence, even identity is embedded in fears of maternal origin. Even in plays where the revenger and his inspiration for revenge are male, they appeal back to a female origin. In Marston's *Antonio's Revenge* (1600), the ghost calls on the goddess of revenge:

> . . . stern Vindicta towereth up aloft
> That she may fall with a more weighty peise
> And crush life's sap from out Piero's brains.
>
> (5.1.4)[4]

The feminization of revenge stems immediately from the feminine Latin noun 'Vindicta', but links back to figures from an older classical tradition: the Furies, the figure of Nemesis, and ultimately the life-giving and consuming earth. The primitive avenging spirits of the Furies (or Erinyes) are part of an ancient and yet natural impulse of revenge. Their powerful influence is shown in Norton and Sackville's play *Gorboduc* (1562), where the King points out that 'nature's force doth move us to revenge' in a pattern of equal reprisal where 'Blood asketh blood, and death must death requite'.[5] The Furies inspire Queen Videna to avenge the death of her son by killing his brother. The stage directions for the dumbshow at the start of Act 4 describe

> *three furies, Alecto, Megaera, and Tisiphone, clad in black garments sprinkled with blood and flames, their bodies girt with snakes, their heads spread with serpents instead of hair, the one bearing in her hand a snake, the other a whip, and the third a burning firebrand: each driving before them a king and a queen; which, moved by the furies, unnaturally had slain their own children. The names of the kings and queens were these, Tantalus, Medea, Athamas, Ino, Cambyses, Althea.*

These grisly 'daughters of the night' (4.2.358) and mothers of revenge have the power to overwhelm both men and women with an implacable desire for violent retribution which leads ultimately to chaos. In *Gorboduc* the Queen's murder of her son is quickly followed by impetuous rebellion on the part of the subjects. In *The Triumphs of Gods Revenge* (1635) by John Reynolds, the female villains are condemned as reincarnations of these monstrous female spirits, in descriptions such as 'like a Fury of hell' or 'like a counterfeit Fury'.[6] The consuming power of vengeance, which can turn mothers such as Medea to kill their own children, is linked ultimately to the cycle of mortality and the mother-earth as both a womb and a grave. Nemesis personifies the connection between revenge and mortality. In emblem books by Hunger (1542) and Alciatus (1621) she is depicted clothed in black and carrying a bit or bridle, with the verbal caution that we should restrain our anger since she 'follows our footsteps' and that 'soon there comes certain revenge and every misdeed expiates itself'.[7] Francis Bacon's *Wisdom of the Ancients* (1609/19) remarked that Nemesis 'signifies revenge or retribution' and terrifies everyone 'with a black and dismal sight', since 'mortals on the highest pinnacle of felicity have a prospect of death, diseases, calamities' which will destroy them.[8] Nemesis is the watchful mother who will ultimately destroy her own children.

Every act of personal vengeance, then, is shadowed by the presence of these ancient maternal spirits. In *The Spanish Tragedy*, the figures of Andrea and a male personification of Revenge oversee the actions of Hieronimo, but the mother behind all these is Proserpine. Andrea tells how she listened to his story:

> And begged that only she might give my doom.
> Pluto was pleased, and sealed it with a kiss.
> Forthwith, Revenge, she rounded thee in th' ear,
> And bade thee lead me through the gates of horn,
> Where dreams have passage in the silent night.
> No sooner had she spake but we were here ...
>
> (1.1.79)[9]

Hieronimo appropriates the biblical tag 'Vindicta mihi' (Revenge is mine) as an act of masculine self-assertion, yet it will be Bel-imperia who kills Don Balthazar. Behind Hieronimo's bluster and artistry, Proserpine remains a silent, unseen presence determining the pattern of vengeance. In another significant reminder of this dark feminine world, we are told that Nemesis has struck down Andrea in battle, as though angry at his male presumption (1.4.16–22).

It is not surprising that revenge is feminized since it is diametrically opposed to the paternal Word, the Law of the Father. The New Testament teaching 'Vengeance is mine, I will repay, saith the Lord' (Romans 12.19) was widely accepted as a divine proscription against individual forms of retribution. In a poem addressed to her sisters, for example, Isabella Whitney cautions them

> Refer you all to him that sits above the skies:
> Vengeance is his, he will revenge; you need it not devise.[10]

Revenge tragedies invariably stage a conflict between this orthodox Christian standpoint and a code of personal reprisal which draws on the Old Testament dictate 'life for life, eye for eye, tooth for tooth' (Exodus

21.23–4) and the ancient tradition. Differences between the two ideologies are implicitly or explicitly gendered. To reject or appropriate God's prerogative on vengeance is to rebel against patriarchal authority and ally oneself with the more disturbing primitive maternal world of the Furies and some infamous female revengers: Juno, Medea, Leto and Artemis, Procne and Philomel, Hecuba, Althea. These chilling examples of ruthless, even unnatural behaviour would have been familiar to many Renaissance playgoers from Golding's translation of Ovid's *Metamorphoses* (1567), English translations of Seneca's tragedies (1581) and from emblem books. For example, in Ovid's *Metamorphoses*, Althea, whose son has murdered her brothers, is torn between the passionate desire for revenge and her maternal feelings. By appealing to the Furies she gains the strength to turn against her son:

> She said: ye triple Goddesses of wreake, you Helhounds three,
> Beholde ye all this furious fact and sacrifice of mee.
> I wreake, and do agaynst all right: with death must death be payde:
> On mischiefe mischiefe must be heapt: on corse must corse be laide.[11]

Equally unnatural behaviour is shown by the protagonist in John Studley's translation of Seneca's *Medea*. Deserted by Jason, Medea overturns patriarchal order and normative gender roles by killing her children on the temple altar:

> Then at the Aulters of the Gods my chyldren shalbe slayne,
> With crimson colourde bloud of Babes the Aulters will I stayne,
> Through Lyvers, Lungs, the Lights and Heart, through every gut and gal
> For vengeance breake away perforce, and spare no bloude at all.[12]

Medea was the epitome of fanatic female vengeance, associated with pagan magic and wilfulness. William Painter's *The Palace of Pleasure* (1567) cites her as an example of destructive female self-possession: 'the eagles flight is not so high, as the foolyshe desires, and conceiptes of a woman that trusteth her own opinion, and treateth out of the track of duety, and way of wisedome'.[13]

The opposition between paternal biblical law and crazy maternal revenge was clearly outlined in Reynolds's *Triumphs of Gods Revenge*, where the mental processes of Lauretia, a young woman bent on killing her lover's murderer, are explicitly condemned as irrational and demonic:

> So as consulting with Choller, not with Reason, with Nature not with Grace, with Satan, not with God, she vowes to be sharply revenged of him . . . yea, the fumes and fury of her revenge are so implacable, yet transport her resolutions to

53

so bloudy an impetuositie, that resembling her sexe and selfe, she inhumanely and sacreligiously darts forth an oath, which her heart sends to her soule, and her soule from Earth to Hell, that if the meanes finde not her, she will find the meanes to quench and dry up her teares for Poligny's death, in the blood of Belville.[14]

By turning to 'Nature', the instinctive, primitive desire to pay back like for like, Lauretia cuts herself off from 'Reason' and 'God', in the 'fumes and fury' of a revenge which is, according to Reynolds, characteristic of 'her sexe and selfe'.

Revenge transformed the figure of Justice, the silent female form who held her sword aloft in the service of patriarchal law, into a frightening independent force. In Renaissance England physically violent punishments were instrumental in legitimating the State, but appropriation of violence by an individual turned it into excess, an excess that defined the law as normative. Revenge is the law's necessary 'supplement' (in Derrida's sense), which guarantees it and simultaneously always threatens to usurp it, to return it to the rule of primordial feminine law.[15] As Bosola tells the Cardinal in *The Duchess of Malfi* (1614):

> when thou kill'd'st thy sister,
> Thou took'st from Justice her most equal balance,
> And left her naught but her sword.
>
> (5.5.38)[16]

Once she stepped off the pedestal in search of what Francis Bacon called 'a kind of wild justice' the armed warrior woman became the embodiment of unruly energies.[17] The sword was no longer a passive symbol of paternal control but a weapon. As Marina Warner notes, the woman who 'tramples, beheads, pierces and otherwise despatches trespassers has lost her innocence. As a figure of virtue she has become saturated with perversity and contradiction'.[18]

In Renaissance England, the opposition between the divine Law of the Father and a feminized personal vengeance was a material reality since women were largely excluded from the legal system. A 1591 emblem noted that a justice was 'the minister of God to revenge in wrath to him that doth evil',[19] but since all lawyers, magistrates, judges, clerks and jurors were male, women had little opportunity of enforcing or applying the law.[20] The legal handbook *The Law's resolution of women's rights* (1632) pointed out 'women have no voice in parliament. They make no laws, consent to none, they abrogate none . . . . The common law here shaketh hand with divinity'.[21] Most women did not have easy access to civil justice as the instrument of divine retribution.

The attraction of private revenge for women is therefore unsurprising. As Jonathan Dollimore notes, revenge can be seen as 'a strategy of survival resorted to by the alienated and dispossessed' which constitutes a rejection of the 'providential scheme which divine vengeance conventionally pre-supposed'.[22] The pamphlet writer Jane Anger openly acknowledges this in her counter-attack to a misogynist tract. She fears 'judgement before trial' for publishing her outspoken opinions, and in the absence of legal justice for the wrongs women have suffered at the hands of men, she recommends a policy of personal reprisal, asking her female readers 'Will the gods permit it, the goddesses stay their punishing judgements, and we ourselves not pursue their undoinge for such devilish practices?' In her comments on male lust, she vows 'Deceitful men with guile must be repaid / And blows for blows who renders not again?'[23] Emilia in Shakespeare's *Othello* puts forward the same argument: 'Why, we have galls; and though we have some grace, / Yet have we some revenge' (5.1.90). Jane Anger's call for revenge speaks directly to the desires of women for self-vindication. Revenge offers an illusion of agency, the power to direct events from a position of apparent impotence. Indeed, Harry Keyishian has argued that in revenge drama it is often presented in positive terms as 'a redemptive declaration of selfhood' with which audiences readily sympathize. Revenge allows characters to 'restore their integrity – their sense of psychic wholeness'.[24] The opportun-ities it offers for rebuilding a damaged self make it very attractive to female characters.

In *The Witch of Edmonton* (1621), for example, Elizabeth Sawyer gives expression to its energizing force, which can transform her from a wretched old woman who has been 'reviled, kicked, beaten' (4.1.77) into a com-manding figure.[25] The play overtly condemns Elizabeth's wish for 'Vengeance, shame, ruin' (2.1.120) since it invokes the Dog, an agent of evil, as her familiar. Nevertheless, Elizabeth is presented more as a victim than a criminal; she effectively turns the accusation of witchcraft back onto those who have injured her, men who 'are within far more crooked than I am, and if I be a witch, more witch-like' (4.1.88). When she exclaims 'A witch! Who is not?' (4.1.103) she gives voice to a communal desire to challenge and avenge the abuses inflicted by male oppressors. As a sympathetic figure whose relationship with the Dog is warmly affectionate, Elizabeth's dedication to revenge still exerts appeal for disenfranchised spectators:

> Revenge to me is sweeter far than life;
> Thou art my raven on whose coal-black wings
> Revenge comes flying to me. O my best love!
> I am on fire, even in the midst of ice,

Raking up my blood till my shrunk knees feel
Thy curled head leaning on them.

(5.1.7)

Francis Bacon noted that 'vindictive persons live the life of witches, who, as
they are mischievous, so end they unfortunate'. By problematizing the
category of 'witch', however, *The Witch of Edmonton* opens a space for
revenge as 'a kind of wild justice' which 'putteth the law out of office'.[26]
Elizabeth's searing critique of male behaviour in the trial scene serves to
remind spectators of the cruelty of Old Banks, the murderous desires of
Frank Thorney and Sir Arthur Clarington's abuse of Winnifrede. She
makes the system of justice that condemns her look corrupt. In such
exceptional cases, revenge could be a viable alternative. As William Perkins
noted in 1606, 'when violence is offered, and the Magistrate absent' or 'no
helpe can be had of him', then 'God puts the sword into the private mans
hands'.[27]

In plays like *The Spanish Tragedy*, *Titus Andronicus* or *The Revenger's
Tragedy*, the protagonists are alienated from regimes whose courts are
corrupt. The revenges these figures enact are destructive since they culmi-
nate in multiple murders, but they simultaneously and paradoxically
constitute a creative response to situations of dispossession. Vindice and
Hieronimo manipulate revenge as an art form, skilfully adopting subservient roles to construct performances that give them the illusion of
control. For female spectators, normally excluded by, and from, the
dominant discourses of Renaissance society, the outlawed agency of the
revenger must have looked exciting. While few women would have dared
to publish a public defence of revenge, some did hint at its dangerous
attraction. In her 'Essay on Adversity' (1580), Mary Queen of Scots noted
'we must endeavor, through all these afflictions, to guard against the sin of
impatience'. She criticizes those who take revenge but ends by acknowledging that she has shared their sins:

> They thrust the law of God on one side, not only to vaunt their own praises but
> to cast away their whole existence for so small a matter as a chance word which
> is but wind, and which, perhaps, he who pronounced it would willingly retract.
> And since this human law is so directly contrary to that of Jesus, alas! how we
> shall have to answer it one day . . . having had, moreover, such strict charge on
> the subject from the great celestial shepherd. God knows that I, for my part,
> have been a great sinner in this respect.[28]

The possibility that stories of revenge could tap into female fantasies of
paying back like for like was recognized by John Reynolds. He anxiously
reminded readers that his examples of avenging women were offered 'not to

your imitation' but 'to the reformation of our lives' and 'to the eternall glory of the most Sacred and Individuall Trinity'.[29] Reynolds's repeated use of theatrical metaphors in *The Triumphs of Gods Revenge* points to an even deeper anxiety about the dramatization of revenge on stage. He remarks: 'I see the Stage whereon these Tragedies are acted and represented, not only sprinkled, but goared with greater variety and effusion of blood.' Since the stories he collected provided source material for at least two revenge tragedies, the comment is all the more resonant. Reynolds tells that, for one of his subjects, love and revenge conspired to 'act two different Scenes upon the Theater of her heart'.[30] Female spectators of revenge tragedy could see their hearts' clandestine desires for vindication played out in the public arena of the theatre.

Kyd's play *The Spanish Tragedy* dramatizes the gendered shift from masculine justice to feminine revenge through the actions of Hieronimo and Bel-imperia. As Knight Marshall, Hieronimo is an instrument of law with access to legal retribution, but the judicial system in the play is deeply suspect. In Portugal, the Viceroy is ready to burn the innocent Alexandro at the stake until news that Balthazar is still alive arrives at the last minute (3.1). This may provide evidence of divine intervention but hardly restores faith in God's deputy on earth. The parallel scene in Spain, where no letter arrives to prevent Pedringano's execution, again shows an uneven kind of justice in action. Pedringano is an unscrupulous murderer, yet after rightly condemning him, Hieronimo discovers that the real villains remain untouched. His decision to 'cry aloud for justice through the court' (3.7.70) will be futile. The ears of the King and his brother remain deaf since their belief in the essential superiority of aristocratic birth makes them privilege the criminals, Lorenzo and Balthazar, above the voice of their socially inferior accuser.

Hieronimo identifies himself with the common people, yet the very sensitivity that makes him a 'gentle' man in the moral sense of the word alienates him from the barbarous values of the ruling order, where wealth and 'violence prevails' (2.1.108). Hieronimo realizes that Horatio's murder will not be answered in the Spanish court, and dedicates himself instead to Proserpine, patroness of a revenge in which he will be a major actor: 'Then will I rent and tear them thus and thus, / Shivering their limbs in pieces with my teeth' (3.13.122). Through artful, feminine performance he will dissemble 'quiet in unquietness' (3.13.30), submitting to the commands of his enemies "Till to revenge thou know when, where and how' (3.13.44).

Bel-imperia is instrumental in transforming Hieronimo into an active revenger. From the beginning of the play, she is committed to taking personal reprisal for Andrea's murder. Her strength of will directs all her emotions towards this goal. She recognizes the limits of her political power because of her sex, but intelligently foresees that she will be matched with Balthazar in a political marriage and uses her position to further her own plans:

> ... how can love find harbour in my breast,
> Till I revenge the death of my beloved?
> Yes, second love shall further my revenge.
> I'll love Horatio, my Andrea's friend,
> The more to spite the prince that wrought his end.
>
> (1.4.64)

Bel-imperia's courtship of a social inferior, Horatio, is deliberately transgressive. She probably stage-manages dropping her glove for him in front of Balthazar, whose tedious wooing she has already mocked, as though to turn her knife in the Prince's wounded pride and annoy her brother (1.4.100). Romance itself can be a form of revenge, as Modleski has noted. Part of the appeal of romantic fiction is the element of 'revenge fantasy ... our conviction that the woman is bringing the man to his knees and that all the while he is being so difficult, he is internally grovelling, grovelling, grovelling'.[31] For Renaissance spectators, Bel-imperia's calculated behaviour constitutes a double revenge on Balthazar and on patriarchal kinship structures in which women are treated as objects of exchange.

The King orders his brother to 'win fair Bel-imperia from her will' (2.3.6), but she remains wilful in her choice of lover. Her feelings for Horatio are not necessarily insincere, but revenge is, consciously or unconsciously, still in her thoughts when she appoints their meeting in the orchard. She imagines the nightingale 'singing with the prickle at her breast' to express their 'delight' (2.3.50). Her allusion recalls the fate of Philomel, who was transformed into a nightingale once she had avenged her rape by Tereus. The mixture of pleasure and pain experienced by the nightingale, who sings pierced by a thorn, suggests Bel-imperia will take a destructive 'delight' in meeting with Horatio. Her plot strikes with deadly accuracy and inaugurates another revenge, the murder of Horatio by Prince Balthazar and Lorenzo. Bel-imperia thus sets off the roller-coaster which will bring together victims and revengers in the final catastrophe.

Once Horatio is dead Bel-imperia cannot use romance as a form of retaliation. Imprisoned by Lorenzo in her father's house, all she can do is to write a letter with her blood to Hieronimo. She has been confined to a role like Andrea's, urging others to act on her behalf. Her physical passivity does not alter her goal. She acknowledges 'I must constrain myself' and 'apply me to the time' (3.9.12), but this patience does not extend to a stoic or Christian acceptance of the situation. She hopes that heaven 'shall set me free' (3.9.14) to pursue her quest, and rushes to Hieronimo with the passion of a Fury (4.1) once she is released. The meeting between Bel-imperia and Hieronimo is a critical turning point. Her vow to murder the villains herself if he will not forces him to translate resolution into action. Her uncompromising energy allows him to believe that even the saints are now soliciting vengeance. The two are bound in a fatal compact that will lead to the destruction of all the protagonists, once she swears to 'Join with thee to revenge Horatio's death' (4.1.48).

Tragically isolated from this conspiracy, and yet still passionately dedicated to revenge, is Isabella. Her mad attack on the arbour where her son was hung makes a striking parallel to Bel-imperia's actions (4.2). In this pathetic, nearly ludicrous scene, the audience are forced to confront the dangers of a culture that excludes women from discourses of knowledge and power. Since she cannot touch the homicides and has no access to justice via the court, Isabella can only attack the place itself and then herself. While her madness is pitiful, her fury is also alarming, warning spectators of an implacable feminine passion, all the more dangerous since there is no immediate outlet for it. The same energy bubbles through Bel-imperia's veins.

Bel-imperia is more than a catalyst to Hieronimo's punitive vendetta. As the personification of feminine vengeance she is instrumental to it. He jokingly tells Lorenzo 'what's a play without a woman in it?' (4.1.97), to which she replies, with no little sarcasm, 'Little entreaty shall serve *me* Hieronimo, / For I must needs be employed in your play' (4.1.97–9) [emphasis mine]. She reminds Hieronimo how much she has had to persuade him to take revenge, and how willing she is to enact it herself. 'Soliman and Perseda' is a fine example of what Kate Saunders defines as feminine revenge: 'an art form; fine, delicate precision engineering, largely beyond male capabilities'.[32] It might have been written for Bel-imperia, since its scenes replay her courtship with Balthazar and she is able to exact payment for the murders of both her lovers. Her lines give concise expression to the subversive undercurrent threatening to erupt through the surface of feminine submission:

Yet by thy power thou thinkest to command,
And to thy power Perseda doth obey:
But were she able, thus she would revenge
Thy treacheries on thee, ignoble prince: Stab him
And on herself, she would be thus revenged.   Stab herself
                                                                                     (4.4.64)

Bel-imperia's use of the conditional 'were she able' works alongside the

metatheatrical effects to define female revenge as a fantasy. She simultaneously enacts the hidden passions of female spectators and contains them
within a fictional framework: the tragedy of 'Soliman and Perseda' and,
beyond that, *The Spanish Tragedy*. What Hieronimo's epilogue chillingly
reminds the audiences on and off stage, though, is that the boundary
between fiction and reality is easily crossed. Whether the story is 'fab-
ulously counterfeit' (4.4.77), performed by actors, or acted out for real
depends upon one's perspective. While the Spanish court see Bel-imperia
stab Balthazar, in the theatre, a boy actor counterfeits what a woman would
do 'were she able'. The actors will 'Revive to please to-morrow's audience'
(4.4.82), while multiple levels of playing and being expose the possibility
of female revenge straying from the theatre into the 'real' world beyond its
doors, just as John Reynolds had feared.

II

While vengeance could promote female agency and insubordination, its
associations with maternal origins gave it an equally disturbing power over
men. Sir Thomas Browne declared that 'since Women do most delight in
Revenge, it may seem but feminine manhood to be vindictive'.[33] The view
that revenge had an emasculating effect went back to Juvenal's thirteenth
Satire: 'vengeance is always the delight of a little, weak, and petty mind; of
which you may straightway draw proof from this – that no one so rejoices
in vengeance as a woman'.[34] For men, a danger of taking personal revenge
was that, rather than being a means of asserting independent subjectivity,
it could be a way of losing one's self. To set out on such a course was an
implicit acknowledgement of one's alienation from patriarchal institutions
and structures of power. As Elaine Scarry notes, a killer 'consents to
"unmake" himself, deconstruct himself, empty himself of civil content'.[35]
The revenger constituted himself as 'other'.

Once in this typically feminine position, he was in danger of losing
touch with the dominant discourses of 'reason' and being overtaken by a
passionate fixation on the injury suffered and the need to avenge it.
According to Thomas Wright, author of *The Passions of the Mind in Generall*
(1604), the imagination locked the subject into dependency on such
passion, to the exclusion of anything else. He defined this emotive realm in
maternal terms:

> The understanding looking into the imagination, findeth nothing almost but
> the mother & nurse of his passion for consideration, where you may well see how
> the imagination putteth greene spectacles before the eyes of our wit, to make it
> see nothing but greene, that is serving for the consideration of the Passion.[36]

Identifying the revenger's blinkered viewpoint with a state of child-like dependency draws attention to the obsessive nature of vengeance, which isolates the individual from the normal social structures governing behaviour. In psychoanalytic terms, the male revenger threatens to regress into a pre-socialized state, a retrospectively re-created identification with a mother figure who feeds his pleasures. He retreats from the Symbolic Order (the social network structured around the Law of the Father) to the illusion of plenitude and of being in absolute control. This imaginary collapse into the maternal womb creates a psychic space of primordial, pre-paternal urges: the instinct to pay back like for like. It is a return to Mother Nature. Scott Wilson observes that Mother Nature as a primordial, savage and nurturing force in plays like *King Lear* looks forward to the ideas of the philosopher Thomas Hobbes. In *Leviathan* (1651), Hobbes sets up an opposition between a paternal 'Civill Law' and 'the condition of meer Nature', where 'the Dominion is in the Mother'. Under the latter, the child 'is first in the power of the Mother . . . and is therefore obliged to obey her rather than any other; and by consequence the Dominion over it is hers'.[37] Trying to return to a maternal space of vengeful passion is inherently dangerous, in spite of the pleasures it holds.

First, revenge threatens to isolate the individual in an idioverse so detached from conventional structures of communication that he or she appears mad. Disidentification with the Symbolic Order confines the subject to a discourse of madness. Most revengers do not regress completely into infantile babble, but their extreme passions raise doubts about their mental states. Revenge and madness are closely associated in many of these tragedies. Hieronimo is described, with some justification, as 'Distract and in a manner lunatic' when he abandons his marshalship, digs his dagger in the earth and vows to avenge Horatio's death (*The Spanish Tragedy*, 3.13.89). After brooding over the skull of Gloriana for nine years, Vindice admits that the 'violence' of his 'joy' in revenge has carried him into a world of apprehension that not even his brother can share (*The Revenger's Tragedy*, 3.5.1–27). By Act 5, his addiction to this violent joy knows no bounds of reason, not even basic self-preservation. Dressing the Duke's corpse in his own disguise, Vindice jokes 'I must sit to be killed, and stand to kill myself' (5.1.5), then launches himself into the murderous masque with complete self-abandon. His proud, suicidal confession to Antonio, ''Twas we two murdered him' (5.3.98), culminates a process of self-destruction that seems an inevitable part of revenge.

As Ford points out in *The Broken Heart*, 'Revenge proves its own executioner' (4.1.139).[38] Paradoxically, the self-assertive action of personal revenge can also devour the individual. For male revengers, the illusion of agency is always shadowed by the danger of self-annihilation, a dissolution

61

of the masculine self into the feminine task. The ghosts of the Furies and of Procne, Philomel and Medea hover in the wings of Renaissance tragedies as silent mothers of the action whose presence can overwhelm the protagonist, dissolve his independent identity as a powerful member of the dominant sex. Revenge pushes male protagonists back towards a female point of origin, creating an illusion of omnipotence, yet at the same time destroying them by absorption. Their journey towards self-loss simultaneously generates pleasure, even erotic pleasure. Georges Bataille argues that since 'desire has loss and danger as its object', literature responds 'in the best possible way to the desire to lose ourselves in the vast movement where beings endlessly lose themselves'.[39] Revenge dramas play out, in nightmarish form, the dangers and pleasures of self-loss in the return to an all-powerful maternal body where horror and desire combine.[40]

A foundation for such tragedies of male self-dissolution is Seneca's *Thyestes*, where the Fury Megaera drives 'rage and fury' through Atreus's house until he is transformed from a powerful prince to a butcher of his nephews who prepares to 'dresse his brother's banquet' and cook the children. His role in the kitchen, supervising 'boyling licour', is a grotesque inversion of feminine domesticity and casts his brother as a monstrous earth-mother who consumes her own children's flesh.[41] English plays such as *Titus Andronicus*, *Antonio's Revenge* and *The Bloody Banquet* build on these prototypes, where gender differences between male revengers and their female equivalents are blurred by revenge action. Marston's *Antonio's Revenge* implicitly identifies the vengeful Antonio as a mother figure when the child Julio tells him 'since my mother died I loved you best' (3.3.9), and Antonio, like Medea or Procne, displays affection towards the child before murdering him to serve to his father.

The Thyestean model is elaborated even more grotesquely in *The Bloody Banquet* (1639), in which the usurper Armatrites discovers his wife having an affair and obliges her to consume the flesh of her lover in the banquet of the title. (Peter Greenaway neatly reverses the gender roles in the final feast scene in his film *The Cook, The Thief, His Wife and Her Lover*).[42] The play draws clear lines between rightful patriarchal rule, God's vengeance and 'proper' gender roles on one side, and the monstrous perversion of these norms in Armatrites's court. The lawful King and Queen of Lydia properly forgive their nephew, Lapirus, who betrayed them. The Queen is poised to kill with thoughts of 'fortunate revenge!' but surrenders the sword and the unconventional power it gives her to Lapirus, enjoining him to 'procure succour to my Babes and me' (l. 343).[43] The King helps Lapirus out of a womb-like pit in which he has fallen seeking food from the 'proud mother' earth (l. 679), and forgives his enemy. The pit symbolizes ravenous, ungoverned appetites associated with revenge, lust and the cycle of mortality represented by the devouring and life-giving earth. The shepherds regard such 'natural' behaviour as female, pointing out that 'the belly of a she wolf is never satisfied till it be damn'd up' (l. 612). The legitimate characters approach the edge of a pit of vengeful desires only to pull back from the edge, but in the court of the tyrant usurper, all are consumed by that feminized unlawful passion.

Armatrites's young Queen recognizes her adulterous lust as 'a Planke on which I runne to hell' (l. 500), but is unable to stop herself. The opinion that women 'have of themselves no entire sway' (l. 462) but are dominated by unruly passions seems borne out by her behaviour. After feasting and enjoying her lover, Tymethes, she shoots him when he disobeys her and discovers her identity. Dedication to revenge makes the other men and women equally unreasonable. Armatrites models himself after Atreus and Procne as an agent of the consuming mother earth. He presents his Queen with the 'fine flesh, course fare' (l. 1720) of Tymethes's limbs, assuring her that she will taste no other food 'Till in thy bowels those Corpses finde a grave' (l. 1723). The perverted nature of his justice is emphasized in the final scene where the bloody banquet is presented to the Queen. The lawful King and his followers, representatives of normative paternal law, enter disguised as pilgrims and are horrified by what they see. Since Tymethes is the King's son, the play carries strong reminders of Seneca's *Thyestes*. As in that play, the fragility of masculine identity and justice are brought to the fore.

Maternal revenge takes on a frightening power in Shakespeare's *Titus Andronicus*, through the parallel tragedies of Titus and Tamora. The play sets up a gendered opposition between patriarchal institutions and clandestine feminine revenge, the resort of the dispossessed. Saturninus opens by addressing the 'noble patricians' (1.1.1) and basing his claim on primogeniture, thus establishing Rome as a centre of male authority. Tamora, the conquered alien, pleads in vain against the sacrificial rites of this patrician state. The execution of her son arouses a maternal fury which may have tuned in to the deep anger and frustrations of female spectators, and which eventually overwhelms Titus. Tamora is identified with Hecuba, not as a symbol of grief, as was conventional, but as a revenging mother:

> The selfsame gods that armed the Queen of Troy
> With opportunity of sharp revenge . . .
> May favour Tamora, the Queen of Goths –
> When Goths were Goths and Tamora was queen –
> To quit her bloody wrongs upon her foes.
>
> (1.1.136)

The allusion to Hecuba here is to the figure in Ovid's *Metamorphoses* whose kingdom is conquered and whose son Polydore is murdered by Poly-mnestor, the Thracian king. Golding's 1567 translation tells 'As though she still had been a Queene, too vengeance she her bent, / Enforcing all her witts too fynd some kynd of ponnishment'. Like a 'Lyon robbed of her whelpes', Hecuba is inflamed to physical violence when she meets her son's murderer. Calling out for 'succor too the wyves of *Troy* at hand', she 'Did in the traytors face bestowe her nayles, and scratched out / His eyes: her anger gave her hart and made her strong and stout'.[44]

Tamora does not have any countrywomen to appeal to for support, but the spirit of maternal revenge she personifies speaks to other dispossessed and furious individuals on and perhaps off stage. Her accomplices Chiron and Demetrius and Aaron are also endemically alien to Roman culture. They are all 'others', united in revenge on the Andronicus family which has subjugated them, although since Chiron and Demetrius are stupid and Aaron has no official position of power, they cannot act without their mother. Tamora's methods are very different from Saturninus's public vows of retribution for the theft of Lavinia. While he retaliates openly, she works covertly. She tells Titus 'I am incorporate in Rome' (1.1.459) and she carefully plots with 'sacred wit' to pursue 'villainy and vengeance' (2.1.121–2). As her plots unfold the overwhelming power of revenge becomes obvious, cautioning female spectators that to unleash it, even in a retrospective act of love for one's children, is violently unnatural.

Titus Andronicus adheres faithfully to Roman values for a remarkably long time. When his sons, Quintus and Martius, are wrongfully accused of murdering Bassianus, he believes that the Tribunes will give him justice, even to the extent of sacrificing his hand. He vows revenge when he realizes he has been tricked, yet even after he discovers the truth of Lavinia's rape, he does not immediately succumb. Marcus is amazed that he is 'yet so just that he will not revenge' and appeals for divine intervention in Titus's cause (4.1.127). In Act 4, Scene 3, Titus's apparently mad project of shooting arrows to the gods again testifies to his faith in divine retribution. Sir Thomas Browne recommended 'Let thy Arrows of Revenge fly short, or be aimed like those of Jonathan, to fall beside the mark'.[45] At this stage, Titus is still sending his arrows too short. It is not until he meets Tamora in disguise that he loses himself to revenge.

The interview between Titus and Tamora, disguised as Revenge, drama-tizes the competitive nature of male and female claims to exact private retribution. Titus and Tamora are mirror images of each other, each trying to outwit the other with deception, role-play and brilliant use of irony. Tamora's assurance that she has come to help Titus 'and right his heinous wrongs' (5.2.4) will be true by the end of the scene since she has provided the means to his end. Her lines 'I am not Tamora / She is thy enemy and I thy friend' (5.2.29) point up the possibility of alliance between them as victims of the Roman state.

Since the audience does not know whether Titus has been taken in by Tamora until she promises to leave her sons, the scene is electric with tension. His confidential aside reassures the audience that he will 'o'erreach them in their own devices' (5.2.144) and turns the parting lines back onto Tamora, as Titus outdoes her at her own witty game of role-play. He bids 'sweet Revenge farewell' (5.2.148), while welcoming her as he plans his own banquet. Titus is not losing revenge but appropriating it. The suppression of female agency in the defeat of Tamora's plots only tells one side of the story. As Marion Wynne-Davies has pointed out, the image of the 'swallowing womb' has considerable power in *Titus Andronicus*.[46] It manifests itself not only in the pit in the forest, or the image of the mother who consumes her own children, but in the emasculating effect of revenge. As Titus takes on Tamora's role, he also assumes her gender attributes. He warns Chiron and Demetrius 'For worse than Philomel you used my daughter, / And worse than Progne I will be revenged' (5.2.193). Titus becomes more like a sister than a father in revenge, playing Procne to Lavinia's Philomel in a dramatization of the Ovidian myth. Golding's translation recounts how the sisters murder Tereus's son and cook his flesh:

> ... And while some life and soule was in his members yit,
> In gobbits they them rent: whereof were some in Pipkins boyled,
> And other some on hissing spits against the fire were broyld:
> And with the gellid bloud of him was all the chamber foyld.
> To this same banket *Progne* bade her husband, knowing nought ... [47]

By enacting a similar scene in his own house, Titus allows Lavinia to become an avenging Philomel. After writing the names of her persecutors in the dust, she can take up the bowl to receive their blood, transforming herself from 'a figure of dismemberment into a figure of agency'.[48] Titus prepares to 'play the cook' (5.2.203) as Procne, and, like the good hostess or mistress of the house, welcomes his enemies. The absurd inversions of this scene were played out in Deborah Warner's 1987 Royal Shakespeare Company production, where Titus came on '*like a cook*', according to the Folio stage directions, accompanied by 'Whistle while you work'. Titus was a monstrous Snow White figure, whose housewifely tasks were simultaneously horrific and comic. The self-destructive nature of Tamora's vengeful plots is illustrated as she consumes her own children. For Titus too, the process is self-destructive. It is the masculine, martial Lucius who will lead the new Rome. The patriarchal state holds no place for Lavinia or for a Titus who is consumed, no less than his victims, by feminized revenge.

The complex relationship between self-annihilation, revenge and maternal power is treated somewhat differently in *Hamlet*. Here, the protagonists strive to define personal acts of retribution in masculine terms, in opposition to feminine passivity. Hamlet curses himself for not acting on the ghost's words:

> I, the son of a dear [father] murdered
> Prompted to my revenge by heaven and hell
> Must, like a whore, unpack my heart with words
> And fall a-cursing like a very drab
>
> (2.2.561)

Licentious female sexuality, the mother's part in Hamlet, corrupts his determination to vindicate himself as his father's son. Suicide offers an alternative form of self-annihilation which looks back to the moment of birth as well as the point of death, to the idealized point of symbiotic unity with the mother before entry into the Symbolic Order constructs and fractures identity. In Hamlet's famous soliloquy, suicide and affirmative vengeful action sit in direct opposition: 'to be or not to be', yet the fact that many male revengers consider suicide attests to the closeness between the two.

John Sym's *Life's Preservative Against Self-Killing* (1637), which drew on a considerable body of earlier writing on suicide, argued that 'the unsatiable desire of revenge' on the part of victims was a motive for '*revenge* against themselves'. Sym defines two types of self-destruction: the first 'when a man labours in a continuall conflict against the execrable *viciousnesse* of his nature' and so tries to 'be revenged upon his wretched flesh and corruption' inspired by 'furious zeale'. The second type of suicide, designed to inflict grief on others, 'is most incident to persons of the weakest *sexe*', such as '*women* and *servants*, and *men sympathizing* with them in qualities'.[49] Seen in this light, Ophelia's suicide, tragic and futile though it is, could have been read by contemporary audiences as a form of revenge on the men who have ruined her life: her overbearing father and brother and the lover who has rejected her. Certainly, if Ophelia's aim was to 'grieve and vexe' Hamlet and 'to deprive him of all benefit and comfort that he might have by her life, and to hurt him by all the evill, that can betide him by her death', then she succeeds.[50]

Hamlet's preoccupation with suicide and female sexuality signals his sympathetic identification with these more feminine types of revenge. To kill himself would be to destroy the whore who unpacks his heart with words, the 'vicious mole of nature' (1.1.18.8) which rebels against the paternal call to revenge.[51] Since Gertrude lives almost by his looks, to kill himself would also be a form of revenge on the mother who had betrayed him and his father by marrying Claudius. Hamlet has to choose between paternal and maternal forms of revenge, and by doing so, also makes choices about his own sense of self. To 'take arms' against Claudius would be to constitute himself in the image of his father, as an independent adult, but to 'take arms' against himself, as a mother's son, would be to embark on a fantasy of annihilating any selfhood apart from her.

The play dramatizes Hamlet's struggle to break away from his maternal origins in order to enact his father's will. He can never construct vengeance in pure, masculine terms. Gertrude's material presence always intervenes between Hamlet and the execution of his task. She contaminates his commitment to revenge with reminders of its threat of self-dissolution, its questionable nature and, on a more practical level, doubts about his own paternity. Both the ghost and Claudius offer themselves as fathers to Hamlet. The fact that Gertrude has had sexual relationships with both kings confuses his sense of whose son he is. Old Hamlet who commands revenge is no more than a ghost or an absence, the immaterial nature of paternity itself. Hamlet can only resurrect the paternal–filial bond through words and images. He must describe his father back into existence in the face of overwhelming odds: the persistent presence of Claudius. Hamlet's determination to address Claudius as a mother illustrates his desire to isolate paternity from the unweeded garden of female sexuality:

HAMLET: Farewell, dear mother.
CLAUDIUS: Thy loving father, Hamlet.
HAMLET: My mother. Father and mother is man and wife, man and wife is
            one flesh, and so my mother.

(4.3.51)

To take revenge by killing Claudius would be to kill the mother who contaminates his identity with 'the woman's part' (*Cymbeline*, 2.5.20). But Hamlet is unable to do this. He recognizes himself in Gertrude and her part in him. Far from being an outraged Fury who inspires him, she chooses the corrupt Claudius above the wronged husband and King. Without her endorsement, Hamlet cannot take reprisal as his father's son.

In contrast to Hamlet, Laertes is unequivocal in his demands for revenge. Regardless of the material or spiritual consequences, he proclaims 'Let come what comes' (4.5.131). His readiness to cut the offender's throat in the church is linked to his own sense of identity:

That drop of blood that's calm proclaims me bastard,
Cries cuckold to my father, brands the harlot

Even here between the chaste unsmirched brow
Of my true mother.

(4.5.114)

Unlike Hamlet, Laertes has no such drops of bastard blood because his
mother is simply absent. This makes revenge a simple bond between father
and son, and thus much easier for Laertes. Whereas the maternal body
persistently troubles Hamlet, Laertes's mother exists only as a disembodied
and idealized spiritual form, a female equivalent of the ghost. Only when
Hamlet is sent away from Elsinore can he strengthen his identity with his
father, and when he returns as 'Hamlet the Dane' (5.1.242), it is with a
commitment to 'special providence' (5.2.157) rather than to revenge: 'If it
be now, 'tis not to come. If it be not to come, it will be now. If it be not
now, yet it will come. The readiness is all' (5.2.158). Even at the end of the
play, Hamlet is not a revenger; he responds to initiatives from Laertes and
Claudius. Only when Gertrude is dead does he finally destroy Claudius.

The hero's resistance to revenge is played out even more fully in
Chapman's *The Revenge of Bussy D'Ambois* (1610). Here, vengeance is a
private feminine task and the female agency which it invokes must be
firmly suppressed.[52] Unlike previous plays, this one relegates the quest for
reprisal to a family context and juxtaposes public scenes depicting a
masculine world of court and military politics. Far from being 'virtually
irrelevant'[53] to the play, the triad of female protagonists embodies the
excess of ungoverned emotions which could overwhelm the hero, Clermont, and push him beyond the law to avenge his brother Bussy's murder.
The Countess represents what could so easily happen to Clermont when he
is betrayed and captured. She collapses into uncontrolled grief, which
blinds her, and vows to attack his enemies with a hundred slashes of a sword
or shots of a pistol, thus playing out the temptation to Clermont to isolate
himself in a blind, introverted passion that would lead to revenge.
Clermont's sister, Charlotte, is vengeance personified, the spirit of outlawed matriarchal power:

Medea
With all her herbs, charms, thunders, lightnings
Made not her presence and black haunts more dreadful.

(4.2.39)

Charlotte makes the revenge of Bussy's murder a condition of her marriage
to Baligny (1.1.82) and refuses to grant him her love until she sees his face
speckled with blood (1.1.117–18). Empowered with a wild madness to
speak and act beyond the submissive behaviour expected of a woman, she
berates Clermont like a Fury to 'revenge a villainy for a villainy' (3.2.96).

Equally passionate is Tamyra's incantation to Revenge to possess her (1.2.1–24), much akin to Lady Macbeth's first soliloquy (*Macbeth*, 1.5.38–52). The spirit of revenge is invoked by and mobilizes a feminist consciousness, from which Tamyra openly criticizes the ways wives are constructed as shadows or appendages of their husbands. Her adulterous love for Bussy D'Ambois is an outright rebellion against a culture in which women are reduced to 'parasites and slaves' (1.2.61). The awakening of feminist consciousness comprises an awareness of one's victimization and a new-found enabling sense of power. The call to revenge is an expression of that strength and rage, inspiring Tamyra to condemn the injustice in so-called loving relationships. She perceptively appropriates the traditional courtly love motif of a besieged castle to expose the underlying brutality of patriarchal oppression:

> So soldiers, tortured
> With tedious sieges of some well-walled town,
> Propound conditions of most large contents –
> Freedom of laws, all former government.
> But having once set foot within the walls
> And got the reins of power into their hands,
> Then do they tyrannize at their own rude swinges,
> Sieze all their goods, their liberties, and lives,
> And make advantage and their lusts their laws.
>
> (1.2.63)

The wooer's conquest over the woman's affections is here rewritten as trickery and tyrannical usurpation. Tamyra implies that the besieged town rightly belongs to its native inhabitants, that woman has an inalienable right to self-government as an autonomous sovereign subject. There is nothing natural about male 'advantage' on which patriarchal 'laws' are based. She redefines the transfer of property in marriage, and the status of the *feme covert* who was subsumed into her husband, as theft and slavery.

Unsurprisingly, Clermont is afraid of the disturbing power this triad of furious women represents. His reluctance to pursue vengeance is part of a wish to deny or suppress such outlawed agency. Clermont is deeply committed to the public world of patriarchal power. In response to Charlotte's appeals for revenge, he asserts 'never private cause / Should take on it the part of public laws' (3.2.114). For him, honour is not a family matter but a code amongst gentlemen. Instead of sweeping to cut the villain's throat in a church, as Laertes vows, he politely presents a written challenge to Montsurry and does nothing further when the latter refuses to acknowledge it. While Clermont is angered by injustice, 'he can contain that fire as hid in embers' (2.1.94) and his stoic acceptance contrasts strikingly with the burning passions of the women, who function as the suppressed, private elements of his being.

In admiration of Clermont's idealism, Charlotte declares 'my brother speaks all principle' (3.2.37). The principles to which he is committed are frustratingly conservative. He condemns the presumption of the active individualist as futile and ungodly, arguing that men should 'willingly obey / In everything without their power to change' (3.4.61). Divinely supervised cooperation is ideal in principle, but under patriarchal practice it oppresses women who have no place in the grand scheme, no power legitimately to change the 'general sway'. They must either 'willingly obey' their overlords or be damned for rebellion. Clermont pointedly excludes women from any active role in the public realm. He tries to distract Charlotte from revenge with promises of a visit from the best beautician in the area. She should 'practice your face' (3.2.28) and attend to her clothing, he advises:

> with these
> Womanly practices employ your spirit;
> The other suits you not nor fits the fashion.
> (3.2.138)

Clermont experiences a crisis of confidence when he is tricked and arrested at Cambrai, and discovers that there is no difference between the public, masculine world and the private, feminine one. Far from functioning by principles of honour and respect for hierarchy, the court works on 'fine hypocrisie' and 'covert practise' (1.1.161–2) to promote selfish interests. Maillard justifies his duplicity in the name of the public 'good', paralleling his devious behaviour for the King's cause and that of widows whose sexual appetite is legitimated in the public bond of marriage (4.1.60–8). Clermont is horrified by this metaphorical invasion of the public realm by women. The ruling hegemony has been effeminized, and to take revenge now would be to descend to the same level.

Only the intervention of Bussy D'Ambois's ghost can redeem revenge and the court from the 'chaos' to which it is 'now returning' (5.1.1–3). The ghost is a commanding figure who begins a rebuilding of patriarchal structures which will finally exclude and subject the women. The spirit of Bussy legitimizes revenge by redefining it in masculine terms. To exact 'punishment and wreak for every wrong', he says, is to enact the Law of the Father: 'To be His image is to do those things / That make us deathless' (5.1.89–93). As a revenger, Clermont will be living in 'His image' rather than that of monstrous foremothers like the Furies.

From this point onwards, women are gradually but inevitably squeezed out of the revenge action by the collusion of men, even enemies. Clermont rejects 'wives, maids, widows, any women' outright, preferring 'friendship chaste and masculine' (5.1.189). The object of his passionate affection, the Duke of Guise, was ironically one of Bussy's murderers! Nevertheless, Charlotte still presents a significant challenge to the male appropriation of revenge. At the end of Act 3, Scene 2 she declares

> I would once
> Strip off my shame with my attire and try
> If a poor woman, votist of revenge
> Would not perform it with a precedent
> To all you bungling, foggy-spirited men.
> (3.2.162)

True to her word, she cross-dresses and sends herself with a letter to Tamyra as Charlotte's chosen instrument of revenge. The arrival of the Countess brings the three women together for the first time. Their power to take reprisal independently provokes anxious interventions from both Renel and the ghost to assert Clermont's exclusive right to 'author this just tragedy' (5.3.46).

The potentially ludicrous nature of much of the final scene serves to illustrate the absurdity of male determination to crush any form of female agency. The complete cowardice of Montsurry provides opportunities for Tamyra and Charlotte to execute the revenges they have so longed to wreak. As each door of opportunity opens, however, the men desperately crowd round to shut it again, even sacrificing their own animosities in favour of the grand patriarchal scheme. When Clermont resigns the abject Montsurry to Tamyra's 'full will' (5.5.50), he finally gets up to fight. Imminent female revenge raises him to his feet to 'ram this same race of Furies' into dust, on behalf of men who have been cuckolded like him (5.5.65). Montsurry's physical acrobatics and the contrast of sword fights and gentlemanly camaraderie raises this scene to the point of ridiculousness. Charlotte poses a second challenge, leaving the spectators' balcony to assert 'I would perform this combat'. The men's surprised question 'against which of us?' points up the idea of male bonding against a female enemy (5.3.91–2). Although she is disguised, she is Charlotte's representative, with 'a mind / Like to my sister' and therefore inherently dangerous (5.3.102). Complete abandonment of the whole revenge task seems preferable to its execution by a woman or her agent.

The strangeness of the final dumb show, in which the ghosts of Bussy, Guise, Cardinal Guise, Chatillon and Monsieur circle the dead body of

Montsurry, has often puzzled critics, but in the context of a gender struggle over revenge its purpose is clear. The play's close completes the marginalization of women. Montsurry and Clermont, supposedly the deadliest of enemies, exchange expressions of mutual admiration as the former dies. The dumb show dissolves differences between the men who form an exclusive circle, victims and murderers alike. News of Guise's death does not inspire Clermont to take revenge since this would be to attack the patriarchal monarchy for which he lives and dies. As a final statement of faith in the status quo, he intones 'there's no disputing with the acts of kings / Revenge is impious on their sacred persons' (5.3.151). His suicide, for the sake of Guise, completes the closed circle. The women can do nothing but retire to a nunnery in order to weep out their griefs. Far from attempting to wreak revenge themselves, they must 'for their wished amends to God complain' (5.3.213). The spirit of female revenge and its empowering potential for self-determination is thus exorcised by the end of the play.

III

In the case of vindictive women, the gender-bending effects of vengeance are as extreme as they are for men. While men are emasculated, female characters often assume a masculine persona in the execution of their tasks. For example, in *The Triumphs of Gods Revenge*, Reynolds recounts that Berinthia 'wisheth her selfe metamorphosed from a Virgine to a man, that she might be revenged of her brother', and she stabs him 'though with a female hand yet with a masculine courage'.[54] Cross-dressing reinforces the crossing of gender boundaries in John Taylor's pamphlet, *The Women's Sharp Revenge* (1640). The 'performers', Mary Tattlewell and Joan Hit-him-home, play on the revenge tragedy tradition and invoke the ghost of Long Meg of Westminster to defend their sex. The gender of the 'ghost', like that of the historical 'Long Meg', is rendered ambiguous by her masculine attire and behaviour. She boasts that her 'sword and buckler' has frightened swaggerers, soldiers and fencers off the stage and defeated the French in the battlefield, so that King Henry declared 'Amongst my brave and valiant men / I knew not one more resolute or bolder'. Meg's weapons are not merely decorative. She has 'cudgeled' her enemies, 'lammed their legs and sides' and treated them to her famous 'blows and knocks'.[55]

The use of violence by female revengers, even to redress the wrongs suffered by the sex, is deeply problematic from a feminist point of view since it often reproduces masculine modes of oppression and possibly even the dominant values of patriarchy. As Angela Carter remarks, the woman who models herself on her male counterparts 'only subverts her own socially conditioned role', not the wider social structures that oppress her. As a 'storm trooper of the individual consciousness' she is isolated from any wider feminist struggle, aspiring only to 'that lonely pitch of phallic supremacy up above the world'.[56] A modern example, from Helen Zahavi's *Dirty Weekend* (1992), focuses attention on how forms of retaliation can implicate women in the very patterns of behaviour that injure them. Bella, a victim of voyeurism and sexual abuse, turns the phallic tools of power back on the men who have ruined her life. When threatened with rape, she becomes excited at the feel of a gun as she 'warmed the metal with her touch', and 'felt her courage grow'. As she pushes the barrel of the gun into the lout who wants to penetrate her, they become indistinguishable:

> They looked at each other, the small one, the still one. The knowing look that passed between them. The look of surprise at the way things turn out. Hunter become quarry. Quarry become hunter. Executioner condemned. Condemned – executioner.[57]

The disturbing picture of the revenger transforming herself into her enemy rapist, and therefore condemning herself, is also found in Renaissance tragedies. In *The Maid's Tragedy* (1610), for example, Evadne becomes a monstrous parody of phallic power in the scene where she murders the King. In the characters of Evadne and Aspatia, Beaumont and Fletcher demonstrate the dangers masculine models hold. The King's decision to take Evadne as his mistress and then marry her to Amintor, beloved of Aspatia, subjects both women to his desires. Though they are very different, their responses ultimately confine each in a self-destructive, patriarchal prison.

Aspatia dedicates herself to grief as a passive sacrifice to the apparent vagaries of male desire. The play teases the audience with the image of a more vindictive figure when she appears in Act 5, cross-dressed and challenging Amintor to a fight. She styles herself as a soldier, draws her sword and resorts to physical violence, kicking Amintor to goad him into action. Even here, however, it is not reparation she seeks but further injury, in the form of a death blow. She tells him 'those threats I brought with me sought not revenge / But came to fetch this blessing from thy hand' (5.3.207). The manly costume has, ironically, reinforced her status as a victim of male cruelty. For all the illusion of self-determination it confers, the weapon she flourishes symbolizes her subjection and reinscribes her as a sacrifice to the dominant values of the court at Rhodes.

Evadne seems to offer a more spirited resistance to prescribed feminine roles, especially in her famous exclamation 'A maidenhead, Amintor, / At my years!' (2.1.190). She confidently advertises her own desire, telling her new husband that her heart holds 'as much desire, and as much will' as that of any other woman (2.1.287), thus implicitly broadening the scope of her subversive behaviour. As she vows to murder the King, she appeals to 'all you spirits of abused ladies' to assist her in her 'performance' (4.1.170–1), but in moving towards revenge, she paradoxically moves away from feminist resistance to be associated more and more closely with her male oppressors. Her brother Melantius is instrumental in transforming Evadne into a masculine revenger, someone who will act for him. By making her confess her adultery as a sin and herself as 'monstrous' (4.1.183), he forces her to internalize the values of the male court. She acknowledges that she can 'do no good because a woman' (4.1.255), so her only chance to redeem herself is to play a man's part of 'one brave anger' (4.1.144) in murdering the King.

Ostensibly, revenge offers Evadne the opportunity to clear her name. If her words to Amintor about her desires are true, though, murdering the King does not so much repay an injury as cut off her pleasure in the interests of her brother, her husband and the spirit of her father, whose sense of honour and possession of her sexuality will be restored. As a revenger, Evadne is merely a projection of male power. She plays a disturbingly pornographic game in the murder scene. She wants to wake the King and 'shape his sins like furies' (5.1.35), as though alluding to her ancient foremothers, yet in stabbing him repeatedly with her knife, she repays and replays his penetrative behaviour all too exactly. As he had bewhored her, so she now ties him to the bed; his response, 'what pretty new device is this?', suggests the erotic frisson her actions hold (5.1.47). Marina Warner notes that 'male repression seeks an outlet in fantasies of phallic power that women are made to bear, reassuring the voyeur of his own potency, and confirming the rationale of his antagonism'. Whatever Evadne's intentions to deliver 'weak catching women' from the plague of tyranny (5.1.93), her actions are a form of rape. The violent delight she experiences in avenging herself is a specifically male form of pleasure: eroticized despoliation. She denies her femininity and tells the King 'I am as foul as thou art' (5.1.74). By reproducing his power for the entertainment, and perhaps even titillation of spectators, Evadne's triumph is an empty one. Revenge patterns like this, for all their dramatic excitement and the illusion of control they grant, 'render women complicit and even instrumental in the violence with which they are seen'.[58] The murder scene in *The Maid's Tragedy* flamboyantly displays this bitter truth to women in the audience.

Evadne's masculinization is made explicit in the reactions of the servants who cannot believe 'a woman could do this' (5.1.127). As Strato remarks, 'she, alas, was but the instrument' (5.1.138). Finally, she is no more than a puppet of Melantius. He longs to acquit the wrongs offered to his family, friend and the court, but quickly recognizes 'to take revenge and lose myself withal / Were idle' (3.2.289). He is committed more to pragmatic self-preservation than passionate schemes of reprisal. By using Evadne to do his dirty work, he can group regicide and private vengeance with infidelity, as specifically feminine sins, and so escape the danger of alienating himself from the centre of power. He justifies his military rebellion against the King as the proper execution of 'mine own justice' in the absence of a proper magistrate (5.2.50).

The masculinized Evadne is also a projection of Amintor's outlawed desires for vengeance. In a moment of insight, he recognizes

> What a wild beast is uncollected man.
> The thing which we call honor bears us all
> Headlong into sin, and yet itself is nothing.
> (4.2.317)

Amintor knows that only a thin line parts him from brutally violent responses to the wrongs he has endured, yet he chooses to 'suffer and wait' (2.1.307), rather like Aspatia. Evadne's actions, ironically, make her more manly than him. Amintor's horror when she appears before him, drenched in blood, is excited by a recognition of something deep in himself, and a combination of shock and shame at her usurpation of his masculinity. The fantasy of phallic power which she bears in the knife does not reassure Amintor of his potency; it emphasizes his loss of control. She asks him 'Am I not fair? / Looks not Evadne beauteous with these rites now?' (5.3.118). He sees in her actions a complete lack of respect for her paternal governors, and interprets them as a prophecy of more transgressive behaviour, namely the murder of himself and the destructive perversion of all loving bonds. Evadne's two questions are simultaneously challenging and resigned, self-assertive and self-effacing, showing the spurious nature of female dominance in revenge. The futility of her action is clear when Amintor rejects her as a wife, saying 'all thy life is a continued ill / Black is thy color now, disease thy nature' (5.3.135).

He cannot completely deny a basic likeness between himself and the bloody Evadne. The ancient impulse to pay back wrong with wrong, which she embodies so vividly in her black and red, calls out to be recognized, and finally drives him off stage:

> Thou dost awake something that troubles me
> And says I lov'd thee once. I dare not stay;
> There is no end of woman's reasoning.

(5.3.165)

Only when Evadne is dead can Amintor return to commit suicide to be with Aspatia, the victim whose passive self-sacrifice he obviously prefers.

The problem of masculinization which destroys Evadne in *The Maid's Tragedy* becomes even more acute in plays where the revenger directs her energies against members of her own sex rather than against men who have injured her. An obvious example is Tamora in *Titus Andronicus*. By becoming 'incorporate' with Rome she has actually taken on the worst extremes of dominant masculine behaviour, its values as well as its violence. In the rape scene, Tamora first proclaims 'Your mother's hand shall right your mother's wrong' (2.3.121) by stabbing Lavinia in return for her insults. Tamora's decision to hand Lavinia over to Chiron and Demetrius instead reduces Lavinia to no more than an object, a possession of her father, whose ruin will injure Titus. Lavinia appeals in vain to Tamora, woman to woman, encouraging the audience to agree that Tamora has betrayed her gendered identity:

> No grace, no womanhood – ah, beastly creature,
> The blot and enemy to our general name . . .

(2.3.182)

Tamora's behaviour is deeply disturbing, her vengeance against Titus allying her more closely with the male rapists and their appetite for erotic despoliation than with the female victim.

Elizabeth Cary's *The Tragedy of Mariam* (1604/6), the first original tragedy written in England by a woman, explores the attractions and dangers of female revenge within a wider tragic arena.[59] John Marston dedicated the 1633 edition of his plays, including *Antonio's Revenge*, to Cary 'because your Honour is well acquainted with the Muses'.[60] Cary meticulously distances herself from any unorthodox attitude to revenge by including an explicit condemnation of it in the fourth Chorus of the play. The Chorus moralizes: 'The fairest action of our human life / Is scorning to revenge an injury' (l. 1), yet, as with many of the Choruses in the play, this prescriptive voice shifts ground from verse to verse, thus implying that the issue is more open to debate than would first appear.

The Chorus argues that gracious forgiveness actually empowers one over an enemy. Then, as if doubting that this point will have persuaded the audience, it goes on to remind spectators that there is 'no honour won' in avenging oneself on someone 'base'. If the enemy is 'worthy', one should naturally yield rather than fighting them (ll. 7–12). Within the Judean court of the play, none of the characters can be defined by these simplistic terms since most are a complex mixture of 'base' and 'worthy' behaviour, so this guideline is unhelpful. To make revenge seem less attractive, the Chorus goes on to point out that brooding on injuries and their reparation is a form of enslavement, to be scorned by the truly 'noble heart' (ll. 19–24). Immediately afterwards, though, it recognizes that the desire for revenge is impossible to eliminate, and is obliged quickly to reconfigure its doctrine of forgiveness as a type of personal reprisal:

> But if for wrongs we needs revenge must have
> Then be our vengeance of the noblest kind.
> Do we his body from our fury save,
> And let our hate prevail against his mind?
>> What can 'gainst him a greater vengeance be,
>> Than make his foe more worthy far than he?
>
> (l. 25)

Thus, while the Chorus reiterates the divine proscription on revenge, it paradoxically and radically rewrites turning the other cheek as a form of vengeance. Cary acknowledges the ineradicable presence of subversive, vindictive energies and daringly suggests to those in her audience that even virtuous behaviour could include mental resistance.

Perhaps this artful appropriation of divine authority and forgiveness is a particularly feminine technique since it is also used by Elizabeth Caldwell, a woman who tried to poison her husband, Thomas, in 1604. Gilbert Dugdale, who obviously sympathized with her, printed her *Letter to Her Husband* in a series of documents relating to her case, giving her a voice to defend herself.[61] Elizabeth reminds Thomas of 'the dissoluteness of your life' and the wrongs he has inflicted on her, thus implicitly defining her own crime as a form of retribution. Since the poisoning failed, she cleverly rewrites herself and her revenge in religious terms, cautioning Thomas to 'make haste ... that you may truly understand the wretched estate and condition of those who, following the lusts of their eyes, wallow in sensuality and so heap up vengeance against the day of wrath' (pp. 144–5). With increasing confidence, she goes on to assure him 'the Lord hath long since taken his sword in his hand to execute his vengeance against all disobedient wretches' and triumphantly ends 'You see the judgements of God are already begun in your house' (pp. 146–7). Elizabeth presents herself as a charitable Christian offering her best advice without rancour, 'for I do love you more dearly than I do myself' (p. 144). Yet from this stance of Christian forgiveness, she is able to take a public form of revenge on Thomas, exposing his crimes which, unfairly, cannot be prosecuted by law, and implicitly justifying her former actions. The presence of revenge within its opposite (forgiveness) alerts us to its pervasive power to unsettle certainties of right and wrong.

Catherine Belsey argues that revenge 'deconstructs the antithesis which fixes the meanings of good and evil, right and wrong', and this is certainly true of the three female characters in *The Tragedy of Mariam* who seek reparation in very different ways.[62] Doris, who has been unfairly deserted by Herod in favour of Mariam, rejects private vengeance in favour of appeals to divine authority. When her son suggests they should poison or stab Mariam's children, she admits that 'revenge's foulest spotted face / By our detested wrongs might be approved' (2.3.66), but fears that Mariam's family are too powerful. Reliance on heavenly retribution thus appears to be a last resort rather than a virtuous choice. Doris asks God to 'stretch thy revenging arm, thrust forth thy hand' (4.8.91), and her curse on Mariam is effective in that Herod kills her. Since it is Herod rather than Mariam who has caused Doris's misery the justice of this resolution seems rather questionable. There is no sense that Doris or her children will be restored to their former positions in Herod's family, so in terms of reparation it is ineffective as well. The Chorus's purported message that vengeance belongs to God is undercut then, since Doris's experience does not promote faith in this idea.

Mariam takes a limited form of active revenge for the murders of her brother and grandfather by Herod. When Herod returns after rumours of his death, she responds by refusing to greet him joyfully. She reminds him that, had he wished to please her, 'my brother nor my grandsire had not died' (4.3.30). Herod is particularly annoyed by her choice of costume, since her 'dusky habits' (4.3.4) proclaim her allegiance to mourning and vengeance rather than to him. Herod's fear of Mariam increases when he discovers that his servant has revealed his plan to have Mariam executed if he should die. He accuses her of adultery and of wanting to poison him: 'And you in black revenge attended now / To add a murder to your breach of vow' (4.4.25). Mariam's moment of greatest power over Herod is also the moment of her downfall since Herod decides to imprison and execute her here. Her plan of non-aggressive and non-violent revenge is therefore also unsuccessful.

The most successful revenger in *The Tragedy of Mariam* is simultaneously the most active and the most villainous. Salome's name recalls the villainy of the biblical Salome, who asked for the head of John the Baptist to avenge his critical remarks about her mother's marriage to Herod (Mark 6.17–28). The dramatic Salome's grudge against Mariam is established early in the play when Mariam and Alexandra insult her in racist and unsisterly terms. Mariam calls her 'base woman' (1.3.17) and 'mongrel issued from rejected race' (1.3.30), the insult 'base' reflecting back on Mariam's own behaviour here. The comparison between Mariam's royal descent from King David, and Herod and Salome's inferior ones, hints at the power struggle which lies beneath these remarks. In Herod's absence, Salome fears for her place at the centre of government, since in the event of his death, the original royal family could reclaim the throne and utterly dispossess her. Salome's obsession with material power is what drives her revenge forward. She picks up on Mariam's insults and turns them back on her. When Mariam glances at Salome's 'shameful life' (1.3.40), or lack of chastity, Salome slanders the tragic heroine to destroy her.

News of Herod's return allows Salome to begin her revenge:

I scorn that she should live my birth t'upbraid,
To call me base and hungry Edomite.
With patient show her choler I betrayed
And watched the time to be revenged by slight.
Now tongue of mine with scandal load her name,
Turn hers to fountains, Herod's eyes to flame.

(3.2.61)

While Mariam 'cannot frame disguise' (4.4.58), Salome is a consummate actor. Her 'patient show' in the face of Mariam's base insults gained her a moral victory over Mariam, though as with the Chorus, forbearance and forgiveness turn out to be their opposites. Salome plays out the subversive undercurrent of the Chorus's paradox, using patience as an artful illusion until she can employ her acting skills to destroy her enemy 'by slight' and to usurp Mariam's powerful position at Herod's side. Bribing the Butler to betray Mariam with lies about her intent to poison Herod, Salome carefully promotes Herod's belief that Mariam is the vengeful and unchaste one. These sins are, of course, her own. By projecting them onto Mariam she disguises her own motives. Salome assumes a powerful matriarchal role as Herod's protector, which allows her, like the ancient maternal spirits, to manipulate him into enacting her revenge. At the same time, she is masculinized. In Stephanie Hodgson-Wright's premiere production of the play, Salome's costume, a white silk shirt with military epaulettes, mirrored Herod's own, and telegraphed her ruthless acceptance of patriarchal values as a means to empower herself.[63]

Herod finally recognizes Salome's vindictive nature, calling her a 'foul mouthed Ate' who has 'made my heart / As heavy with revenge' (4.7.155–63). To the Greeks, Ate symbolized moral blindness, though in Shakespeare's plays she is associated more with the passion of a Fury, as in *Julius Caesar* where Antony imagines 'Caesar's spirit ranging for revenge / With Ate at his side come hot from hell' (3.1.273). Salome's behaviour is moral blindness, utterly condemnable in Christian terms. Interestingly, though, the Chorus does not single her out as a villain, and the play quietly shows that while Mariam fails, Salome's reprisal invisibly succeeds. Instead of defying male authority, Salome relies on it. Her revenge is based on a belief that the competitive rivalry which patriarchy sets up between women can actually be a means to self-advancement. Cary's play thus presents a bleak vision of female self-determination within the confines of Renaissance society. Salome's success re-creates her in the image of her brother as a petty dictator over the rest of her sex.

Competitive relationships between women are the basis of revenge again in James Shirley's *The Maid's Revenge* (1626), although here the context is romantic love.[64] The rigid family hierarchy in which fathers bestow their daughters according to seniority rather than affections is the cause of revenge and of tragedy in this play. The first revenge plot is initiated by the suitor Antonio's preference for Count Vilarezo's younger daughter, Berinthia. The attraction is mutual but, as she points out to a rival suitor, she has no power to follow her affections:

> Alasse, what ist to owne a passion
> Without power to direct it, for I move
> But by a higher rapture, in obedience
> To a father.
>
> (1.2, p. 9)

While recognizing the power of paternal authority, she does pursue a clandestine courtship with Antonio which immediately excites the jealousy of her sister, Catalina. In the source for the play, one of the stories in Reynolds's *Triumphs of Gods Revenge*, the two sisters are clearly contrasted: 'In a word, *Catalina* was of humour extreamely imperious, ambitious, and revengefull and *Berinthia* modestly courteous, gracious and religious'.[65] In the play, audience responses to Catalina are made more complex by the juxtaposition of lines which prove her a villain, and details about the family hierarchy which creates competitive relations between the sisters. Her father points up the sense of shame Catalina ought to feel at being 'out runne' by her younger sibling (2.5, p. 27), and, in a telling soliloquy, she says she feels trapped in an antagonistic relationship with Berinthia: 'I cannot be / Friend to my selfe, when I am kinde to thee' (2.5, p. 28).

Nevertheless, Catalina's initial plot to expose the relationship to her father indicates the emergence of a dangerously ungoverned will. She suggests that the rival suitor, Valasco, should inform her father, and he praises her as his 'safe guiding starre'. Catalina is not content to remain a patron of male interests. In soliloquy, she confesses 'I shall prove a wandering starre, I have / A course which I must finish for my selfe' (2.3, p. 24). Valasco is not her protégé but her 'instrument' (2.3, p. 24). When Catalina is entrusted with the imprisonment of her sister in the house, Berinthia and Antonio's relationship continues to flourish by letter. Catalina's discovery of a letter poisons her mind again and leads to a more vicious revenge. Again, she employs Valasco, suggesting that he should snatch Berinthia from her bedroom and Antonio's love. In addition to this plot, which would release Antonio for Catalina herself, the elder sister plans a secret revenge. She will pay back the poison of the letter by poisoning Berinthia. The competition between them has become so intense that Catalina can find 'no quiet in my selfe' while her rival lives (3.1, p. 32).

Antonio's servant, Diego, overhears Catalina and quickly disperses any sympathy her lament may elicit by condemning her as a suitable mate for the devil to 'furnish Hell' with evil spirits (3.1, pp. 32–3). With prior warning, Diego and Antonio are able to thwart Catalina's plots by abducting Berinthia before Valasco arrives. In Reynolds's narrative, God's intervention to prevent the tragedy results in the poison being consumed by Diego's spaniel, which 'instantly sweld, and dyed', and then by Catalina's unfortunate parrot, which 'swells and dyes before them'.[66] Shirley obviously thought better of trying to dramatize these gruesome details! In the play, Catalina, still expecting the poison plot to work, turns truly villainous in the audience's eyes as she rejoices in 'revenge beyond / My expectation', anticipating her sister dying in her lover's arms. Her moral world is inverted as she believes virtue is only for the weak and dedicates herself to 'mischief' (3.6, p. 46). Her clever performance contrasts with the extravagant protestations of revenge made by the men in the household when Antonio and Berinthia's flight is discovered. Alvarez sees in Catalina only 'vertue' and innocence, while his younger daughter's transgression makes her 'ambitious', a 'disordered branch' who disgraces 'the faire tree she springeth from' (4.2, p. 54). The father's pride in his position as head of the family and dynasty makes him utterly blind to the behaviour of his daughters. His inversion of their virtue and vice raises the possibility that, had their positions been reversed, they would have been as they seem to him now.

The possibility that Catalina's villainy could be the creation of the patriarchal family rather than a vindictive nature is increased by the second revenge plot. The play's title should be *The Maids' Revenge*, since its latter part dramatizes the younger sister's quest for reprisal on the family. Berinthia has been characterized throughout the first four Acts as a modest, generous and defenceless lady. She is stolen from her father's garden like a tender flower, and greeted as a 'double Daisie', a 'gillowflower' by Antonio's friend, Sforza, who assures her 'th'ast a wall of brass about thee / My young Daffodill' (4.1, pp. 46–7). Antonio's house provides a brief haven from the destructive pressures of the dynastic family. Here, Berinthia is welcomed warmly by Antonio's sister, Castabella, and their affectionate relationship suggests the sisterly love which could have flourished between Catalina and Berinthia. Men's rigid loyalties to their dynasties are also briefly relaxed to allow room for friendship in this oasis. Sebastiano, Berinthia's brother who has been sent to avenge her abduction, is persuaded not to duel immediately with Antonio. Their deep friendship, soon to be strengthened by the marriages with Castabella and Berinthia, looks forward to new household alliances where affection is allowed to flourish peacefully.

The paternal will and pride of the old household invades the new to destroy its harmony, as Vilarezo forces his son to kill Antonio in revenge for abducting Berinthia. The women watch helplessly, their loyalties torn, as their brothers and their husbands-to-be are forced to confront each other. Grief for the loss of Antonio transforms Berinthia from the 'young Daffodill' into an even more furious, passionate agent than her elder sister. She appeals to the Furies to infuse her with the power to avenge her wrongs, uncover her 'buried' nature, which has been frozen under a snowdrift of feminine conformity, and re-create her as an 'Element of fire' (5.2.62):

> Those furies which doe wait on desperate men,
> As some have thought, and guide their hands to mischiefe:
> Come from the wombe of night, assist a maide
> Ambitious to be made a monster like you;
> I will not dread your shapes, I am dispos'd
> To be at friendship with you, and want nought
> But your black aid to seale it.
>
> (5.2, p. 63)

The images of rebirth point to the terrifying new sense of self Berinthia enjoys as a revenger. She explodes into her father's house like a 'bearded Comet, threatning death and horror' (5.2, p. 62), pays back Catalina by poisoning her and stabs her brother to death as he had stabbed Antonio. Berinthia's enjoyment of revenge reaches beyond its retributive aspect. Having 'court[ed]' revenge for justice, she falls in love with its wild energy. She imagines herself consumed like a shooting star and looks forward to bathing in the flames of vengeance, fully conscious that its destructive power will consume and kill her. The imminent loss of self also carries an erotic charge, as in her celebration of Catalina's death: 'my soule / Ravish thyself with laughter' (5.3, p. 66). Berinthia's power is terrifying, especially to her father. Vilarezo is irked at being upstaged by his daughter, to have 'no part' in the 'direfull Tragedy' which has destroyed his house. Berinthia is now the 'Tragedian' who has seized control of the plot and he tellingly describes her as 'mother of all this Horror', alluding back to the ancient maternal spirits who have inspired her revenge (5.3, p. 67). In a desperate attempt to reclaim authorship and control, Vilarezo is forced to acknowledge his responsibility for the deaths of his children. The play thus ends with a blistering critique of the patriarchal family. It is the cause of tragedy, but at the same time, as in so many plays considered here, male authority proves very brittle in the face of revenge. Drawn from the primitive energy of the Furies, revenge has the power to consume and dissolve gendered identities, to elevate women to new heights of self-determination in its pyrotechnic and destructive splendour.

Notes

1 M. C. Bradbrook, *The Rise of the Common Player: A Study of Actor and Society in Shakespeare's England* (Cambridge University Press, Cambridge, 1979), p.130.

2 Cyril Tourneur [?], *The Revenger's Tragedy*, ed. Brian Gibbons, New Mermaids (Ernest Benn, London, 1967).

3 Katherine A. Rowe, 'Dismembering and Forgetting in *Titus Andronicus*', *Shakespeare Quarterly* 45 (1994), 279–303; p. 297.

4 John Marston, *Antonio's Revenge*, ed. W. Reavley Gair, Revels Plays (Manchester University Press, Manchester, 1978).

5 Thomas Norton and Thomas Sackville, *Gorboduc*, in Ashley Thorndike (ed.), *Minor Elizabethan Drama. Volume One: Pre-Shakespearean Tragedies*, Everyman (Dent, London, 1958), pp. 1–53 (4.2.106 and 4.2.365).

6 John Reynolds, *The Triumphs of Gods Revenge against the crying and execrable sinne of (wilfull and premeditated) Murther* (1635), pp. 14, 26.

7 Andreas Alciatus, *Emblemata* (Padua, 1621), no. 27, in Peter M. Daly (ed.), *Andreas Alciatus: Emblems in Translation*, 2 vols (University of Toronto Press, Toronto, 1985), and Hunger, *Emblemata* (Paris, 1542), no. 13, in Peter M. Daly et al. (eds), *The English Emblem Tradition*, 2 vols (University of Toronto Press, Toronto, 1993). Quotations are from the Hunger emblem motto.

8 *The Wisdom of the Ancients*, in *Bacon's Essays Including his Moral and Historical Works* (Frederick Warne, London, n.d.), p. 311.

9 Thomas Kyd, *The Spanish Tragedy*, ed. J. R. Mulryne, New Mermaids (Benn, London, 1970).

10 Randall Martin (ed.), *Women Writers in Renaissance England* (Longman, London, 1997), p. 285.

11 *Shakespeare's Ovid: Being Arthur Golding's Translation of the Metamorphoses*, ed. W. H. D. Rouse (Centaur Press, London, 1961), p. 172 (Book 6, l. 624).

12 Thomas Newton (ed.), *Seneca His Tenne Tragedies, translated into English* (1581), 2 vols (AMS Press, New York, 1967), vol. 2, p. 57.

13 William Painter, *The Palace of Pleasure*, ed. Joseph Jacobs (David Nutt, London, 1890), vol. 3, p. 54. On Medea as a model for feminist revengers see John Kerrigan, *Revenge Tragedy: Aeschylus to Armageddon* (Clarendon Press, Oxford, 1996), pp. 315–42.
14 Reynolds, *The Triumphs of Gods Revenge*, p. 138.
15 René Girard, *Violence and The Sacred*, trans. Patrick Gregory (Johns Hopkins University Press, Baltimore, 1977), p. 22.
16 John Webster, *The Duchess of Malfi*, ed. Elizabeth Brennan, New Mermaids, 3rd edn (A & C Black, London, 1993).
17 Brian Vickers (ed.), *Francis Bacon* (Oxford, Oxford University Press, 1996), p. 347.
18 Marina Warner, *Monuments and Maidens: The Allegory of the Female Form* (Pan Books, London, 1987), p. 154.
19 P. S. (Parradin), *Devises* (London, 1591), no. 29, in Daly et al. (eds), *The English Emblem Tradition*, vol. 2.
20 Anne Laurence, *Women in England 1500–1700: A Social History* (Weidenfeld and Nicolson, London, 1994), pp. 263–4.
21 Kate Aughterson (ed.), *Renaissance Woman: Constructions of Femininity in England, A Sourcebook* (Routledge, London and New York, 1995), p. 134.
22 Jonathan Dollimore, *Radical Tragedy: Religion, Ideology and Power in the Drama of Shakespeare and His Contemporaries*, 2nd edn (Harvester, Hemel Hempstead, 1989), p. 29.
23 Jane Anger, *Her Protection for Women* (1589), in Simon Shepherd (ed.), *The Women's Sharp Revenge: Five Women's Pamphlets from the Renaissance* (Fourth Estate, London, 1985), pp. 31, 32, 34.
24 Harry Keyishian, *The Shapes of Revenge: Victimization, Vengeance and Vindictiveness in Shakespeare* (Humanities Press, New Jersey, 1995), pp. 2–3.
25 William Rowley, Thomas Dekker and John Ford, *The Witch of Edmonton*, in Peter Corbin and Douglas Sedge (eds), *Three Jacobean Witchcraft Plays* (Manchester University Press, Manchester, 1986).
26 Vickers (ed.), *Francis Bacon*, p. 347.
27 *The Whole Treatise of the Cases of Conscience...By Mr M. W. Perkins* (1651 edn), cited in Fredson Bowers, *Elizabethan Revenge Tragedy 1587–1642* (Princeton University Press, Princeton, 1940), p. 36.
28 Betty Travitsky (ed.), *The Paradise of Women: Writings by Englishwomen of the Renaissance* (Columbia University Press, New York, 1989), p. 203.
29 Reynolds, *The Triumphs of Gods Revenge*, p. 45.
30 Ibid., pp. 16, 138. Book 1, History 4 is a source for Middleton and Rowley's *The Changeling*, while Book 2, History 7 was dramatized by Shirley as *The Maid's Revenge* (see below).
31 Tania Modleski, *Loving With a Vengeance: Mass-Produced Fantasies for Women* (Routledge, New York, 1988), p. 45.
32 Kate Saunders (ed.), *Revenge* (Pan Books, London, 1993), p. vii.
33 Sir Thomas Browne, *The Major Works*, ed. C. A. Patrides (Penguin, Harmondsworth, 1977), p. 458.

34 *Juvenal and Persius*, trans. G. G. Ramsay (William Heinemann, London, 1918), pp. 260–1 (ll. 189–92).

35 Elaine Scarry, *The Body in Pain: The Making and Unmaking of the World* (Oxford University Press, Oxford, 1985), p. 122.

36 Cited in Charles Hallet and Elaine S. Hallet, *The Revenger's Madness: A Study of Revenge Tragedy Motifs* (University of Nebraska Press, Lincoln, NB, and London, 1980), p. 67.

37 Scott Wilson, *Cultural Materialism* (Blackwell, Oxford, 1995), pp. 165–8. Thomas Hobbes, *Leviathan*, ed. C. B. Macpherson (Penguin, Harmondsworth, 1985), p. 254.

38 John Ford, *The Broken Heart*, ed. Brian Morris, New Mermaids (Benn, London, 1965).

39 Georges Bataille, *The Bataille Reader*, ed. Fred Botting and Scott Wilson (Blackwell, Oxford, 1997), pp. 261–2.

40 The disturbing connection between revenge and maternity is suggested in Artemisia Gentileschi's remarkable picture, *The Murder of Holofernes* (1619), which shows the avenging Judith and her maidservant beheading Holofernes. Marcia Pointon has convincingly argued that the figures are arranged like a birth scene, with Judith and her maid as midwives and Holofernes giving birth to himself at his moment of execution. See Marcia Pointon, 'Artemisia Gentileschi's *The Murder of Holofernes*', *American Imago* 33 (1981), 343–67.

41 Newton (ed.), *Seneca His Tenne Tragedies*, vol. 1, pp. 58, 81.

42 *The Cook, The Thief, His Wife and Her Lover*, written and directed by Peter Greenaway (Erato Films, Allard Cook Ltd, 1989).

43 Anon, *The Bloody Banquet*, ed. Samuel Schoenbaum, Malone Society Reprints (Oxford University Press, Oxford, 1962).

44 *Shakespeare's Ovid*, ed. Rouse, pp. 264–5 (Book 13, ll. 654–7, 672, 673–7).

45 Browne, *Major Works*, ed. Patrides, p. 457.

46 Marion Wynne-Davies, '"The Swallowing Womb": Consumed and Consuming Women in *Titus Andronicus*', in Valerie Wayne (ed.), *The Matter of Difference: Materialist Feminist Criticism of Shakespeare* (Harvester Wheatsheaf, Hemel Hempstead and New York, 1991), pp. 129–51.

47 *Shakespeare's Ovid*, ed. Rouse, p. 135 (Book 6, ll. 813–18).

48 Rowe, 'Dismembering and Forgetting in *Titus Andronicus*', p. 300.

49 John Sym, *Life's Preservative Against Self-Killing*, with an introduction by Michael MacDonald, Tavistock Classics in the History of Psychiatry (Routledge, London, 1988), pp. 232–6.

50 Ibid., p. 236.

51 The Norton text (which derives from the Oxford) uses the First Folio as the control text for *Hamlet* but incorporates this passage from the second quarto version of the play (Q2) as an insert after line 18 of the Folio text. I have followed the Norton lineation here.

52 George Chapman, *The Revenge of Bussy D'Ambois*, in Katherine Eisaman Maus (ed.), *Four Revenge Tragedies*, The World's Classics (Oxford University Press, Oxford, 1995), pp. 175–248.

53 Maus (ed.), *Four Revenge Tragedies*, p. xxvi.

54 Reynolds, *The Triumphs of Gods Revenge*, pp. 127, 123.

55 Shepherd (ed.), *The Women's Sharp Revenge*, p. 163.

56 Angela Carter, *The Sadeian Woman: An Exercise in Cultural History* (Virago, London, 1979), pp. 133, 143–4.

57 Helen Zahavi, *Dirty Weekend* (Flamingo, London, 1992), pp. 158, 161.

58 Warner, *Monuments and Maidens*, p. 175.

59 Elizabeth Cary, *The Tragedy of Mariam*, ed. Stephanie J. Wright (Keele University Press, Keele, 1996). See chapter 4 for a fuller consideration of the play.

60 Marston, *Antonio's Revenge*, ed. Reavley Gair, p. 159.

61 *A Letter Written by Elizabeth Caldwell to Her Husband*, in Martin (ed.), *Women Writers in Renaissance England*, pp. 142–7. Subsequent page references are to this edition.

62 Catherine Belsey, *The Subject of Tragedy* (Methuen, London, 1985), p. 115.

63 Stephanie Wright, dir., *The Tragedy of Mariam*, Tinderbox Theatre Company, Bradford Alhambra Studio, October 1994. See Alison Findlay, Gweno Williams and Stephanie Hodgson-Wright, '"The Play is Ready to Be Acted": Women and Dramatic Production 1570–1670', *Women's Writing,* special issue, ed. Marion Wynne-Davies, vol. 5 (forthcoming).

64 James Shirley, *The Maid's Revenge: A Critical Edition*, ed. Albert Howard Carter (Garland Publishing, New York and London, 1980). References are given by Act, Scene and page number.

65 Reynolds, *The Triumphs of Gods Revenge*, p. 106.

66 Ibid., pp. 113, 116.

CHAPTER 3

'I please my self': Female Self-fashioning

Moll Frith, the heroine of *The Roaring Girl* (1611), confidently declares: 'I please my self, and care not else who loves me' (5.1.349).[1] Setting out to construct a life around one's own desires or pleasures was inimical to the model of feminine behaviour laid down in Renaissance conduct books, and at odds with the traditional roles allotted to women as nurturing figures who serve the interests of others in the household. In Vives's *The Instruction of a Christian Woman*, for example, the ideal woman was to 'be content with a little, and take in worth that she hath, nor seek for other that she hath not'.[2] Moll's self-assertion contrasts dramatically with the pattern of self-denial set out here, where woman's virtue is equated with passivity, contented acceptance of 'a little' rather than any personal endeavour to improve her circumstances or 'seek for other that she hath not'.

For Renaissance women, the very act of going to the theatre was, according to moral commentators, a singularly selfish pleasure or pastime and an opportunity for self-display outside the home. John Northbrooke argued 'what safeguarde of chastitie can there be, where the woman is desired with so many eyes, where so many faces looke upon hir, and again she uppon so manye? She must needes fire some, and hir selfe also fired againe, and she be not a Stone'.[3] What seems to concern Northbrooke is that, in addition to being the object of so many male gazes, the female spectator would find 'hir selfe' inflamed by passions, transformed from a stone to an active, eroticized being. Stephen Gosson similarly warned the gentlewomen citizens of London that by going to plays, they were open targets for Cupid: 'The little god hovereth above you, and fanneth you with his wings to kindle fire ... Desire draweth his arrow to the head and sticketh it uppe to the fethers, and Fancy bestireth him to shed his poyson through every vayne.'[4] Drama that presents women who are determined to follow their desires tunes into the Renaissance theatre's potential to transform female spectators into wilful subjects who will please themselves. This chapter considers plays where women's experiences of self-fashioning are central. The first section concentrates on romantic love, while the second looks at how the city offered a range of pleasures and opportunities to women.

I

'Your wrongs do set a scandal on my sex' complains Helena to the man she loves in *A Midsummer Night's Dream* (1595). Demetrius's neglect of her in favour of a new mistress has put her into an impossible position. She must either lose him or pursue him, behaviour which sets a scandal on her sex because it moves her into the role of active subject. Helena exclaims 'We should be wooed and were not made to woo' (2.1.240–2), drawing on conventional ideas about women's silence and modesty, and the model of romance in Castiglione's *Book of the Courtier*. This very influential book, translated into English in 1561, recommended that women should be extremely cautious about revealing their affections because 'men may with a great deale lesse daunger declare themselves to love, than women'.[5] Helena's behaviour impeaches her 'modesty too much' (2.1.214) not because she follows Demetrius into a wood beyond the walls of civilized Athens, but because she chases him there, loudly protesting her love. She tries to rewrite her role as the heroine of a romantic quest instead of the male hero's destination and prize. Speaking from the position of suitor, she tells Demetrius

> The more you beat me I will fawn on you.
> Use me but as your spaniel; spurn me, strike me,
> Neglect me, lose me; only give me leave
> Unworthy as I am, to follow you.
> (2.1.204)

Helena's helpless self-abasement is typical of the courtly love tradition, but what her situation shows quite clearly is that the conventional status positions of lover and mistress are the wrong way round. It is the woman who is left at the mercy of male whims of affection. It is she rather than he who is unable to help herself or further her romantic interests.

Texts in which heroines are the central subjects of romantic quests raise unsettling questions about the social configurations of love to support a gender hierarchy that designates women a secondary place. In Lady Mary Wroth's romance *The Countess of Montgomerie's Urania* (1621), for example, the writer's appropriation of Petrarchan love tropes constitutes a subtle but unmistakeable exposure of the real power relations between men and women in Renaissance England. In the mouth of a woman, the helplessness of the lover acquires new resonance, as when Antissia laments 'Obedience, fear and love do all conspire / A worthless conquest gained to ruin me', or when Pamphilia styles herself as the victim of oppressive, phallocentric definitions of love, asking 'Must we be servile? doing what he list?'[6]

In spite of such deeply felt frustrations with the conventions of romance, in Renaissance England, as today, women were the primary consumers of romantic fiction. Caroline Lucas has shown how, in the second half of the sixteenth century, the rise in female literacy was accompanied by an increase in the publication of popular romances that were addressed to women readers. Although these texts often reinforced patriarchal prescriptions, they simultaneously offered an escape by presenting heroines who did have 'greater autonomy' and whose thoughts, actions and emotions were 'accorded a worth and significance beyond anything likely to have been experienced by the women reading'.[7] The fantasy of power created by prioritizing female experience is an enduring characteristic of the genre that has attracted women readers, as feminist scholars have shown. In the case of stage plays, a wish to satisfy the needs of female customers may have been one factor motivating dramatists to explore 'stories of great love' (as Wroth calls them) from a different, feminine perspective.[8] We can see how romantic dramas could be read in feminist ways by approaching them via a female audience. Women spectators could resist the plays' patriarchal messages by favouring more liberating elements in their own creative interpretations.

Lady Mary Wroth's play *Love's Victorie* (*c.*1620) offers a good example of a feminist reinterpretation of romantic conventions. The play was written for a domestic arena and was possibly performed at one of the Sidney houses, a very different kind of theatre to the commercial stage. Nevertheless, it provides an especially illuminating parallel to the love stories dramatized there: a female perspective on romance. *Love's Victorie* focuses special attention on the experiences of female characters and, at the ending, shows women's power to create love's victory, to 'shape destiny as well as to endure it', as Carolyn Ruth Swift observes.[9] By paralleling the emotional experiences of male and female lovers, Wroth gives dramatic expression to the other side of the conversation in courtly love. The heroine Musella tells the hero Philisses 'it may be for your love she feels like pain', to which he responds 'Like pain for me!' (4.1.58–60).[10] His surprise is a less arrogant version of Orsino's belief that no woman's heart can hold a passion like his own (*Twelfth Night*, 2.4.91–4). Wroth's play shows emphatically that this view is mistaken. She dramatizes the pain women experience in courtship in the characters of Climeana and Simeana (both in love with Lissius) and Phillis and Musella (in love with Philisses). Even the chaste Silvesta, who has dedicated herself to chastity, has experienced 'endless pain' (1.2.193) in loving Philisses. Simeana and Musella eventually find their loves requited, but in Climeana and Phillis Wroth gives stark examples of the helplessness of unrequited love. Unlike the male Forester who hopelessly protests his passion to Silvesta, Phillis has remained absolutely silent about how she loves Philisses:

> And ever would though he did me despise
> For then, though he had ever cruel proved
> From him, not me, the fault must needs arise.
> (3.2.72)

In contrast, Climeana declares her love to Lissius and is rejected. Her radical behaviour in leaving her family to pursue her first love, then shifting her affections to Lissius, and finally wooing him herself, is criticized. Simeana believes Climeana's 'scope to change and choose' (3.2.125) makes her love inferior. Lissius upbraids her in just the same way that Demetrius does Helena:

> Is this for a maid
> To follow and haunt me thus? You blame
> Me for disdain but see not your own shame!
> Fie, I do blush for you! A woman woo?
> The most unfittest, shameful'st thing to do!
> (3.2.184)

Nor can this conservative attitude be dismissed as the opinion of a short-sighted man since the other female characters and the play itself seem to endorse it. Dalina could be quoting from *The Book of the Courtier* when she advises Climeana and Simeana 'Rather than too soon won, be too precise / Nothing is lost by being careful still' (3.2.164). Her words are proved right when Lissius chooses the 'careful' Simeana rather than her outspoken rival. It is possible that Wroth may be 'admitting or at least acknowledging guilt' for her own sexual licentiousness (she had two illegitimate children) by displacing it onto transgressive female figures like Climeana.[11]

In the Musella love plot the heroine is just as reserved as Simeana. The play demonstrates that love's victory comes by following courtly conventions while transgressions threaten it. Philisses mistrusts the Musella 'who such passion proves' (3.1.72) by talking to Lissius about him. Her animated discussions lead him to believe she loves Lissius. Even though a declaration of her true affections would clear up the misunderstanding, both Musella and Silvesta reject this option:

MUSELLA: Sometimes I fain would speak, then straight forbear
              Knowing it most unfit; thus woe I bear.
SILVESTA: Indeed a woman to make love is ill.

                         (3.1.77)

By Silvesta's careful direction Musella is placed where she can overhear Philisses's own declaration of love and then respond to it, so preserving her feminine modesty and gradually revealing to Philisses that his feelings are reciprocated. After this happy resolution, though, Wroth introduces a new threat to their love in the form of an arranged marriage for Musella. Musella's mother moves swiftly to ratify the betrothal because she has been deceived into believing that 'Musella wantonly / Did seek Philisses' love' (5.5.128). Presumably she feels that wantonness on Musella's part would threaten marital prospects with Philisses or Rustic, the husband her father's will has selected for her. In its presentation of courtship, then, the play follows a conventional line and shows the problems this creates for women. It is through the powerful character of Silvesta and the cooperation between women that Wroth makes room for manoeuvre within romance conventions. Silvesta and Venus create love's victory from the seemingly tragic circumstances in which Musella and Philisses are trapped. The tragi-comic aspect of the play's ending and its focus on sisterly solidarity has strong parallels with Shakespeare's *All's Well That Ends Well* (1604), although the class relations in the latter play cast a different light on the relationship between the heroine and her beloved.

In *All's Well*, Helen both appropriates and rejects the Petrarchan conventions of romance to suit her own purposes. She first assumes the role of the courtly lover, declaring 'I am undone' by passion for the unattainable Bertram (1.1.79) and making full use of the tropes of sickness and idolatry. Helen's view of Bertram as a star whose 'bright radiance' shines down on her from another 'sphere' is appropriate given his aristocratic birth (1.1.80–4). Like the medieval troubadour, she is of a distinctly inferior social station. Her quest to win Bertram's hand can be read as emblematic of a wider shift in Renaissance society under James I, when the creation of new knighthoods and the increasing power of the merchant classes put in question a hierarchy based on aristocratic blood. Julie Soloman argues that *All's Well* explores the socially constructed nature of erotic attraction to show how society is 'transformed by authority's need to address previously unaddressed desires'.[12] Some of these are class based: the testing of class

91

boundaries and the value of noble birth are major concerns of the play. Equally important, however, are women's previously unaddressed desires.

In her first and second soliloquies Helen's explicit acknowledgement of her social inferiority is matched by an equally significant silence about her gender. Her decision to take control of her emotional destiny as the subject of ardent passion would have appeared extraordinary. As Wroth's play shows, women knew that such immodest behaviour would inevitably cast doubt on one's chastity. Robert Burton warned that a woman would 'be reputed to be malapert and wanton' if she made her own choice of husband 'for she should rather seem to be desired by a man than to desire a man herself'.[13] Helen's declaration of her feelings in the privacy of soliloquy gives public expression to female passions in the theatre. As Susan Zimmerman argues, the theatre 'served as a medium for the release of transgressive erotic impulses'.[14] Spectators from across the broad panorama of social classes could have identified with Helen's frustrations and longings from the common ground of gender. Her quest to marry Bertram plays out the fantasies of the lower or middling sort who dreamed of marriage as preferment. At the same time, Helen voices the frustrations of those higher up the social order whose affections had to be subordinated to the financial and social interests of a family or even a nation.

In the absence of writing about love by women from the lower classes it is difficult to construct patterns of response to Helen's behaviour, although their romantic fancies probably found expression in popular ballads of the time such as 'Patient Griselda' and 'Child Waters'.[15] In the latter, Ellen, the low-born heroine, is made pregnant by her beloved Lord, cross-dresses as a page, and follows him to his castle. As in *All's Well*, the Lord's mother (or sister) plays a vital role in helping the heroine, seeing through her disguise and sending him to investigate when Ellen gives birth in the stable.[16] The fairy-tale structure of *All's Well*, in which a heroine performs amazing feats, draws on the ballad tradition of popular romance. A paradigm for middle-class identifications with Helen is offered in *The Copy of a letter . . . , by a younge Gentilwoman: to her unconstant Lover* (1567) by Isabella Whitney. Whitney's probably semi-autobiographical poem suggests that women of the middling sort could have easily sympathized with Helen's sense of helplessness in winning Bertram's love. The 'younge Gentilwoman' castigates her unfaithful lover, asking him to keep his promise and 'take me to your wife', but later presents herself as his jilted victim:

> But if I can not please your mind
>   for wants that rest in me:
> Wed whom you list, I am content
>   your refuse for to be.[17]

However resigned she says she is, the 'gentlewoman' uses her writing to make her lover confront the harsh reality of his actions. Her determination to fight against her fortune echoes that of Helen in *All's Well* when Bertram rejects her after the betrothal. Helen's resourcefulness is appealing because it constitutes a vigorous rejection of misogynist constructions of woman as a commodity or disposable 'refuse'. Daughters or wives of merchants and citizens may have seen in Helen a pioneering figure of their own wishes for self-determination.

Helen's exchange with Paroles on the subject of virginity marks her change from passivity to agency. Paroles is also a social entrepreneur trying to win a place amongst the nobility, so their conversation dramatizes a struggle over the ownership of female sexuality amongst the middling sort. Helen challenges his definition of virginity as the starting point and guarantee of male reproduction, a 'commodity' which is more or less 'vendible' (1.1.142–3). She will not accept Paroles's view that, irrespective of her wishes, a man will 'undermine you and blow you up' (1.1.113). Instead, she retaliates 'Is there no military policy how virgins might blow up men?' (1.1.115). While Paroles is a coward, Helen is courageous and daring in the pursuit of her goals.

The examples of romantic writing we have from high-born women such as Wroth, Mary Queen of Scots and even Queen Elizabeth suggest that Helen's story could also have engaged the interest of wealthier spectators trapped by their good fortunes and plagued by passions for those seemingly out of reach.[18] The Countess's reactions to Helen provide an example to such members of the audience. As well as legitimizing Helen's actions on-stage, the Countess endorses sympathetic identification with a social inferior. She begins 'Even so it was with me when I was young / If ever we are natures these are ours' (1.3.113), inviting agreement from women who have experienced passion and tried to conceal it. The Countess's inter-rogation of Helen in Act 1, Scene 3 is aggressive only in appearance. In spite of the dramatic tension between them, the women work cooper-atively. Helen's cheeks and gestures, 'the proclamation of thy passion', are a language that the Countess can read and, from the safety of her objective position, translate in words (1.3.158). Her insistent questions are necessary to push Helen to declare her own feelings.

The value of a female audience for declarations of love is also shown in Wroth's *Love's Victorie*. The safety of all-female company gives Dalina, Phillis, Climeana and Simeana the chance to confess their 'passions past' and current feelings since 'None can accuse us, none can us betray / Unless ourselves our own selves will bewray' (3.2.4–6). Silvesta and Simeana have a similar scene in which they share their feelings (3.1). It is interesting to speculate on whether Wroth imagined or produced *Love's Victorie* for an all-female audience, which would duplicate that gossip-like atmosphere, or whether the female confidences would have been displayed in a more 'public' arena with a mixed-sex audience.[19] In either case, this scene (or Helen's confessions) may have given women spectators a sense of cathartic release as passions are brought safely out into the open.

In the exchange between older and younger woman in *All's Well*, the articulation of desire is reached via the safer forms of maternal and sisterly love (though Helen is frightened by the incestuous implications of the latter). Different kinds of love are woven together in the play, suggesting that the masculine, eroticized version of romance offers only a narrow perspective from which to express women's emotional needs. The Countess differentiates between Helen's erotic attraction to Bertram and her own maternal affection, but Helen's description of her passion as self-sacrificing and boundless aligns them. She says she pours the waters of her love into the 'sieve' of Bertram's affections 'and lack[s] not to lose still' (1.3.186–8), words which are borne out by her subsequent actions. In spite of Bertram's cruelty, she continues to adore him, even to sacrifice her own happiness for his safety. It is difficult to reconcile the resolute Helen who wins the man she wants with the Helen who vows to give him up and leave Roussillon so that he can return from the danger of the battlefield. In the context of a love which combines maternal and erotic elements, however, Helen's contra-dictory behaviour is understandable.

Nor was that mixture of emotions peculiar to Helen. If Lady Mary Wroth's play and sonnets are indicative of other women's experiences of romance, they suggest a natural sympathy between female spectators and Helen. In *Love's Victorie* Musella advises Simeana to take a distinctly maternal, caring attitude to her lover Lissius (4.1.285–6), and her own concern for Philisses's welfare is likewise nurturing (4.1.47–50). Wroth makes frequent use of maternal imagery in her poems, characterizing Cupid as a demanding child who enslaves the speaker: 'Give him, he the more is craving, / Never satisfied with having' (p. 96). She cannot resist the temptation to protect and nurture him:

> Late in the forest I did Cupid see
> Cold, wet and crying; he had lost his way,
> And, being blind, was farther like to stray,
> Which sight a kind compassion bred in me.
>
> (p. 119)

In spite of the kindness Wroth's sonnet persona shows, Cupid, like Bertram, returns injury for care: 'Burning my heart, who had him kindly warmed' (p. 119). The Petrarchan mode of masochistic love is modified into a 'natural' form of maternal self-sacrifice by the female speaker. Helen's illogical pursuit of the cruel Bertram works in a similar way. She suffers abuse in a process of education and redemption by which Bertram will be socialized as a cooperative member of the courtly community.

Helen's success is not simply the result of an intense and enduring passion for Bertram. It relies on a series of non-sexual relationships with her surrogate mothers and sister. The pursuit of desire depends heavily on an unspoken understanding between the women, seen first between Helen and the Countess. Once the Countess has established that Helen loves Bertram the real reason for her journey to cure the King hangs as an unspoken secret between the women. The Countess promises to 'pray God's blessing into thy attempt' (1.3.241), knowing full well that the 'attempt' is to win her son's hand in marriage. This is the first of many scenes of female conspiracy in the play where intentions are understood rather than made explicit, a dramatic technique that makes the play especially receptive to the projected wishes of female spectators. *All's Well That Ends Well* contains significant gaps as to the motivation of the characters, the most obvious example being when Helen leaves Roussillon to become a pilgrim. It is impossible to know whether here, as before, her purported reasons for travel disguise a more self-interested agenda, a quest to find Bertram rather than the shrine of St Jacques le Grand. Instead of reading Helen's soliloquy as a declaration of self-sacrificing love, spectators could see her determination to 'steal away' in the dark like a 'poor thief' as the pursuit of a covert, driving passion (3.2.29). As Susan Snyder remarks, 'indefinition opens space for multiple interpretations', in which the audience can fill in the gaps with their own assumptions and needs.[20] Beneath the coincidental, fairy-tale plot, or the idea of divine providence governing the action, women spectators could weave a more subversive, feminist narrative. The subtext of the play traces the subtle but unstoppable workings of female desire, its consummation through self-determination and sisterly cooperation. Such energies are inherently dangerous to a society based on the principle of male superiority. Their presence becomes obvious in the final scene, where the King notes anxiously 'all yet seems well' (5.3.329).

Helen's negotiations with paternal authority are dramatized at the French court. Since Bertram is the King's ward, she must win his approval for the match just as a male suitor would have to. Soliciting paternal approval is more complex for Helen, though. She trades her father's cure for the right to choose a husband, for the King's sanction of romantic advances which would normally be thought of as immodest. Helen is well aware of the dangers to her reputation. She tells the King that if the cure fails, she will lay herself open to

Tax of impudence
A strumpet's boldness, a divulgèd shame;
Traduced by ballads, my maiden's name
Seared.

(2.1.169)

Curing the King and declaring her passions are curiously linked in Helen's mind. The nature of the King's sickness reinforces the connections. His fistula is symbolic of the disease which affects the French court and Bertram in particular: an obsessive form of homosocial bonding based on fear of female passion. Mars and Venus are diametrically opposed for the French courtiers, most extremely in the minds of Paroles and Bertram. Ironically, by seeking military valour on the battlefield, Bertram is running away from the unknown world of mutual heterosexual desire to the more familiar territory of all-male camaraderie, in which women are no more than objects of male lust. The King is, indirectly, the source of such exclusive male bonding. His memories of Bertram's father (1.2.24–67) hark back nostalgically to a golden age of male companionship; his court is peopled by lords, soldiers and doctors unable to cure its disease of introverted narcissism.

Helen uses her father's knowledge to break into that claustrophobic world and open its abscess. Lafeu's comments about the King's transformation suggests there is something sexual about the cure (2.3.25 and 38). Its effects are certainly physical since the King is carried off the stage and returns dancing like a lover. He and Helen both attribute the 'miracle' to divine intervention, the 'showing of a heavenly effect in an earthly actor' (2.3.22), and critics have seen references to God's purpose as an attempt to reinscribe Helen's power within a larger patriarchal framework. For example, Lisa Jardine proposes that Helen's dangerous, secret knowledge and active sexuality are finally transmuted into the chaste duty of 'the knowing, ideal wife'.[21] Such readings do not take adequate account of Helen's plotting and sexual self-fulfillment in the latter part of the play. *All's Well* rewrites the relationship between knowledge and sexuality from a distinctly feminist perspective.

In Act 2, Scene 1 Helen's expertise challenges the male monopoly on learning enjoyed by the doctors. When her help is refused, the 'Doctor She' (2.1.77) then goes on to challenge the King himself by referring to the higher authority of God:

Inspirèd merit so by breath is barred.
It is not so with him that all things knows
As 'tis with us that square our guess by shows.

(2.1.147)

96

Helen suggests that the power of royal 'breath' is being abused since it bars or prevents the workings of divinely inspired merit like her own. Attributing her power to God and to her father does seem conservative at first, but in claiming access to a knowledge beyond mortal understanding, Helen initiates another feminist reinterpretation of the narrative of Eden, like that explored in chapter 1. The appearance or 'show' of women under the gaze of patriarchal ideology is deceptive, Helen argues. She asks the King to make a leap of faith, to see her from God's perspective as man's equal, and to trust that women have the capacity for knowledge whose effects are beneficent rather than evil. The price of her knowledge is respectful recognition of female sexuality and its regenerative power. She asks the King 'will you make it even?' (2.1.190), demanding public acknowledgement of her skill in the form of a gift which will satisfy her sexual desires. Her cheeks tell her '"We blush that thou shouldst choose"' (2.3.67), but the King's supportive voice dissolves the oppressive force of convention to let her speak and act for herself.

These tentative steps towards a more understanding relationship between the sexes are brutally shattered by Bertram. Refusing Helen's love is a rejection of female desire within romance. Even though Helen offers herself in subjection, Bertram finds the betrothal ceremony shocking because it feminizes him as a commodity, a gift from father to suitor, as Carolyn Asp points out.[22] The audience may well hold some sympathy for the Bertram who is surprised by having a wife thrust upon him. When the power dialectic in betrothal is reversed it seems that his desires are now being ignored, a brilliant exposé of the ways women were often treated. Promises of a large dowry and a title cannot make Helen sexually attractive in Bertram's eyes, blinded as he is by his own preconceptions about proper feminine behaviour. Helen's tentative request for a kiss makes it clear how far from achieving her goal she still is:

BERTRAM: What would you have?
HELEN: Something and scarce so much: nothing indeed.
I would not tell you what I would, my lord. Faith, yes:
Strangers and foes do sunder and not kiss.
BERTRAM: I pray you, stay not, but in haste to horse.

(3.1.78)

This poignant exchange shifts audience sympathy back to Helen. The frank confession of her sexual appetite snatches happiness away even as it seems to lie within her grasp. One of Lady Mary Wroth's sonnets captures Helen's pain exactly:

97

Eyes, having won, rejecting proves a sting,
   Killing the bud before the tree doth spring;
   Sweet lips, not loving, do as poison prove.

(p. 25)

Winning Bertram's hand does not bring Helen the happy ending of fairy tale. The harsh reality of Renaissance sexual mores which permeates the play makes her advances repellent to him.

Helen must undertake a second quest to win Bertram's heart by cleverly usurping the position of disdainful chastity that he finds so attractive. Diana's goddess of chastity is the opposite of Helen's deity of desire, Venus, yet Helen must perform Diana's role to give Bertram the illusion of virile sexual conquest which the unconventional betrothal denied him. In effect, the bed trick disempowers Bertram as he is passed between the women in exchange for a dowry for Diana. It is his virginity which is commodified in the symbolic exchange of rings, as Diana gives his to Helen and she gives her own ring to Bertram in bed. Instead of being undermined and blown up by a man, Helen endows her body 'to her own liking' (1.1.140). In contrast, Bertram's ignorance of his partner in the bed trick is metaphorical as well as literal. He cannot see beyond Helen's unconventional behaviour to know and value her, however much he may know her carnally. The exposure of Paroles, and the home truths he speaks, inaugurates a slow process of self-recognition for Bertram which must continue if all is really to end well.

The play shows that collaboratively, women can subvert the male-dominated world they are forced to inhabit. Diana, her mother and Helen use feminine ingenuity to unmask the corrupt artifice of masculine romance. Having listened to Bertram's adulterous vows, Diana says

My mother told me just how he would woo
As if she sat in's heart. She says all men
Have the like oaths . . .
Marry that will; I live and die a maid.

(4.2.70)

The three women represent an empowering trinity of female love which can re-create Helen from the annihilation to which Bertram's hate has doomed her. Diana determines to 'live and die a maid' (4.2.75) but will risk her reputation to help Helen. Her mother's knowledge, like that of the Countess, offers a protective love. Helen is the intermediate Christ-like figure who is transformed by 'death': the Passion or orgasm which marks the death of her virginal self and rebirth into sexual knowledge and maternity. In a comment rich with innuendo we learn that Helen 'made a groan of her last breath and now she breathes in heaven' (4.3.51). The female solidarity which these characters represent contextualizes erotic love within what Carolyn Asp calls 'the larger sphere of female affectivity'.[23]

The appeal of a wider emotional range in romance is also shown in Wroth's work. The happy ending of *Love's Victorie*, for example, depends on a romantic dissolution of competitive relations between women. Silvesta, whose love for Philisses was rejected, bears no grudge towards her rival, Musella. Like Shakespeare's Diana, she dedicates herself to chastity:

> I with Dian stand
> Against love's changing and blind foolery
> To hold with happy and blessed chastity.
> (1.1.88)

She tells Musella that, out of love for her, she will offer any 'service which to your content may tend' in winning Philisses's love (3.1.52). Like Diana in *All's Well*, Silvesta leads the romantic heroine and her lover through 'death' to rebirth when her happiness is threatened by another contract. She gives Musella and Philisses what she says is poison to escape the arranged marriage, and is prepared to be burned alive for the deed in a striking display of female friendship. Although tragedy and punishment seem imminent, female agency is a positive force in this play. The goddess Venus miraculously restores the lovers to life and rewards Silvesta with 'Immortal fame and bands of firmest love / In their kind breasts where true affections move' (5.7.73). Silvesta is, Venus says, 'my instrument' (5.5.71), just as Diana becomes the willing instrument to Helen's Venus. In both plays, love's victory is won by powerful maternal figures who work in concert with chaste sisters.

The final scene of *All's Well* dramatizes a shift from death to life, from ignorance to knowledge, in which women are the controlling figures. Knowledge is in their hands and the men are helpless to counter their accusations or undo their riddles. Helen's appearance as mother-to-be symbolizes the fruitful combination of erotic and maternal energies which have allowed her to achieve her goal. As the riddle states, 'one that's dead is quick' (5.3.300). The fulfilment of Helen's desires is a self-created miracle. She embodies the power to counter mortality in her own self-resurrection and in her life-giving womb. Female knowledge and self-possession, the source of Eve's subjection, are rewritten in a narrative of redemption and renewal. The men are slow to learn this new knowledge. As Adam's sons, they cling to traditional readings of Genesis and of woman. Diana's riddling wisdom makes the King impatient, and although his promise of a husband seems to revalidate Helen's actions, it also betrays his blindness to Diana's wish to remain a maid (he does not even consider this as a possibility). Similarly, although Bertram seems repentant, his reformation is yet to come. At the end of the play the men are uncertain. For the daughters of Eve, however, it is a triumphant celebration. The primacy of female knowledge and the regenerative female body return them to a new beginning. In the rebirth of Helen as the knowing, controlling mother-to-be, female spectators see an affirmation of their own desires for self-expression, agency and equality in difference.

While Helen, the physician's daughter, struggles to win the love of her lord, aristocratic female characters face different restrictions on their desires. 'The misery of us that are born great', says Webster's Duchess, is that 'We are forced to woo, because none dare woo us' (2.1.357).[24] Tragedy in *The Duchess of Malfi* (1614) centres on the fact that, for the noble elite, female sexuality determines ownership of property and blood. The need to protect these material and metaphorical assets resulted in rigorous enclosure of the female body and a tendency to fossilize it in the service of the family. The image of the Duchess of Malfi as a 'figure cut in alabaster' who 'kneels at [her] husband's tomb' (1.2.370) is just what her brothers want to protect their own conservative interests in the estate. In the dynastic family model, active sexuality is displaced onto the figure of the whore. Since female orgasm was considered a vital element in conception, aristocratic women's passion was necessary for dynastic renewal but could not easily be reconciled with the ideal of disembodied chastity.[25] The first description of the Duchess draws attention to the problem:

> For her discourse, it is so full of rapture,
> You only will begin, then to be sorry
> When she doth end her speech . . .
>
> > whilst she speaks
> She throws upon a man so sweet a look,
> That it were able to raise one to a galliard
> That lay in a dead palsy; and to dote
> On that sweet countenance: but in that look
> There speaketh so divine a continence,
> That cuts off all lascivious, and vain hope.
> Her days are practis'd in such noble virtue,
> That, sure her nights, nay more, her very sleeps,
> Are more in heaven, than other ladies' shrifts.
>
> > > (1.2.112)

Antonio's admiring words break the Duchess into two halves that threaten to dissolve into each other. The woman who opens her mouth to speak has a tongue and discourse which produce 'rapture' in her listeners. Her knowing looks seem to have the same sexually provocative power as Helen's magical cure of the King in *All's Well*. Having dwelt on these sensual pleasures, Antonio swiftly cuts off all 'lascivious' associations to redefine the Duchess in spiritual terms as a model of heavenly virtue. He tries to 'case the picture up' (1.2.129), to recontain her as a silent object rather than a sexually enticing subject.

The Duchess's brothers are even more anxious to control her sexuality. She is a widow who 'know[s] already what man is' (1.2.215), so her erotic appetite is a disturbing presence. Leonard Tennenhouse rightly observes that the aristocratic lady is a dangerous figure on the Renaissance stage because her body 'produces either a desirous or desiring self'. She is either the object of passions which threaten the aristocratic community's boundaries or she is the subject of clandestine desire. The latter is particularly disturbing since it undoes gender as well as class distinctions. Passionate ladies are monstrous since they 'bring an extra member into the body politic' by integrating lower-class lovers and by taking on 'the features of masculine desire themselves'.[26] The Duchess's love for Antonio pollutes the aristocratic female body in precisely this way. As Bosola remarks, the 'pretty art' of 'grafting' or intercourse has dissolved the difference between noble and ignoble blood (2.1.148–9). Beneath the Duchess's majestic costume kicks the unborn child of a servant, an incorporation of the low by the elite, the 'young springal cutting a caper in her belly' (2.1.155).

The ring is an important symbol for female sexuality in this play and its meaning is ambiguous. As an unbroken circle, it represents the enclosed chastity which guarantees and isolates aristocratic elitism, distinctiveness. At the same time, however, the ring (like the vagina) is glaringly open, a hole to be penetrated by lower-class fingers like Antonio's. When the Duchess offers him her wedding ring he tells her 'There is a saucy and ambitious devil / Is dancing in this circle' (1.2.329). *The Duchess of Malfi* depicts the struggle to open or close the ring of the female aristocratic body. The romance of Sydelia in Lady Mary Wroth's *Urania* provides a useful parallel text to suggest how women spectators might have responded to the play. It splits elements of the Duchess's story between two aristocratic women whose affections for the hero, Antonarus, are frustrated by the intervention of a powerful male rival, the villain Terichillus.[27]

The Duchess is, as Frank Whigham observes, 'an exogamous family pioneer',[28] navigating by the compass of her own will and pleasure rather than duty to the dynasty into which she was born. She opens up the circle to create a new kind of family which defies distinctions of gender and class. She recognizes that by planning to propose to Antonio, she is entering 'a wilderness / Where I shall find nor path nor friendly clew / To be my guide'

(1.2.278). Her boldness contrasts favourably with the more restrictive passions of Julia, who mistakenly believes that her sexual attraction gives her power over men. Julia regards modesty as 'a troublesome familiar' to ladies (5.2.167) and solicits Bosola, telling him that 'great women of pleasure' such as herself do not waste time with 'unquiet longings' but enjoy the 'sweet delight' of consummation instantly (5.2.189–94). This very liberal attitude represents only an illusory freedom. The Cardinal torments Julia with guilty thoughts about the 'giddy and wild turnings' in herself (2.4.12). Her verbal and sexual openness proves her undoing when he finally poisons her.

The Duchess's proposal to Antonio is more subtle yet it disturbs the gender hierarchy much more deeply. Giving her ring to Antonio is an autonomous act, as she wittily acknowledges by telling him 'I am making my will' (1.2.295). Whereas Antonio 'took the ring' in the 'sportive' action of the joust (1.2.6–10), now the Duchess uses it to manoeuvre him into marriage. Her adroit control of the situation disguises any emotional hesitation, but both Antonio and Cariola recognize the dangers of her actions. In the Sydelia story of Wroth's *Urania,* tragedy is the direct result of such unconventional behaviour. The Austrian noblewoman who is beloved of both Antonarus and Terichillus expresses her love to the former, 'most prizing worth' like Webster's Duchess. However, out of love for his friend, Antonarus leaves and Terichillus intercepts the lady's letter proposing marriage, replying in Antonarus's place 'that he despised her forwardness'. The lady's heart breaks. When she meets Antonarus on her deathbed, she asks pardon for declaring her love 'since I feare my former boldness made you despise me'. Discovering the truth, she sends Antonarus her ring in a moment that recalls Webster's play:

> then taking a ring from off her finger (which was a pointed Diamond she ever wore, & had vowed to doe so, till she died or married) charged her [woman] to give it *Antonarus*, then turning to her other side, tell him (said she) I bequeath this my truest love and last love to him, & so I conjure him to keepe these.[29]

Such lines suggest that female spectators or readers of *The Duchess of Malfi* would have quickly picked up the more sinister undertones of the betrothal scene, to read a certain doom in the Duchess's determined making of her 'will'. The death knell resounds as surely as a heartbeat when the Duchess kisses Antonio with the words 'I sign your *Quietus est*' (1.2.380). Women spectators who were surrounded by cultural prohibitions on their behaviour were probably sharply attuned to a sense of self-destruction attendant on the audacity of the Duchess's self-determination.

In open defiance of dynastic politics, and perhaps with tragic prescience, the Duchess creates a ring with her arms to embrace Antonio, wilfully carving out a private space in which their love can blossom. As well as challenging her brothers' authority, the clandestine marriage allows her to maintain her high-status position as Antonio's mistress. She does not submit to his husbandly authority. The inversion of gender roles is emphasized when Ferdinand brings her a poniard, which she calmly accepts from him with the self-possession of 'a prince' (3.2.71). In contrast, Antonio arrives late and flustered onto the scene and is frightened by the sword. Instead of taking it up as her protector, he suggests the Duchess should defend him:

> This hath a handle to't
> As well as a point: turn it towards him, and
> So fasten the keen edge in his rank gall.
>
> (3.2.152)

The swapping of traditional chivalric roles is almost comic as the Duchess endeavours to hurry Antonio and their eldest son away to safety.

The Duchess's chief weapon is her tongue, which gives her freedom to govern and dispose of her own property, including her self. Throughout the play her power of speech unsettles patriarchal family values. By declaring that 'Diamonds are of most value / They say, that have pass'd through most jewellers' hands' (1.2.220), she aligns herself more closely with the whore than the chaste, disembodied wife. Her rhetorical cleverness allows her to manipulate Bosola into declaring it is wrong 'rather to examine men's pedigrees, than virtues' (3.2.260), thus pre-empting any criticism of her choice of husband. Similarly, she easily unravels Ferdinand's riddles about wanting Antonio's *'heart'* or *'head in a business'* to see the literal threats they pose (3.5.27–45). Ferdinand perceives his sister's tongue as a treacherous instrument and so advises her to cut it out (3.2.109). The way he has her murdered is therefore not surprising. As he says, 'strangling is a very quiet death' (5.4.33); it silences the self-proclaiming female voice.

The play positions Ferdinand as the male reflection of his twin sister. Interestingly, he is the younger twin rather than the first-born, and the Duchess's claim to independence is profoundly threatening because it destabilizes his identity as a primary subject, or origin of authority. Throughout the play, Ferdinand struggles to reconstruct her as a reflection or projection of himself. His intensely introverted tendencies appear as incestuous desire. As Whigham remarks, Ferdinand's incest is social as much as sexual. It is 'elite paranoia', an obsessive wish to close off the aristocratic family, an inward-looking disease that culminates in the lycanthropy where Ferdinand feels his skin 'hairy ... on the inside' (5.2.17).[30] That such paranoia fastens its desires on the Duchess confirms the social and political importance of the aristocratic female body. From a feminist perspective, the way Ferdinand tries to destroy the Duchess's self-fashioned identity is even more important.

While the Duchess strives to move outside the patriarchal family circle, Ferdinand longs to bind her within it, as is clear when he returns her wedding ring 'for a love token' on the dead man's hand (4.1.47). The petrifying nature of his desire is proved by the fact that he can only repossess her by imprisoning and killing her. It is founded on denial rather than a wish for enjoyment, specifically a denial of her new subjectivity. As he confines the Duchess to smaller and smaller 'presence chamber[s]', she grows more beautiful in his eyes as a silent 'shape of loveliness' and suffering (4.1.7). Ferdinand's torture chamber is a magnificent palace where he re-creates her as an object indistinguishable from the grotesque mannequins of her husband and children, or from her 'picture in the gallery', which Cariola says is 'a deal of life in show but none in practice' (4.2.32).

The terrifying power of Ferdinand is echoed in the second part of Wroth's tragic romance where Sydelia, Terichillus's sister, falls in love with Antonarus and secretly marries him. Terichillus is incensed, has Antonarus murdered, and forces Sydelia to ride with his corpse back to the city 'as the substance and demonstration of my miserie'. The heroine responds to such perversity with composure, not unlike the Duchess, and the reader is invited to condemn the tyrannical brother as 'unkind and cruell', 'unnatural' and unbalanced.[31] Nevertheless, his destructive malice cannot be withstood. In *The Duchess of Malfi* Ferdinand's possessive love of his sister is equally unnatural and his destructive power equally irresistible. To female spectators, he may have represented their worst nightmares about the controlling figures in their own lives. Ferdinand denies the Duchess the right to exist as a living woman of 'flesh and blood' (1.2.369), reconstructing her as 'some reverend monument', like the alabaster statue at her husband's tomb (4.2.34). He pulls the concentric circles of the patriarchal family tighter around her until they stop her breath (the wedding ring and the noose is paralleled in Cariola's murder). 'Is she dead?' he asks, to which Bosola tellingly replies 'She is what / You'll'd have her' (4.2.251).

Nevertheless, the Duchess maintains faith in herself and the right to love as she chooses. 'I am the Duchess of Malfi still' (4.2.139) is not a declaration of social status since she scorns to be 'shot to death with pearls' (4.2.212–14). Her sense of self is linked to the 'excellent company' (4.2.208) of the man she has chosen as a companion in marriage and their children. The details about her son's cough and her daughter's prayers reaffirm, even in the face of death, the domestic sphere she created with the ring of her arms (4.2.200). The 'integrity of life' (5.5.119) which Delio celebrates in the closing lines of the play is a fitting description of the Duchess, whose end does crown her self-fashioned identity. In spite of Ferdinand's attempt to silence her 'last woman's fault' (4.2.222) of speech, her voice returns in the echo that speaks to Antonio. Ferdinand's fear of his own shadow, wanting to 'throttle it' (5.2.38) because it haunts him, shows that he is still threatened by the power of the twin whose indomitable spirit challenges his own primacy. Bosola too feels he is haunted and, at the end of the play, the Cardinal makes reference to another brooding female presence that will spell the end of the patriarchal dynasty:

> None of our family dies, but there is seen
> The shape of an old woman, which is given
> By tradition, to us, to have been murther'd
> By her nephews, for her riches.
>
> (5.2.89)

The return of the repressed female spirit, crushed in the interests of masculine self-possession, will always trouble the men in power.

Female-driven romance ends in tragedy for Webster's Duchess but leads to more transgressive behaviour in Thomas Drue's *The Duchess of Suffolk* (1624). Like the Duchess of Malfi, the eponymous heroine of this drama chooses to marry her steward. The character is based on the historical Duchess of Suffolk, persecuted for her Protestant faith during the reign of Mary Tudor. The play opens with the Duchess publicly rejecting the suits of the King of Poland, the Duke of Northumberland and the Earl of Erbaigh in favour of her servant Bertie. She vows to be 'Queene of my rich desires in marrying thee' (B1). This 'madcap' (B2) assertion of will does more than fulfilling her erotic wishes; it marks out the Duchess as a kind of superwoman who will combine traditional female roles with masculine ones in her struggle against Mary's Catholic bishops. The emotional haven of the nuclear family with a mother at its centre lies at the heart of *The Duchess of Suffolk*.[32] The Duchess is a loving wife and a devoted mother, tenderly carrying her infant daughter through the streets of London in an escape to the continent. She is next depicted heavily pregnant, yet not even the onset of labour in the middle of a thunderstorm or an attempted rape by robbers can dampen her spirits. Soon after giving birth to a son in a church porch, she eludes Mary's bishops by leaving the city hidden in a hearse with her new baby. By setting the Duchess's exceptional dangers alongside those risked by all women in pregnancy and childbirth, these scenes advertise the resilience of the female body, its strength to endure suffering, as heroic. Although the Duchess is 'a Princesse' (F3), important details link her experiences with other classes of female spectators. She escapes *'like a*

Citizens' wife' (D1), loses her wealth in the robbery (F2) and gives birth like a pauper in 'a homely place' without even a couch or curtains (F3).

The Duchess excels in more unconventional skills as well; she is a deft swordswoman who, like the Duchess of Malfi, outdoes her husband in terms of martial bravery. When attacked by soldiers, she cries 'Then farewell woman weaknes, welcome sword, / For once Ile play the man, to save my lord. *She fights, beates them off*' (H2v). The Duchess's remarkable courage and tenderness, in addition to some very lucky breaks, are explained as the result of her faith. The model of staunch Protestantism she presents to female spectators is certainly not a conventional one, however. Under the celebration of religious integrity, women in the audience could also read a more subversive celebration of self-integrity, a woman's ability to mould herself, her family and her own heroic quest.

For female characters in more traditional romance structures, masculine costume offers a means to express feelings of love like the sex who were 'made to woo' (*A Midsummer Night's Dream*, 2.1.242). Romantic comedies which feature cross-dressed heroines can radically destabilize conventional gender roles, though for the heroines, masculine attire is as problematic as it is enabling. In *As You Like It* (1599), Rosalind exclaims 'what shall I do with my doublet and hose!' (3.2.200) once she discovers Orlando is in the forest, and in *Twelfth Night* (1601) Viola's costume as Caesario does not free her voice to declare her love to Orsino. Her initial choice of masculine identity is significant, as Stephen Orgel remarks.[33] Having noted that Orsino is a 'bachelor' (a potential marriage prospect), and having discovered that Olivia's house is closed to visitors, Viola decides to present herself to the Duke as 'an eunuch' (1.2.52). The eunuch, who is physically incapable of expressing desire through intercourse, personifies bottled-up passion. Viola's new persona therefore duplicates her sexual frustration rather than offering a release. The Captain says 'Be you his eunuch and your mute I'll be' (1.2.58), hinting at how the disguise will silence Viola.

Viola is not completely silenced, of course. The play's numerous references to her 'maiden's organ' suggest she appropriates the eunuch's voice in her guise as page, as Kier Elam has pointed out.[34] Viola's feelings find lyrical expression in the willow cabin speech where she promises to sing 'loyal cantons of contemnèd love' (1.5.239). The fact that she never does sing on stage emphasizes the perpetual deferral of satisfaction to a point beyond reach and, paradoxically, provokes desire in the eyes of the beholder. Olivia reads Viola's spontaneous departure from her conventional wooing 'text' (1.5.204) in relation to her own attraction to Caesario. To whom and as whom is Viola speaking at this point? The 'babbling gossip of the air' who will cry out '"Olivia"' (1.5.243) is an allusion to the female Echo, and the play poses the possibility that if the only safe audience for women's romantic declarations is that of other women, then erotic attraction between them will inevitably present itself as an alternative.

The appeal of the cross-dressed heroine for female characters and spectators need not necessarily be erotic, of course. It could involve identification *with* as well as longing *for*. Having listened to Caesario, Olivia is encouraged to declare her own feelings, excusing her boldness with the reasoning that 'Love sought is good but given unsought is better' (3.1.147). In Shakespeare's comedies the multi-layered persona of a boy actor playing a female character (Viola/Rosalind) disguised as a boy (Caesario/Ganymede) makes his/her relationships with other characters and spectators ambiguous, creating space for a multiplicity of desires in which subject and object positions are constantly shifting.[35] Sexual identities as well as gender identities are redefined as constructs of performance in plays whose titles invite characters and audience to read romance as they like it or according to what they will. Female tastes are as important as male: the epilogue to *As You Like It* appeals to women to 'like as much of this play as please you' (Epilogue.11).

While cross-dressing does allow the expression of female desire, it also threatens to eclipse it under the overbearing shadow of homoerotic attraction, as Rosalind's name 'Ganymede' makes explicit. Rosalind and Viola enjoy freedom in male clothes but each is obliged to re-create herself in fictional form in order to be both the subject and object of desire. Ganymede tells Orlando that 'he' will pretend to be Rosalind. Viola as Caesario creates another persona who is a return to her feminine identity:

VIOLA: My father had a daughter loved a man
As it might be, perhaps, were I a woman
I should your lordship.
ORSINO: And what's her history?
VIOLA: A blank, my lord. She never told her love,
But let concealment, like a worm i'th' bud,
Feed on her damask cheek. She pined in thought,
And with a green and yellow melancholy
She sat like patience on a monument
Smiling at grief.

(2.4.106)

Why does Viola refuse this invitation to give another version of her willow cabin speech? It is possible that she only presents a blank because she has internalized the prescriptions on female modesty so deeply that she cannot speak her love, even at two removes of sister-persona and disguise. The other possibility is, of course, that she recognizes her costume could present attractions for Orsino as well as for Olivia, that Orsino will fall in love with her as a boy or as a eunuch. The wooing scenes here and in *As You Like It* are alive with homoerotic possibilities and in each case the male costume imposes restraint rather than freedom. Counterfeiting to be a 'Rosalind' of 'a more coming-on disposition' (4.1.96) brings Rosalind temptingly close to the fulfilment of her longings, yet when Orlando offers to kiss her she quickly replies 'nay, you were better speak first' (4.1.63). Rosalind's refusal of what she desires, out of modesty or fear of discovery, disguises a much deeper fear that 'she' may not be what Orlando wants, that he may want to kiss a boy.

In *Twelfth Night* the sexual allure of the eunuch threatens Viola's romantic interests just as much as the homoerotic attraction of the boy because the eunuch personifies the tantalizing but unconsummated love which Orsino wallows in so luxuriously. For Orsino to fall in love with his eunuch would be to become trapped in a fantasy of self-love rather than love of another. His unrequited passion for Olivia would be mirrored in the perpetual deferral of satisfaction personified by the eunuch. The boy actor whose lip is 'smooth and rubious' though 'semblative of woman's part' (1.4.31–3) keeps both the boy and the eunuch alive as alternative objects of Orsino's passion. Even in the final lines of the play, Orsino takes Caesario's hand and Viola and the actor remain in masculine attire. The satisfaction of Viola's passion is still out of reach. For all the appearance of liberty, then, cross-dressing seems to gesture to fulfilment beyond the pastoral retreats of Shakespearean comedy. At the end of *As You Like It* Rosalind steps out of Arden and into the realm of the audience at the edge of the stage. The city offers different kinds of 'liberty' for cross-dressing and other types of female pleasure.

II

The city is a crossroads or market place in which traditional gender roles and even sexual identities can be exchanged and interrogated. A foreign visitor to Renaissance London remarked that 'the women there have much more liberty than perhaps in any other place; they also know well how to make use of it'.[36] *A Letter Sent by Maydens of London* (1567) demonstrates how women valued and used the liberty that the city afforded them. In this pamphlet six maidservants (Rose, Jane, Rachell, Sara, Philumias and Dorothy) reply to an earlier anti-feminist attack on their activities. The legal references in the *Letter* suggest that its real author was male, yet the equally precise details about domestic service argue for a woman's contribution, so perhaps it was composed collaboratively.[37] The maidservants appeal to their 'matrons and mistresses' to support their rights to 'our lawful libertie' in the city. Liberty to spend their leisure time in 'talkes, meetings, drinkings, going to playes and sporting &c' (p. 296) leads to greater liberties to choose their husbands. The maidens argue that 'sith love should be the principall cause in mariage, why shold we be blamed, for chosing wher we most love and fansie?' Their own 'liking' or physical attraction to a partner is of the utmost importance. The advice of parents is to be disregarded if 'we can not frame our selves to love the partie that our parentes have provided for us' and they defend the value of 'privie contracts' with their lovers (pp. 300–1). Such outspoken ideas on the rights of women to assert their erotic preferences seem to be generated by the range of leisure activities offered by the city. The maidens staunchly defend their freedom to spend their hard-earned wages 'in good chere and banketting', eating and drinking in public houses, and in attending plays where they can 'bothe take learning and pleasure' (p. 301).

The 'Liberties' of Renaissance London, where theatres were located, offered special opportunities for pleasurable pastimes in which gender conventions could be challenged. The Liberties were nominally under the authority of the City Fathers but were 'in a limited sense, places of literal "liberty" opened within the city by the contradictions between its legal structure and its material life', as Susan Wells remarks.[38] Plays that were set in the city as well as being performed in that culturally liminal space could expose contradictions between the ideals of feminine behaviour and the emergence of proto-feminist demands for equality, based on women's material experiences. In the *Letter*, the maidens claim that 'under those six names' are 'above six thousand of us' (p. 297), suggesting an enormous appetite for such entertainment.

Jonson's *Epicoene* (1609) opens with an explicit acknowledgement of the need to cater for the particular tastes of its female spectators. The prologue announces that the poet has taken care to serve a variety of local delicacies to please all:

> Though there be none far-fet, there will dear-bought
> Be fit for ladies; some for lords, knights, squires,
> Some for your waiting-wench and city wires,
> Some for your men and daughters of Whitefriars.
> (Prologue.20)[39]

The luxurious tastes of ladies, the delights of fashionable citizens ('city wires'), the wishes of those in domestic service, and even the needs of 'daughters of Whitefriars' (probably prostitutes), can be served by Jonson's menu. He self-consciously eschews 'far-fet' exotic settings in favour of

London to give a sophisticated demonstration of how his female spectators' tastes and pleasures have been constructed by the city. This play, the prologue assures, will give them food for thought as they leave the theatre.

In *Epicoene*, London is a centre of extravagant consumption. The play's witty dramatization of commerce offers to instruct as well as entertain those women in the audience with money to spend – either as housekeepers or as wage-earners.[40] Karen Newman's astute analysis of the play argues that in images of female speech, sexuality and commodities, Jonson shows how 'women enter the sphere of early seventeenth century London by going to market, both to buy and sell'.[41] Dekker's *Gull's Hornbook* (1609) claimed 'The theatre is your poets' Royal Exchange', and the prologue's image of female spectators as guests at an inn links their purchasing power as playgoers with that of the female characters who go shopping 'to the china houses or to the Exchange' (4.3.22).[42]

Since china and expensive fabrics say more about the purchaser's tastes than her material needs, the consumption of luxury goods in Renaissance London can suggest 'the existence of a subculture, in which women were able to express themselves' through their possessions. Feminist historians have been eager to uncover evidence of such a subculture, although the nature of household inventories makes this difficult.[43] However, personal letters and journals offer glimpses of women as consumers. For example, correspondence from Joan Thynne to her husband is filled with details of various luxury items from the capital. In 1576 Joan reports that she has bought a 'nightcap of red satin' and has been pricing 'crystal buttons'. In 1595 she has received clothes and 'pomegranates' – ornamental fastenings or decorations. She requests cloth of 'some other pretty colour' to make the children clothes for Christmas, and 'cambric thread, silver and spangles' are bought to decorate the gowns of her daughters in 1601.[44] Even the extremely pious Lady Margaret Hoby went shopping on a visit to London, reporting in her diary 'I went with Mrs Thornborough to the Exchange' and 'I went with my mother to see the glass house', where Venetian glass was made and sold.[45]

Lorna Weatherill has tentatively argued that women's ownership of 'new and decorative goods' in the later seventeenth century may indicate their 'independence to acquire what they wanted and to satisfy their own tastes'.[46] In the early seventeenth-century London of Jonson's play, the women exercise just such independence in their purchase of expensive objects to decorate themselves and their houses. The Collegiates and Mistress Otter are inveterate shoppers and in these caricatures, the play offers female spectators an exaggerated image of their own power as consumers. Truewit warns Morose that if he marries a wife she must have a rich gown for such a great day, a new one for the next, a richer for the third; be served in silver; have the chamber filled with a succession of grooms, embroiderers, jewellers, tire-women, sempsters, feathermen, perfumers; while she feels not how the land drops away, nor the acres melt.

(2.3.101)

The insatiable quality of women's appetite for goods is made manifest in the figure of Mistress Otter, whose damask tablecloth, black satin gown, wire and ruff, and crimson suit are disposable, to be replaced with newer and better items once they are damaged (3.2.60–70). To the patriarchal hierarchy of Renaissance England she is the nightmare of uncontrolled inflation. Her ambitions for more expensive possessions are linked to inflated ideas of her social status and to monstrous dominance in the little commonwealth of the family. Mistress Otter rules as a Princess over the finances and her husband. It is she who allows him 'maintenance', clothes and pocket money while he must be her 'subject' and 'obey' (3.1.30–9).

The characters' power as consumers does present a problem for the feminist critic since their choice of costumes and accessories to make themselves attractive threatens to recodify them as objects of male desire. Truewit argues that women should repair nature with art, that they should devote all their attention to the enhancement of what would appear attractive in male eyes, and to the concealment of anything that would offend the male gaze (4.1.31–48). *Epicoene* warns that the woman addicted to commodities is herself in danger of being commodified. The most explicit example is in Otter's description of his wife as 'a great German clock', composed of pieces which come from all over the city (4.2.83–90). Spectators are invited to see how their tastes are, in fact, constructed from outside. Mistress Otter's commanding appearance dissolves instantly when confronted by the phallic power of Morose, who *'descends with a long sword'* and terrifies her 'with a huge long naked weapon in both his hands' (4.3.2). As this moment graphically illustrates, the empowerment of women as consumers may only be illusory.

Awareness of how a commodifying culture represents a trap and an opportunity for self-expression is not exclusive to recent Marxist or feminist analysis. Isabella Whitney's poem *The Manner of Her Will and What She Left to London*, published in 1573, shows remarkable insight into how money, goods and identities are constructed in relation to each other.[47] Her mock legacy is an assertion of personal control over the city and its goods, all the more ironic since she has to leave London because of unemployment. Wilfully ignoring her material realities, Whitney claims intellectual ownership of the markets. She recognizes that 'many women, foolishly / Like me and many mo' have been drawn by the city's magnetic

111

power, only to be ruined (p. 289). She leaves Cheapside and the Royal Exchange specifically to ladies:

> ... plate to furnish cupboards with
> Full brave there you shall find,
> With purl of silver and of gold
> To satisfy your mind;
> With hoods, bongraces, hats or caps
> Such store are in that street
> As, if on t'one side you should miss,
> T'other serves you feat.
> For nets of every kind of sort
> I leave within the Pawn,
> French ruffs, high purls, gorgets, and sleeves
> Of any kind of lawn.
> For purse or knives, for comb or glass,
> Or any needful knack,
> I by the Stocks have left a boy
> Will ask you what you lack.

> (p. 293)

The illusion of choice proliferates with shops 'on either side', in the Pawn or covered arcade of the Royal Exchange and the Stocks Market place. Nevertheless, as the poem hints, there are 'nets of every kind of sort' in the shops; literally hairnets but, metaphorically, forms of entrapment. The profusion of goods constructs the women in terms of 'lack'. Combs and mirrors become as 'needful' as purses and the money necessary to buy into the beauty culture. Whitney's understanding of how values and identities are negotiated in the city's commercial traffic suggests that Renaissance women could have read the play's consumer culture from a feminist perspective.

Epicoene offers no feminist utopia beyond the city but shows how women can work within its confines to their own advantage. Even though Mistress Otter is a slave to fashion herself, 'the rich china-woman' seems to have profited from other women's addiction to china goods (1.4.25). Lady Haughty and her Collegiates are supremely conscious of their depreciating value in a market place constructed round male desire. With the same grim realism as the Rosalind who tells Phoebe 'Sell where you can. You are not for all markets' (*As You Like It*, 3.5.61), they know that age will wither them so they must make the most of their beauties (4.4.37–56). The Collegiates use commodities to enhance their sexual appeal, earning power to command 'with most masculine or rather hermaphroditical authority'

112

(1.1.76). Their use of male names signals their personal investment in the prevailing sexual economy, as they spend their sexual favours with as much freedom as their husbands' money. Knowing how the system works gives the Collegiates an intellectual purchase on the culture in which they are obliged to operate, just as Isabella Whitney's knowledge of London allows her to exert her 'will' even though she is materially powerless. As shrewd manipulators, the Collegiates can even destabilize masculine authority. Truewit claims that a successful courtier must learn to dress himself for the female gaze, according to her tastes (4.1.88–115), a reversal of conventional subject–object positions in romance.

The Collegiates' active engagement in the market of romance destabilizes courtship patterns, whose perils for women are made explicit in the speeches of Truewit. In Truewit's opinion, women must be wooed: 'They would solicit us, but that they are afraid. Howsoever they wish us in their hearts, we should solicit them' (4.1.71). *Epicoene* makes a radical exposé of this romantic convention as disabling and dangerous for women since it sanctions rape:

> TRUEWIT: Though they strive, they would be overcome.
> CLERIMONT: Oh, but a man must beware of force.
> TRUEWIT: It is to them an acceptable violence, and has oft-times the place of the greatest courtesy. She that might have been forced, and you let her go free without touching, though she then seem to thank you, will ever hate you after.
>
> (4.1.77)

Fortunately, the behaviour of the Collegiates gives the lie to Truewit's opinion of female modesty. Lady Haughty, Centaure and Mavis have no hesitation in expressing their sexual interests. Solicited by offers from all three ladies, Dauphine remarks 'I was never so assaulted' (5.2.49). Their sexual precocity may be comic, but for female spectators it offers a far more attractive alternative than being mapped as the passive territory for male desire to measure and conquer, as in Sir Jack Daw's fantasy of mapping Epicoene (5.1.16–23).[48] By the end of the play, female desire must be publicly acknowledged in Morose's confession that he has wronged 'your whole sex' by marrying Epicoene and then being unable to satisfy her sexually 'by reason of frigidity' (5.4.33–44). In spite of his ability to wield a 'huge long naked weapon' (4.3.2), Morose's physical 'infirmity' humiliates him in front of the 'lady' whose 'longings' represent those of her sex, and demand to be recognized (5.4.48).

As Richard Dutton observes, paradox is the dominant structural principle in *Epicoene*, the most extreme examples being Morose, the man with

phallic power who is simultaneously 'no man', and Epicoene, the supposedly silent woman who proves to be neither silent nor a woman.[49] These
two characters are pivotal tools by which the play explores the instability of
gender constructs. The play recognizes that the 'stiff piece of formality'
(1.1.138) which polarizes men and women as active subject and passive
object is already in decline in the new city environment where social and
financial exchange makes everything, including gender identity, fluid. All
the characters are somewhat epicene in nature, an effect highlighted in
performance where the roles would have been played by boy actors of the
Whitefriars company.[50] Dauphine (whose very name suggests femininity),
his page and the boy who plays Epicoene are able to shift gender roles with
the time, exerting their own erotic appeal for the women on stage and
possibly in the audience as well. In contrast, Morose clings adamantly to
the old order of binary opposition, which makes him inevitably brittle in
the city. His use of pillows, cushions and padded doors is a physical
reminder of the fragility of an ideology which, since it cannot bend with
the time, must be broken.

Morose's attempt to monopolize speech, relegating his wife and servants
to silence, is rightly perceived as monstrous since speech is central to self-
fashioning. The arbitrary construction of woman as chaste, silent and
obedient is highlighted in Daw's 'madrigal' (2.3.111–20). The audience
already know that there is more to Epicoene than meets the eye, since 'she'
promised Dauphine 'ample conditions' (2.4.41) in return for the marriage.
Rather than a model of female behaviour then, Epicoene's silence and
deference looks like a performance to secure a husband. If women in the
audience had been obliged to use the same technique, their response to
Epicoene's winning modesty may have included admiration of 'her' ability
to keep up the role, as well as a shared awareness of its performative nature.
In Jane Cavendish and Elizabeth Brackley's later play, *The Concealed Fancies*
(*c.*1645), the heroines are contemptuous of the prescribed forms of deference which reduce a woman to 'such a mechanical wife', and yet each
exploits insincere performances of obedience to maintain independence
within marriage.[51] To such spectators in the Whitefriars theatre, the comic
reversal where Epicoene triumphantly casts off 'her' role after the wedding
would have been eagerly anticipated and would have had an extra sense of
comic release:

> Why, did you think you had married a statue? or a motion only? one of the
> French puppets with the eyes turned with a wire? or some innocent out of the
> hospital, that would stand with her hands thus, and a plaice mouth, and look
> upon you?
>
> (3.5.34)

Contempt for the ideal woman is expressed in strikingly similar terms by Hic Mulier, the cross-dressed, mannish woman in the 1620 pamphlet *Hic Mulier*:

> because I would not stand with my hands on my belly like a baby at *Bartholemew fayre* ... that am not dumbe when wantons court mee, as if Asse-like I were ready for all burthens ... am I therefore barbarous or monstrous?[52]

Though such a remark seems to apply more immediately to Jonson's *Bartholomew Fair*, its relevance to *Epicoene* is also clear. Like the cross-dressed Epicoene, this cross-dressed female speaker clearly rejects the model of feminine behaviour as infantile and ridiculous. Putting on the clothes of the opposite sex gives insight into the performative nature of gender and simultaneously displays that to an audience. What both speakers point out is that the silent woman is a crazy male invention, inevitably doomed to collapse in the presence of 'woman's chiefest pleasure', her tongue (2.5.40). As the rest of the play demonstrates, the Epicoene who emerges as a barbarous or monstrous 'Semiramis' (3.4.51) is just as much a male construct.

Epicoene shows that there is no place outside male-dominated discourse in which women can define themselves. Women's voices are completely excluded from the play, as its stunning dramatic climax highlights. When Epicoene's real identity as a boy actor is revealed the Collegiates are reduced to silence. Truewit remarks 'Madams, you are mute upon this metamorphosis!' (5.4.227). As Tracey Sedinger observes, at such moments of exposure, the cross-dresser reframes our impression of the surrounding dramatic action in a process which Žižek calls re-marking: 'the thing itself in its immediacy does not change; all that changes is the new modality of its inscription in the symbolic network'.[53] At the end of *Epicoene* the boy actor is simultaneously re-marked within the symbolic networks of the play and the London of the audience, forcing spectators to acknowledge that all the female characters on stage, from monstrous Penthesilias to silent women, are male representations. Although female spectators still have no official voice to intervene, the unnaturalness of such a situation is heightened and the authority of male discourse is significantly undermined. Most importantly, the unmasking of Epicoene weakens Truewit's authority. Earlier he had remarked 'he that thinks himself the master-wit is the master fool' (3.4.46) and Dauphine's trick fools him as well as the Collegiates. Truewit's lengthy verbal constructions of ladies as monstrous, artful, unable to express their desire, turn out to be delusions. Ironically, he ends up having to condemn 'common slanders' to the sex and their reputations at the end of the play (5.4.219). Thus, although Jonson's

Epicoene confines female spectators as silent women, it offers them a sparkling illustration of how their voices, tastes and apparent freedoms were circumscribed by an ideology that was as insubstantial as theatre itself.

Unlike *Epicoene*, Middleton and Dekker's play *The Roaring Girl* (1611) does not use cross-dressing as a disguise. There can be no *coup de théâtre* in revealing that either Moll or Mary is a woman since characters and audience already know. Cross-dressing remains a powerful means to interrogate constructions of gender, though. Moll publicly adopts masculine attire to campaign for liberty in the city, liberty for herself, for the young lovers and for the merchants' wives. She even liberates Jack Dapper from the sergeants so that he can continue to spend his father's money. Combined with the liberty for which she strives is a deep sense of social responsibility, or 'honesty', which Moll values in herself and expects in others. This explains the simultaneously radical and conservative nature of Moll's role within the play.

Like the speakers in *A Letter Sent by Maydens of London*, Moll defends the liberty to marry for love rather than according to parental choice. As Sebastian says, "Twixt lovers' hearts she's a fit instrument / And has the art to help them to their own' (2.2.198). The 'art' Moll uses includes getting her tailor to dress Mary Fitzallard as a page, an unnecessary precaution in terms of the plot, but a vital one in giving Mary the freedom to express her love. Although Mary is dutifully submissive for the majority of the play, in male attire she kisses Sebastian 'Never with more desire and harder venture' (4.1.44). Sebastian obviously finds such 'manly' or overt expressions of passion attractive. He tells Moll that he relishes drinking 'from such an outlandish cup' (4.1.54) and believes that each kiss Mary gives him 'in this strange form is worth a pair of two' (4.1.56). On one level, the doubled kiss signals the homoerotic appeal of the boy actor beneath the female character. Moll remarks 'How strange this shows one man to kiss another' (4.1.45). At the same time, Moll's presence on stage suggests another kind of doubling, between the two cross-dressed women. In the kisses, Sebastian enjoys both the 'outlandish' female assertiveness personified by Moll, the masculine 'instrument', and the more submissive aspects of Mary.

Marjorie Garber argues that by doubling these two female characters who share the same name, the play demonstrates that what society labels as transgressive in Moll is also present in the socially acceptable Mary. Attempts to split and pigeonhole the two, and to marginalize Moll, are the defence mechanism of a culture anxiously preoccupied 'about the ownership of desire'. By putting on male clothes Moll and Mary claim and proclaim themselves as eroticized subjects, apparently democratizing erotic energies.[54] Even when worn in a claim to equality though, these masculine garments prescribe limits to women's desire, as we shall see. In 1611, Mary Fitzallard's romantic cross-dressing would have been an especially resonant signal of female transgression, since in June of that year, Lady Arbella Stuart had escaped from house imprisonment disguised as a man, with boots and a rapier, in order to meet her husband William Seymour after King James had forbidden their marriage. In a letter to James, Arbella defends her marriage with the words 'my good likeing to this gentleman that is my Husband, and my fortune, drew me to a contract before I acquainted your Majesty'.[55] Her disobedience in following her 'likeing' links her with Mary, who pleases herself in defiance of Sir Alexander Wengrave, the most powerful patriarch in the play.

Lady Arbella Stuart's letters also demonstrate attempts to assert herself as an autonomous subject, which allies her with Moll. In an earlier controversy, she told the counsellor Henry Brounker, 'if you leave me till I be my owne woman . . . then your trouble and mine too will cease'.[56] Moll echoes the words, saying of herself, 'My spirit shall be mistress of this house / As long as I have time in't' (3.1.138). Like Arbella, Moll is determined to remain her own woman, as was the historical Moll (Mary Frith) when she leapt up on the stage of the Fortune Theatre 'in the publique viewe of all the people there presente in mans apparrell & playd upon her lute & sange a songe'.[57] Arbella Stuart and Mary Frith were at opposite ends of the social scale, but their assertion of independence strikes a common chord, one which sounds again in the voice of Isabella Whitney in *The Manner of Her Will and What She Left to London*. In Whitney's poem, the pronoun 'I' inserts itself into each district of the city and rings throughout as a strong affirmation of identity as she moves through the streets with the same freedom as Moll.

Voices like these suggest that the dramatic character of Moll can indeed be seen 'as a metaphor for the changing condition of women in early modern England', as Mary Beth Rose argues. Moll is by no means unique, the prologue notes, 'for of that tribe are many'. They include women who frequent taverns, prostitutes and proud citizens' wives, a social range probably not unlike that represented in the audience (Prologue.16–24). Nor was Moll's cross-dressing unique. In Renaissance London, wearing male attire seems to have been quite a fashionable phenomenon for women in the upper and middle classes in the years leading up to 1620, when King James publicly denounced it.[58] The play's sanitization of the historical Moll, to which the prologue draws attention, legitimizes identification with the character on the part of more 'respectable' female playgoers or readers.

Cross-dressing symbolizes Moll's claim to equality with men, both in social and sexual terms. Dressed as a man, or with articles of male attire,

Moll shows that a woman can move freely about the city and address people from all social classes with confidence. When Laxton proposes an amorous assignation, she reads it as an invitation to fight for her cause. She appears as an Everywoman championing her sex:

> In thee I defy all men, their worst hates
> And their best flatteries, all their golden witchcrafts
> With which they entangle the poor spirits of fools:
> Distressèd needlewomen and trade-fallen wives –
> Fish that must needs bite, or themselves be bitten –
> Such hungry things as these may soon be took
> With a worm fastened on a golden hook:
> Those are the lecher's food, his prey. He watches
> For quarrelling wedlocks and poor shifting sisters:
> 'Tis the best fish he takes.
>
> (3.1.92)

Moll defends women as the victims of male deceit, male lust and economic necessity. They are not the sexually insatiable monsters of men's worst fears. Her acquaintance with the poverty of the city is shared by Isabella Whitney, whose *Will* dwells vividly on the plight of the destitute. Like Moll, Whitney sees honest women driven to prostitution by monetary need or greed rather than sexual voracity:

> They oft shall seek for proper girls
>   (And some perhaps shall find)
> That needs compel or lucre lures
>   To satisfy their need.
>
> (p. 295)

In contrast to such victims, Moll in *The Roaring Girl* is self-sufficient, as though her masculine clothes give her financial independence. This is a rare privilege not enjoyed by any of the other subordinate characters and puts Moll on a par with Sir Alexander Wengrave, Sir Davy Dapper, Goshawk and the three male shopowners. It makes her into a powerful icon, a projection of the fantasies of all those who depended on male superiors. Women like Whitney, who were unable to survive alone in London, were probably thrilled to hear Moll reject Laxton's ten gold pieces: 'I scorn to prostitute myself to a man, / I that can prostitute a man to me' (3.1.111). Neither Moll nor Isabella Whitney conduct vicious attacks on men because of their sex. Their sympathies are roused more by those in need and their angers are directed against those who are dishonest. Whitney points out

For maidens poor, I widowers rich
  Do leave, that oft shall dote,
And by that means shall marry them
  To set the girls afloat.
And wealthy widows will I leave
  To help young gentlemen,
Which when you have, in any case,
  Be courteous to them then,
And see their plate and jewels eke
  May not be marred with rust,
Nor let their bags too long be full,
  For fear that they do burst.

(p. 298)

Whitney's wish to give the poor maidens financial security demonstrates her awareness of her sex's vulnerability. At the same time, her concern for the young men as much as the widows shows a genuine wish for openness and equality in the city, a goal shared by Moll. When she counsels Sebastian against choosing her as a wife, Moll contrasts her own honesty in speaking 'against myself' with that of 'cozening widows' who fool impoverished younger brothers into marriage, only to cheat them out of any inheritance (2.2.60–3). Moll rates honesty above loyalty to her sex. Her wish that 'every woman would deal with their suitor so honestly' (2.2.59) is strong testament to her sense of fairness and strengthens her claims for equality.

Moll announces confidently 'I please my self, and care not else who loves me' (5.1.349), a lower-class claim for agency which rings with the same power as Webster's 'I am the Duchess of Malfi still', though liberty for Moll means remaining single rather than choosing a husband. She rejects marriage under the present social conditions, telling Sebastian, 'a wife, you know, ought to be obedient, but I fear me I am too headstrong to obey, therefore I'll ne'er go about it' (2.2.37). Her wish for autonomy cannot be accommodated so her sexuality remains free-floating. The importance Moll places on honesty means that she will not have sex outside marriage because this would confirm her reputation as a whore. A secondary meaning therefore applies to her words 'I please my self, and care not else who loves me'. As Jean Howard's fine essay argues, Moll's viol-playing in Act 4, Scene 1 is an image of masturbatory pleasure: 'her viol suggests her own sexual instrument', which she strokes and fingers in 'a final defiance of patriarchal, phallus-oriented sexuality'.[59] Since sex outside and inside marriage is unsatisfactory, Moll chooses to please herself.

Her choice does not isolate her as a purely self-interested character.

119

Moll's involvement with the citizens' plot and the romantic plot is part of a quest to redeem women's reputations and to assert their rights as desiring subjects within marriage. She attacks, in Laxton, all those who unjustly slander 'our sex' with a 'blasted name' (3.1.81–2), asserting her right, or that of any woman, to 'sport', to be 'merry' and 'jest' (3.1.104) freely without the imputation of sexual immorality. Given this feminist goal, her behaviour towards the citizens' wives in Act 2, Scene 1 seems surprising. She appears a masculine *'frieze jerkin'*, takes tobacco and is eager to buy a shag ruff, all signalling what seems to be the adoption of male attitudes. Of Mistress Tiltyard, she says 'The purity of your wench would I fain try: she seems like Kent unconquered, and I believe as many wiles in her' (2.1.314). She then argues that there are more whores 'of their own making than of any man's provoking' (2.1.318–21). These are just the misogynist attitudes she later criticizes in Laxton.

Nevertheless, as Moll's costume – half masculine and half feminine – suggests, she wears her jerkin with a difference. Like Openwork and Laxton, she does want to test the sexual honesty of the citizens' wives but it is to clear them from the oppressive prejudice, abuse and suspicion that arises from men's fear of women as eroticized subjects. By publicly displaying her own free-floating sexuality as a symbol of male desire and paranoia she helps to put the other women on trial in a purging process, hoping to prove their honesty or cure their dishonesty and to redeem her own reputation at the same time. Her goal is to win them freedom to pursue their own pleasures, to 'sport' and be 'merry'. Proving their honesty is the only way to do this; the sexist culture is such that wives must be 'thoroughly tried' so that they can be cleared as 'throughly honest' (2.1.319). Moll is, perhaps unwittingly, involved in Openwork's plot to test his wife and Goshawk. Her timely appearance in Openwork's shop, then meeting him to go for a drink, promote his scheme of pretending to keep a whore in the suburbs (2.1.223–30, 388–91). Of course the success of Moll's role depends precisely on Rosamond Openwork's mistaken assumption that Moll is a whore (2.1.233–5).

As the wives' fidelity comes to trial in Act 4, Moll's continued involvement with the plot is signalled in the bawdy songs she sings to the viol. The first relates to Mistress Gallipot's failure with Laxton and, indirectly, to Moll's own situation as one who 'goes unto her sisters', but 'never comes at any', that is, plays on her sexual reputation but remains chaste (4.1.102–9). The boat references in the second song point to Rosamond's temptation to 'hoise up sail' (4.2.33) with Goshawk. Its lyrics also reveal Moll's contempt for the hypocrisy of adulterous wives who accuse her of being a whore. As Moll's dreams, the songs are intimately connected to her own fears and desires, including her concern for her sisters' reputations and sexual fulfilment. After the songs, Mary says 'No poison sir, but serves us for some use / Which is confirmed in her' (4.1.48). This comment seems odd from Mary but in relation to the citizens' wives it explains Moll's wish to cure any imperfections in her sex through a potentially harmful process.[60] As their names suggest, Rosamond Openwork and Prudence Gallipot respond with different degrees of honesty to the possibilities of adultery and are rewarded accordingly. The former's openness with her husband allows her to return to a happier marriage, convinced that husbands are the more valuable men who can satisfy their wives' desires (4.2.50–3). Openwork welcomes Goshawk back into the house not in preference to his wife but as a declaration of faith in her fidelity: 'Seeing, thus besieged, it holds out, 'twill never fall!' (4.2.234). This new faith brings Rosamond both freedom and respect.

Prudence Gallipot's economy with the truth does not produce such a happy resolution. Her continued betrayal of her husband, with lies about a broken contract to Laxton, brings slander not sexual rewards. It confirms Laxton's view that women are daughters of Eve, 'apple eaters all, deceivers still!' (3.3.265). Only his impotence preserves her chastity, though when she rejects him in Act 4, Scene 2 it is possible that in conversation with Mistress Openwork she also begins to appreciate the value of her husband's love. She does confess her lies and stealing but not her desires. It is this sexual dishonesty for which she is punished. Laxton says that he was keen to challenge a 'she-citizen' (4.2.317) who maintained that city wives were the victims of male slanders and

> for her own part,
> She vowed that you had so much of her heart,
> No man by all his wit, by any wile
> Never so fine spun, should yourself beguile
> Of what in her was yours.

> (4.2.307)

Mistress Gallipot's behaviour patently does not match up to this ideal model and Moll shares Laxton's contempt for such hypocrisy: 'How many are whores in small ruffs and still looks?' (5.1.344). However, Laxton's further lies that Prudence repulsed his advances gives her a starting point for a more honest sexual relationship based on the lessons she has learnt. The play suggests that until she does confine her desires within the proper sphere of marriage, she will not be rewarded with a husband who will give her 'deeds' rather than words and who can satisfy her 'in her kind' (3.2.24–7).

Paradoxically, what makes *The Roaring Girl* an ultimately conservative play is the liberties it offers to female characters and spectators. The final scene, in which all the female characters appear, suggests distinctly subversive possibilities within the play's endorsement of marriage. The swapping of the cross-dressed Moll, the Moll in women's clothes, and Mary as brides for Sebastian shows the presence of more radical politics and sexual energies beneath the apparent conformity of wives. Sir Alexander unwittingly remarks of Moll 'Just of her pitch was my first wife, his mother' (5.2.132). The citizens' wives are welcomed as paragons of virtue 'whose sparkling presence / Are glories set in marriage, beams of society' (5.2.259), but Moll's presence as an independent woman on stage suggests that their sparkle is due to their autonomous identities. She gives female spectators a different perspective from which to pay tribute to these women whose ingenuity and skill make them valuable contributors to the economy of their households.

The problem with the autonomy or liberty which Moll represents is that it carries a price tag. Her help for Sebastian and Mary is conditional on the fact that their 'loves are honest' (4.1.40), that they will marry. If young women are given liberty to pursue their own passions in 'privie contractes', to quote the *Maydens of London*, they must police their own behaviour responsibly. Similarly, wives like Mistress Openwork and Mistress Gallipot may enjoy the freedom to choose lovers outside marriage but the play teaches them to renounce those personal pleasures in the interests of the common good. The donning of male clothes may give women liberty to express themselves as freely as a man, but in this play patriarchal values are sewn into the fabric. Even Moll, the single or free woman on stage, is limited to an isolated form of auto-eroticism in pleasing herself and looking forward to a time when she can marry. While liberating female desire, she ultimately recontains it by producing subjects who will willingly confine themselves to socially acceptable practices. What all these plays show, then, is that for Renaissance women liberty came in a questionable shape; it meant both freedom and restraint. Within male-dominated spaces, the freedom to woo men, to cross-dress or to spend in the city could lead into traps: difficult marriages, persecution, reinscription into subordinate positions. The plays offer examples of heroines whose intelligence, drive and personal integrity allow them to fashion themselves even within those hostile arenas. Their courage in pursuing this difficult task is inspiring testimony to the stirrings of a feminist consciousness in Renaissance England.

Notes

1 Thomas Middleton and Thomas Dekker, *The Roaring Girl*, ed. Paul Mulholland, Revels Plays (Manchester University Press, Manchester, 1987).

2 Kate Aughterson (ed.), *Renaissance Woman: Constructions of Femininity in England, A Sourcebook* (Routledge, London and New York, 1995), p. 71.

3 *A Treatise Wherein Dicing, Dauncing, Vaine Playes or Enterluds...are reproved* (London, 1577), cited in Jean E. Howard, *The Stage and Social Struggle in Early Modern England* (Routledge, London, 1994), p. 25.

4 Stephen Gosson, *The Schoole of Abuse* (1579), reprinted for The Shakespeare Society (London, 1841), p. 49.

5 Baldesar Castiglione, *The Book of the Courtier*, trans. Sir Thomas Hoby (Dent, London, 1937), pp. 236–42; p. 238.

6 Lady Mary Wroth, *Poems*, ed. R. E. Pritchard, Renaissance Texts and Studies (Keele University Press, Keele, 1996), pp. 134, 37. All further page references to the poems are to this edition.

7 Caroline Lucas, *Writing for Women: The Example of Woman as Reader in Elizabethan Romance* (Open University Press, Milton Keynes and Philadelphia, 1989), p. 26.

8 Wroth, *Poems*, ed. Pritchard, p. 126.

9 C. R. Swift, 'Feminine Self-definition in Lady Mary Wroth's *Love's Victorie* (c.1621)', *English Literary Renaissance* 19 (1989), 171–88; p. 177.

10 Lady Mary Wroth, *Love's Victorie*, in S. P. Cerasano and Marion Wynne-Davies (eds), *Renaissance Drama By Women: Texts and Documents* (Routledge, London, 1996), pp. 96–126. All references are to this edition.

11 See Heather Dubrow's *Echoes of Desire: English Petrarchanism and its Counterdiscourses* (Cornell University Press, Ithaca, NY, 1995), p. 157 for a discussion of this technique in Wroth's sonnets.

12 Julie Robin Soloman, 'Morality as a Matter of Mind: Towards a Politics of Problems in *All's Well That Ends Well*', *English Literary Renaissance* 23 (1993), 134–69; p. 159.

13 Robert Burton, *The Anatomy of Melancholy*, Everyman (Dent, London, 1932), Book 3, p. 238, cited in Carolyn Asp, 'Subjectivity, Desire and Female Friendship in *All's Well That Ends Well*', in Gary Waller (ed.), *Shakespeare's Comedies* (Longman, London, 1991), pp. 175–92; p. 179.

14 Susan Zimmerman, 'Disruptive Desire in Jacobean Comedy', in Susan Zimmerman (ed.), *Erotic Politics: Desire on the Renaissance Stage* (Routledge, New York and London, 1992), pp. 39–63; p. 42.

15 See Bernard Capp, 'Popular Literature', in Barry Reay (ed.), *Popular Culture in Seventeenth Century England* (London, Routledge, 1988), pp. 198–243; pp. 211, 214.

16 Francis James Child (ed.), *The English and Scottish Popular Ballads* (Cooper Square, New York, 1965), vol. 2, pp. 83–100 (Child 63B).

17 Betty S. Travitsky (ed.), *The Paradise of Women: Writings by Englishwomen of the*

Renaissance, Morningside edition (Columbia University Press, New York, 1989), pp. 119–20.

18 See, for example, Mary Queen of Scots' sonnets to Bothwell and Queen Elizabeth's poem 'On Monsieur's Departure', in Travitsky (ed.), *The Paradise of Women*, pp. 193–8 and p. 20.

19 Roberts suggests that the play may have been performed at Penshurst, the Pembroke family home. See Josephine A. Roberts, 'The Huntington Manuscript of Lady Mary Wroth's play *Love's Victorie*', *Huntington Library Quarterly* 46 (1983), 156–74; p. 163.

20 Susan Snyder, '*All's Well That Ends Well* and Shakespeare's Helens: Text and Subtext, Subject and Object', *English Literary Renaissance* 18 (1988), 66–77; p. 75.

21 Lisa Jardine, 'Cultural Confusion and Shakespeare's Learned Heroines: "These are old paradoxes"', *Shakespeare Quarterly* 38 (1987), 1–18; p. 11.

22 Asp, 'Subjectivity, Desire and Female Friendship', p. 183.

23 Ibid., p. 188.

24 John Webster, *The Duchess of Malfi*, ed. Elizabeth M. Brennan, New Mermaids, 3rd edn (A & C Black, London, 1993).

25 Coppelia Kahn, 'Whores and Wives in Jacobean Drama', in Dorothea Kehler and Susan Baker (eds), *In Another Country: Feminist Perspectives on Renaissance Drama* (Scarecrow Press, Metuchen and London, 1991), pp. 246–60; p. 251.

26 Leonard Tennenhouse, 'Violence Done to Women on the Renaissance Stage', in Nancy Armstrong and Leonard Tennenhouse (eds), *The Violence of Representation* (Routledge, London, 1989), pp. 77–97; pp. 88, 90.

27 I am grateful to C. R. Swift for drawing attention to the parallel in her article 'Feminine Identity in Lady Mary Wroth's Romance *Urania*', *English Literary Renaissance* 14 (1984), 328–46.

28 Frank Whigham, *Seizures of the Will in Early Modern English Drama* (Cambridge University Press, Cambridge, 1996), p. 201.

29 Lady Mary Wroth, *The Countess of Montgomerie's Urania* (London, 1622), Book 2, pp. 230–1.

30 Whigham, *Seizures of the Will*, pp. 194–5.

31 Wroth, *Urania*, pp. 234–5.

32 Albert H. Tricomi, *Reading Tudor-Stuart Texts Through Cultural Historicism* (University Press of Florida, Gainesville, 1996), pp. 136–56, skilfully compares the power of familial affectivity in this play and *The Duchess of Malfi*.

33 Stephen Orgel, *Impersonations: The Performance of Gender in Shakespeare's England* (Cambridge University Press, Cambridge, 1996), p. 54.

34 See Kier Elam, 'The Fertile Eunuch: *Twelfth Night*, Early Modern Intercourse and the Fruits of Castration', *Shakespeare Quarterly* 47 (1996), 1–36.

35 See Valerie Traub, 'Desire and the Difference It Makes', in Valerie Wayne (ed.), *The Matter of Difference: Materialist Feminist Criticism of Shakespeare* (Harvester Wheatsheaf, Hemel Hempstead and New York, 1991), pp. 81–114, for an excellent account of the shifting nature of erotic desire in the plays.

36 John Dover Wilson (ed.), *Life in Shakespeare's England* (Penguin, Harmonds-worth, 1968), pp. 116–17.

37 F. J. Fehrenbach, 'A Letter sent by Maydens of London (1567)', *English Literary Renaissance* 14 (1984), 285–304. All references to the *Letter* are to page numbers of the text in this article.

38 Susan Wells, 'Jacobean Comedy and the Ideology of the City', *English Literary History* 48 (1981), 37–60; p. 42.

39 Ben Jonson, *Epicoene or The Silent Woman*, ed. R. V. Holdsworth, New Mermaids (Benn, London, 1979).

40 On the variety of, and changes in, waged work for women see Alice Clark, *The Working Life of Women in the Seventeenth Century* (Routledge and Kegan Paul, London, 1982), and Anne Laurence, *Women in England 1500–1760: A Social History* (Weidenfeld and Nicolson, London, 1994), pp. 125–41.

41 Karen Newman, 'City Talk: Women and Commodification', in David Scott Kastan and Peter Stallybrass (eds), *Staging The Renaissance* (Routledge, New York, 1991), pp. 181–95; p. 184.

42 Thomas Dekker, *The Gull's Hornbook*, ed. R. B. McKerrow (De La More Press, London, 1905), p. 59.

43 Lorna Weatherill, 'A Possession of One's Own: Women and Consumer Behavior in England 1660–1740', *Journal of British Studies* 25 (1986), 131–56; pp. 155–6.

44 Alison D. Wall, *Two Elizabethan Women: The Correspondence of Joan and Maria Thynne 1575–1611*, Wiltshire Record Society, vol. 38 (Devises, 1983), pp. 3–4, 11, 13, 19, 16.

45 From *The Diary of Lady Margaret Hoby*, in Randall Martin (ed.), *Women Writers in Renaissance England* (Longman, London, 1997), pp. 201–2.

46 Weatherill, 'A Possession of One's Own', p. 156.

47 Isabella Whitney, *The Manner of Her Will and What She Left to London*, from *A Sweet Nosegay or Pleasant Posy* (London, 1573), in Martin (ed.), *Women Writers in Renaissance England*, pp. 289–302. Subsequent references are to page numbers.

48 As if in response to such attempts to map the female body, Madame de Scudéry's French romance *Clélie* (1654) contains a map of the Pays de Tendre, the emotional territory to be traversed by lovers. See J. J. Jusserand, *The English Novel in the Time of Shakespeare* (Benn, London, 1966), p. 359.

49 Richard Dutton, *Ben Jonson: To The First Folio* (Cambridge University Press, Cambridge, 1983), pp. 102–5.

50 Eric Partridge, *The Broken Compass* (Greenwood Press, Westport, CT, 1958), p. 58.

51 Jane Cavendish and Elizabeth Brackley, *The Concealed Fancies*, in Cerasano and Wynne-Davies (eds), *Renaissance Drama by Women*, pp. 131–54 (Epilogue.40). On the play's extensive use of performativity to explore gender see Alison Findlay, 'Playing the "scene self": Jane Cavendish and Elizabeth Brackley's *The Concealed Fancies*', in Viviana Comensoli and Anne Russell (eds), *Enacting*

Gender on the English Renaissance Stage (University of Illinois Press, Urbana, 1998), pp. 154–76.

52 *Hic Mulier* (London, 1620), cited in Mary Beth Rose, 'Women in Men's Clothing: Apparel and Social Stability in *The Roaring Girl*', *English Literary Renaissance* 14 (1984), 367–91; p. 376.

53 Slavoj Žižek, *For They Know Not What They Do: Enjoyment as a Political Factor* (Verso, London, 1991), pp. 77–8, cited in Tracey Sedinger, '"If sight and shape be true": The Epistemology of Cross Dressing on the London Stage', *Shakespeare Quarterly* 48 (1997), 63–79.

54 Marjorie Garber, 'The Logic of the Transvestite: *The Roaring Girl* (1608)', in Kastan and Stallybrass (eds), *Staging The Renaissance*, pp. 221–34; pp. 229–31. On the democratization of desire, see Zimmerman, 'Disruptive Desire', p. 55.

55 Lady Arbella Stuart, *The Letters of Lady Arbella Stuart*, ed. Sara Jayne Steen (Oxford University Press, Oxford, 1994), pp. 68–9, 254. The behaviour of another court lady, Elizabeth Southwell, provided an earlier example of romantic cross-dressing since in 1605, she had disguised herself as the page of Robert Dudley and fled to Italy to marry him in spite of the fact that he already had a wife and children in England.

56 Ibid., p. 168.

57 Extract from the *Consistory of London Correction Book*, in *The Roaring Girl*, ed. Mulholland, p. 262.

58 Rose, 'Women in Men's Clothing', pp. 390, 371.

59 Jean E. Howard, 'Sex and Social Conflict: The Erotics of *The Roaring Girl*', in Zimmerman (ed.), *Erotic Politics*, pp. 170–90; p. 185.

60 The idea that poison could have beneficial effects, put forward by Paracelsus, was familiar to medical practitioners. Lady Grace Mildmay's medical recipes made use of toxics like arsenic and mercury. See Linda Pollock (ed.), *With Faith and Physick: The Life of A Tudor Gentlewoman, Lady Grace Mildmay 1552–1620* (Collins and Brown, London, 1993), p. 105.

CHAPTER 4

Household Tragedies

In the writings she left as a legacy to her grandchildren, Lady Grace Mildmay (1552–1620) summarized her ideas on the household:

> A private household of family (which may resemble a whole commonwealth), consisting of the master and mistress, the husband and the wife, children and servants, all of one mind in love, fear and obedience, being all well chosen, instructed and governed with true judgement. That house may be called the house of God. But if the master and mistress and the family be careless of their own duties to God and one towards another and in the education of their children, or in what company they converse, or in the choice of their servants, whom they bring into their house, there is nothing to be looked for but confusion.[1]

The picture is two-sided: the home could be a paradise of harmony or a storm of disorder. Lady Mildmay's description is typical because the household is a trope characterized by ambiguity in Renaissance culture. It is public and private, peopled by servants as well as kin; both material and ideological, a physical building and a model of the 'whole commonwealth'. It is a peculiarly female sphere and yet it is dominated by a male governor. For the people who inhabited it, the Renaissance household had a protean quality with the potential to nurture and to destroy. Its enclosing walls were designed to protect those within from harm, but their embrace could also be suffocating. The hothouse atmosphere of the domestic arena could intensify destructive emotions as much as protective ones. In one of her spiritual meditations Lady Mildmay discusses the darker side of family life, remembering how she suffered 'violence and wrong in mine infancy and swaddling clouts', and that as an adult, 'in mine own house amongst my servants and family', proper relations of love masked much deeper enmity: 'mine adversaries being those which should have been my chiefest friends, even fathers, sisters and brothers, notwithstanding their protestation of friendship and love'.[2]

The drama of the period picks up on many of the paradoxes built into the fabric of the early modern household to magnify fault lines in the wider social order. Tragedies set in a domestic realm depict crises where the nearest kindred prove the greatest adversaries, where insiders inflict emotional or physical violence on each other in ways which throw the well-ordered household into confusion. Since the family was a microcosm of 'a whole commonwealth', such disorder necessarily represented a threat to the wider community. The legal classification of domestic crimes reinforced the parallels between 'private household' and state. The master of a household who killed his wife, children or servants was charged with murder, but subordinates who perpetrated the same crime on their governor were presented for petty treason, equating their domestic insurrection with rebellion against the monarch. Plays that centred on the family and home were therefore always essentially political in nature.[3] These plays invariably scrutinize the relationship between gender and agency by dramatizing, often in microscopic detail, the opportunities offered to men and women to style roles for themselves in the household and the world beyond.

Experiences of the household were significantly different for men and women. For both sexes setting up house was a form of advancement. After the Reformation a broader range of social classes became property owners and enjoyed the superior social status conferred by the title of householder. The focus on middle class or minor gentry in domestic tragedy concurs with this changing pattern.[4] For men, ownership of a house provided the means to develop subjectivity, autonomy and responsibility as an adult. The master had absolute authority to govern his wife, children and servants. Householders depicted on the Renaissance stage invariably share a sense of self-satisfied complacency in their status as property owners. In Heywood's *A Woman Killed With Kindness* (1603), for example, Frankford celebrates the delights of being the master of a house:

> How happy am I amongst other men
> That in my mean estate embrace content.
> I am a gentleman, and by my birth
> Companion with a king; a king's no more.
> I am possessed of many fair revenues,
> Sufficient to maintain a gentleman.

(4.1)[5]

Frankford's comparison of his estate to a monarchy draws on the popular idea that the Englishman's home is his castle. As the eminent lawyer Sir Edward Coke remarked, 'the house of every one is to him his castle or fortress, as well for defense against injury and violence as for his repose'.[6] The appeal to the master's ego is powerful, suggesting, as it does, that within his own walls he is completely autonomous, subject to the commands of no one. Domestic tragedy on stage is often intrinsically subversive because it undermines that image of individual patriarchal power, exposing it as an illusion (or delusion) suffered by the master. In *A Woman Killed With Kindness*, Master Frankford's contented soul and house is shattered by the adultery of his wife and best friend. Far from being a haven from 'violence and injury', the household is the space where such violence is enacted. The anonymous *Arden of Faversham* (1591) shows how Master Arden is murdered in his own home by the very subordinates who should provide the sanctuary of protection.

For male householders, the apparent autonomy conferred by property ownership was also qualified by responsibilities. Nowhere is this more clear than in the play *A Yorkshire Tragedy* (1605), where the Husband (otherwise unnamed, as if to emphasize the emblematic quality of his role) laments how his prodigal life has caused the decline of his house:

> Mine and my father's and my forefathers', generations, generations. Down goes the house of us; down, down it sinks. Now is the name a beggar, begs in me. That name, which for hundreds of years has made this shire famous, in me and my posterity runs out. In my seed five are made miserable besides myself. My riot is now my brother's jailor, my wife's sighing, my three boys' penury, and my own confusion.
>
> (4.73)[7]

The destructive effects of the patriarchal family structure are obvious in relation to those whom it disempowers, such as women, but the Husband's lines remind us that even those who wield power within the household are subject to its oppressive paternal authority. 'Generations' of forefathers weigh down on the present owner. The need to pass on, if not improve, a patrimony puts huge pressure on the head of the family. It was a sense of duty to past and future generations rather than selfish niggardliness which often motivated insensitive treatment of family members in arranged marriages or the refusal of requests for financial assistance. In *A Yorkshire Tragedy* the Husband is driven mad by a belated sense of responsibility. Personal responsibility for his actions cannot be denied. Unlike its source, or George Wilkins's dramatic adaptation *The Miseries of Enforced Marriage* (1607), this play pays little attention to the Husband's previous betrothal or a doubly contracted marriage as a cause of the tragedy.[8] Instead, it shows how he has single-handedly ruined the lives of his subordinates. His wife, brother and children appear as largely helpless victims of his extravagance.

A Yorkshire Tragedy demonstrates the dangers of male authority by showing that absolute control of the family leads to complete loss of self-control. The Husband is possessed: first by a passion for gambling, then by barbaric savagery. Having realized that he has destroyed his family socially and financially, he determines to destroy it literally by murdering his wife and children. Such tyrannical and socially reprehensible behaviour on the part of the governor obviously undermines the conventional family structure. To circumvent criticism of male authority, conduct books and court cases involving murderous husbands stressed that such men were not true governors but had lost their reason.[9] For example, William Gouge commented that men who attacked their wives were 'either blinded in their understanding, or possessed with a devill', since to do so was to mutilate their own flesh and 'no man but a franticke, furious, desperat wretch will beat himselfe'.[10] *A Yorkshire Tragedy* seems to follow this line by presenting the Husband as demonically possessed. He is the 'serpent of his house' (9.7) and the Wife depersonalizes his actions with the words 'Murder has took this chamber with full hands / And ne'er will out as long as the house stands' (7.39). This deflects critical attention from a particular male governor only to redirect it to the whole paternal model as the source of evil. The play subversively suggests that the house and the line of ancestors stretching back through history are responsible for the murders. Within its walls, the Husband is seized, overwhelmed with his sense of duty to these forefathers, and acts as their agent. Spatial position is bound up with perception. Only when he moves outside the building can he see, as do his dependents and neighbours, how unnatural his actions are. As he passes his doorway, he recognizes 'I am right against my house, seat of my ancestors' (9.36). The patriarchal family is self-destructive, for in following his duty to his ancestors, the Husband has destroyed his kin. His sons' bodies on the threshold physically mark the tragedy of his introverted preoccupation with, and metaphorical confinement within, the 'walls' or values of his house. The sons cannot pass beyond the threshold to set up new houses. In this play, as in so many domestic tragedies, the dramatist explores the fragility of the male householder's position as a privileged ruler, showing how tensions intrinsic in the family structure can easily turn the well-governed house into confusion.

For women as for men in Renaissance England, setting up a household (which was the only real career option for most) represented advancement. Marriage was 'preferment' since it transformed the utterly dependent daughter into a wooed mistress and finally into mistress of her own home with command over servants and children. The diary of Lady Margaret

Hoby (1571–1633) gives ample evidence of the wife's power as a manager of economic, social and spiritual affairs in the domestic microcosm. She kept a 'Household book' of accounts, paid wages to servants, sewed linen, ordered the meals and sometimes helped in the kitchen, preserving fruit or baking. She managed livestock, sowed seeds and supervised her own team of workmen, distinct from those of her husband, it seems. During Sir Thomas Hoby's frequent absences on business to York or London she was solely responsible for running the estate. In addition, she also educated the young gentlewomen sent to wait on her, led discussions of the sermon with her neighbours, entertained visitors, and treated the illnesses of members of the household and the community in Hackness.[11] In spite of the apparently high status of a mistress like Lady Hoby, the 'preferment' of marriage could prove to be illusory because, finally, the house was not hers at all but her husband's. As a wife, she was subject to her husband and unable to manage affairs at home according to her will if it differed from his. She therefore occupied a liminal position in the household between the governor and the governed. Lady Grace Mildmay's description of the 'master and mistress, the husband and the wife' in the family distinguishes between domestic and marital roles. The status of woman as both mistress and subject was ideologically awkward, as the writers of conduct books recognized. Thomas Gataker's marriage sermon *A Bride Bush* (1617) remarked, somewhat uneasily:

> As first for reverence, the wife owes as much of that to her husband as the children or servants do to her, yea, as they do to him: only it is allowed that it be sweetened with more love and more familiarity. The wife should not think so erroneously of her place as if she were not bound equally with the children and servants to reverence her husband: all inferiors owe reverence alike. The difference is only this: she may be more familiar, not more rude than they, as being more dear, not less subject to him.[12]

The contradiction between the woman's two positions as both superior and inferior, ruler and ruled, creates a gap in which female self-determination can develop. Domestic tragedies invariably explore this gap and the consequences of a budding sense of agency on the part of women within the household.

The dramatic presentation of domestic tragedy drew attention to a further paradox in the household: its contradictory nature as a public and private space. The presence of servants, its openness to neighbours, kin and visitors, meant that it could never be the totally private domain of the nuclear family. Lady Margaret Hoby's diary illustrates how both public and private realms coexisted within her house. Devotion took the form of both communal or 'publeck' prayers and solitary meditations, the latter taking

131

place in her closet, 'wher I praied and Writt som thinge for mine owne privat Conscience'.[13] Outside the closet, Lady Margaret Hoby's home and time were invaded by numerous claims on her attention, as on 17 January 1599, where she records 'som strangers Came which held me tell Diner time, and after, tell 3 a cloke: then I went forth to some workmen, and after dispatched busenes in the house tell night'.[14] As Lena Orlin notes, not all women had access to a retreat like Lady Margaret Hoby's closet.[15] Plays such as Heywood's *A Woman Killed With Kindness* and Elizabeth Cary's *The Tragedy of Mariam* (1604/6) dramatize their heroines' lack of privacy by self-consciously exposing them to the critical gaze of on-stage and off-stage spectators.

The playhouse reproduced the structure of the household in that it was fenced off from the outside world by walls and entry to it was therefore privileged, but once inside, entrants still experienced a public arena. Even the 'rooms' and galleries to which wealthier members of the audience withdrew were subject to the scrutiny of all the spectators. Indeed, in some cases the so-called 'private' rooms were intended precisely for the public display of the occupants. The only really private places in the playhouse were those that the audience were not permitted to enter unless invited: the tiring house and the discovery space (if this was used in performance); and, beyond these, the imaginary spaces created by the actors' performances as, for example, Frankford and Anne's bedroom in *A Woman Killed With Kindness*. These spaces exist only in the imagination of actors and audience and in that sense they are really private since each person's room will be different. In his study of the poetics of space, Gaston Bachelard argues that our responses to fictional rooms or houses is essentially idiosyncratic, in that 'the reader who is "reading a room" leaves off reading and starts to think of some place in his own past'. According to Bachelard, the house is a focal point of our memories and dreams and 'appears to move elsewhere without difficulty', so that the dwelling places in our lives, past and present, constantly penetrate our consciousness.[16] By inviting the spectator into a space of intimacy, then, domestic drama paradoxically alienates him or her, sending the audience off into their own intimate worlds, the houses of their own imagination and memory.

The oneiric quality of the house is emphasized in the theatre. Unlike real houses, concrete entities with solid walls and rooms, the stage world offers only a skeleton of the house's geographical reality: a platform, doors and canopy. It is the audience's imaginary forces that must fill out the bare bones of this structure with their memories, fantasies and nightmares. The prologue to *A Woman Killed With Kindness* advertises the starkness of 'a barren subject, a bare scene' to be presented and invites the audience to furnish the household with their own materials and banquets (Prologue.4).

As Mark Girouard has shown, the late sixteenth and early seventeenth century witnessed a reconfiguration of the communal spaces of the medieval manor house into a series of private chambers or 'privy lodgings'. Smaller houses gave less opportunity for the physical privatization of space, but those further down the social scale could still make a mental series of retreats to the dwelling places of their own lives.[17] If Bachelard's theory about the power of the house over human life is correct, the audience's creative engagement with domestic drama must have been intensely private, even though it took place in a very public arena.

Like plays, households had their audiences. Neighbours, friends and relations as well as servants constantly scrutinized the behaviour of families. While such attention may offend our modern sense of privacy (and may have irritated our ancestors as the strangers did Lady Hoby), the connections between the household and the community had important positive effects. Susan Amussen has pointed out that domestic violence was a public issue and to some extent the critical gaze of outsiders was able to protect or censure those within any house where confusion or tyranny seemed to reign. The practice could help the most vulnerable members, wives and children, by attempting to control patriarchal power, though it was not always effective in time to prevent tragedy.[18] When domestic tragedies were represented on stage, the Renaissance audience occupied the position of the censoring community. We do not know to what extent spectators intervened in performances and presumably they did not prevent the tragic outcomes, but they were certainly placed in a position of critical surveillance. Entry to the theatre formed them into a temporary vigilant community. By repositioning them in the roles they were accustomed to play at home, the plays implicitly obliged them to accept some responsibility for the events on stage. The spectators' wish to protect subordinate family members would have been checked by a shared need to maintain a 'proper' sense of order, so even female spectators would be unlikely to give unequivocal support to rebellious wives or daughters. As playgoers who had abandoned their proper domestic sphere to go to the theatre, women in the audience shared some of the characteristics of these rebellious figures, laying themselves open to criticism. They would be unlikely to express approval of unorthodox behaviour openly, whatever private sympathies they held.

The community played a vital part in monitoring shifts of power within the family. Betrothal was an especially critical moment since it involved the breaking up of one household and the establishment of another. Since most spectators would have direct experience of this fracture point, as parents, children or as interested parties, it is not surprising that dramatists often use it as a starting point for domestic tragedy. The power parents or children should have in the choice of marriage partners was a matter of debate in which dramatists and their theatre companies were actively engaged.[19] There was much flexibility over betrothal practices across the social scale in Renaissance England, though one common feature differentiates the earlier situation from our own: negotiations and selection of partners usually centred around generational relationships between parents and children rather than erotic relationships between lovers.[20] In tragedies which stem from betrothal situations audiences oversee conduct within the household as the community does: censoring or approving the behaviour of dramatic characters from different critical, ideological and emotional standpoints. Early modern women's experiences, as transmitted to us through selected writings, can illuminate how those plays might have appealed to some female spectators.

In betrothal the daughter moved into a liminal position between her father and her husband-to-be and paternal authority became necessarily fragmented as a new governor strove to establish himself. In the space between the old household and the new the circulation of desire threatened to disrupt the well-ordered family. The daughter was not only the source of potentially anarchic passions, temporarily outside the absolute authority of her male governors; she was also the focal point on which they converged. In anthropological terms daughters are 'outsiders', destined to be given away by the father to the son of another family. In Lévi-Strauss's model of kinship relations, the exogamous exchange of women is motivated by the incest taboo, and on a psychological level, the daughter is a focus for both outlawed incestuous desire (from her father or brothers) and exogamous desire of her suitors. Lynda Boose has argued that the ritual of giving away a daughter in marriage is vitally important to the harmonious breaking up of one family and establishment of a new one. The father's need to protect his family, to stand at the centre of its bonds of love and duty, makes it very difficult for him to accept the loss of a daughter. In extreme cases, this can lead to a semi-incestuous love for the daughter and a resentment of suitors whose intervention will inevitably destroy the enclosed family circle. The ritual of giving the daughter away offers the father a means of managing the situation, literally and emotionally. As Boose remarks, 'the bestowal design places the daughter's departure from the father's house and her sexual union to another male into a text designed by obedience to her father – not preference for an outside male. So long as this strategy operates, the loss of a daughter can be psychologically mitigated, and defeat by a rival male constructed into public rituals that redefine this as the father's magnanimous gift'.[21]

This system can only function smoothly if the daughter remains a gift, an object of male desire. In fact, far from serving the wishes of the woman at their centre, the economic and social exchanges of betrothal redirect the erotic energy of the triangle to promote homosocial desire between men, something which the drama repeatedly draws attention to.[22] In Renaissance England, where betrothals were a vital element in the creation of new social and economic alliances, the daughter's acceptance of her role as gift was materially as well as psychologically important. When daughters took choice into their own hands, in defiance of convention, the happy ending of marriage could easily collapse into domestic tragedy.

'I would the fool were married to her grave!' says Lady Capulet, enraged that Juliet should defy parental authority regarding the choice of her marriage partner (3.5.140). The words prove ominous, but as in many staged betrothal situations the play remains ultimately equivocal about where blame for the tragedy should lie. In one sense, Juliet, like Romeo, is an innocent victim of the feud between their powerful fathers. At the same time, her independent choice of Romeo and her haste to marry would have attracted criticism from at least some members of the audience. 'The grave's a fine and private place / But none, I think, do there embrace' declares Marvell to his coy mistress, yet Romeo and Juliet try to do just that, penetrating even the Capulet tomb in a quest for privacy in which to enjoy their love.[23] As Baz Luhrmann's film version demonstrates, their endeavour will always be frustrated by the invasive gaze of the society around them, ever anxious to delve into family affairs and make them the stuff of public entertainment. From its prologue onwards, Shakespeare's play dramatizes the conflict between public and private, affairs of the heart and the household, and does so with a particular focus on female experience: Juliet's role is larger than Romeo's, her strength of will and her journey to maturity are dramatized more fully. The growth of passionate commitment between the protagonists and the possibility of familial reconciliation is always shadowed by a sense of doom, introduced in the advance publicity of 'their death-marked love, / And the continuance of their parents' rage', before the play's events begin (Prologue.9). The prologue to Baz Luhrmann's film, a television news report complete with headlines from the text and summary shots of the story even before it has been shown, suggests that the lovers' predestined fate is the creation of a media-centred society. Rather than modernizing Shakespeare beyond recognition, Luhrmann brilliantly recaptures the essentially public nature of family politics and alliances in Renaissance England, an essential dimension of the play.[24]

It seems likely that Shakespeare drew on a contemporary case of public family feuding and clandestine marriage in his dramatization of Brooke's 1562 poem, the main literary source for the play. As Alison Wall has shown, details in Shakespeare's *Romeo and Juliet*, especially its deviations from the poem, correspond closely with the intricacies of the feud between the Thynne and Marvin families of Wiltshire.[25] Fights between them from 1589 to 1592 were well known at court, and in October 1594 important allies of both sides were killed in another major skirmish (possibly the source for the confrontation between Mercutio, Tybalt and Romeo). Lord Hunsdon, the Lord Chamberlain and Shakespeare's patron from 1594, was involved in the dispute as a Privy Councillor and later through the marriage of his son into the Danvers family, allies of the Marvins, so Shakespeare may have learned inside details. Somewhat remarkably, given the rancour between the factions, in early 1594 the Romeo figure, Thomas Thynne (eldest son of the family), went with two friends to a supper held by some of the Marvins at the Bell Inn in Beaconsfield. Here he met his 'Juliet', Maria Audley, granddaughter and sole heir of Sir James Marvin, head of the rival household. Having apparently fallen in love at first sight, Thomas and Maria were married by candlelight in an upstairs room.

The wedding was kept secret from the Thynnes until April 1595 but, in contrast to the situation in Shakespeare's play, Maria's mother, Lady Lucy Audley, was present at the marriage. Indeed, she seems to have encouraged it. Joan Thynne, Thomas's mother, later informed her husband 'after the contract she caused a pair of sheets to be laid on a bed and her daughter to lie down in her clothes and the boy by her side butted and sported for a little while, that it might be said they were abed together'.[26] Lady Audley's part in the conspiracy, especially her interest in getting the couple into bed, may have found its way into the play in the role of Juliet's Nurse, who acts as go-between, bringing the rope ladder for Romeo to climb to the marriage bed. Financial considerations probably influenced Lucy Audley's promotion of the match, but her more noble intentions, outlined in a letter to Joan Thynne, also liken her to Shakespeare's Friar Lawrence. She says her offence 'rested more in manner than matter', and tells Joan she hopes 'between your good disposition and mine own good desert' that reconcilement can be achieved, 'the band being indissoluble that should tie our affections together, and withal the reason so unlike reason, that should divide when cause hath so nearly joined' (p. 26). Shakespeare may have been motivated to write the play to further a reconciliation, though Lucy Audley's hopes came to nothing. Neither Thomas nor Maria were driven to the tomb, but the rift between the two families was not healed. The correspondence of Joan Thynne and her daughter-in-law Maria offers insights into female perspectives on the play, especially its presentation of Juliet.

Romeo's description of love as a 'misshapen chaos of well-seeming forms' (1.1.170) is an apt motto for the two rival households, particularly the Capulet home where seeming order, in the careful matching of Juliet with Paris, causes chaos and tragedy. A wealth of realistic detail in the Capulet settings creates the impression of an ordered household community. The servants have names and specific tasks to carry out; we hear of trenchers, cupboards, spices, dates and quinces. There is a genuine sense of bustle when the wedding preparations are under way and Capulet proclaims he will 'play the housewife' for once (4.2.43). The prosaic tone of such scenes gives a tangible sense of normality, which contrasts with the heightened rhymed verse and extravagant feelings of love and hate that drive the plot forward.

Juliet's words to Romeo, 'I should kill thee with much cherishing' (2.1.228), are likewise an apt motto for the Capulet house since they point to an excess which characterizes not only her love but that of her father. The strength of Capulet's attachment to his daughter does not compare with Lear's for Cordelia but, nevertheless, he is unwilling to relinquish her to Paris at the beginning of the play. He seems to invite Paris to the feast in the hopes of deflecting his interest to some other beauteous lady of merit, whose 'reck'ning' may be more than Juliet's (1.2.22–31). Although he tells the hopeful suitor that Juliet's 'scope of choice' (1.2.16) will command his consent, in the event he relies exclusively on the ritual of gift-giving. Without consulting her, he makes a 'desperate tender' of Juliet's love (3.5.12) and when she refuses to accept his choice, he reduces her to a piece of property:

An you be mine, I'll give you to my friend,
An you be not, hang, beg, starve, die in the streets,
For, by my soul, I'll ne'er acknowledge thee,
Nor what is mine shall never do thee good.

(3.5.191)

If Juliet refuses to be a gift, she loses her position as heiress in the Capulet household. Only by constructing herself as another Capulet asset can she inherit that property for her husband-to-be. Self-possession means dispossession in Capulet's eyes. His attitude may not seem like that of a 'careful father' (3.5.107), especially to a modern audience, but his preoccupation with Juliet's match, read on both practical and psychological levels, suggests otherwise. Writings like the Thynne family correspondence give evidence of a strong emotional attachment between parents and children in the period, suggesting that a child's betrothal was emotionally as well as materially significant. No documentation detailing Maria's father's reaction to the marriage survives, but in Joan Thynne's letters to her husband and to Lucy Audley there is a real sense of hurt as well as outrage at the loss of her son, 'that I once loved more than myself' (p. 28). She confesses 'my fault in loving him too well above the rest, for which I fear I have offended mighty God' (p. 10). Fathers could be equally upset at daughters whose will or desire eclipsed their duties. Sir Christopher Hatton declared that his daughter, 'who was the chiefest cause of my care and my greatest hope of comfort', had driven him to the grave by contracting a marriage 'directly contrary to my mind, as wilfully bent in the frowardness of her heart to disobey me, and violently as it were, to carry me into my grave with tears'.[27] Such lines suggest that parents watching *Romeo and Juliet* might well have sympathized with Capulet's position when his daughter resists his will and later when she is stolen from him by death.

Juliet's independence, which so shocks her parents in this scene, is a striking feature of her character. Even at the beginning of the play, when Paris is first proposed as a suitor, Juliet's reply makes her duty to her parents dependent on her own emotions: 'I'll look to like, if looking liking move' (1.3.99). When she meets Romeo, she is not afraid to use the conceit of pilgrimage to ask for a second kiss (1.5.107), and her open declaration of her 'true-love passion' in the orchard is, as she knows, unconventional (2.1.146). Far from blushing, she asks him outright 'Dost thou love me?' (2.1.132) and follows up her frank admission with a proposal of marriage (2.1.185–90). The strength of Juliet's passion for Romeo and the same outspokenness are found in Maria Thynne's letters to Thomas. Like Juliet, she abandons blushes in favour of an eager anticipation of sexual pleasure, when she receives his 'kind wanton letters':

> My best beloved Thomken, and my best little Sirrah, know that I have not, nor will not forget how you made my modest blood flush up into my bashful cheek at your first letter, thou threatened sound payment, and I sound repayment, so as when we meet, there will be pay, and repay, which will pass and repass . . . . Even so, being as melancholy as a red herring, and as mad as a pilchard and as proud as a piece of Aragon ling, I salute thy best beloved self with the return of thine own wish in thy last letter, and so once more fare ever well, my best and sweetest Thomken, and many thousand times more than these 1 000 000 000 000 000 000 000 000 00 for thy kind wanton letters
> Thine and only all thine
> Maria
>
> (pp. 37–8)

Maria's bawdy allusions and thousands of farewells (like the thousand good nights at the end of the orchard scene) demonstrate the same wilful passion that motivates Juliet's behaviour. The daughter who has moved out of the role of gift to follow her own desires occupies an incongruous position in her father's household. Once married through her own choice, Juliet's sense of autonomy brings her into direct conflict with her father. Capulet reads her refusal of Paris as a form of petty treason, threatening to drag her 'on a hurdle' to church, thereby positioning her as both a traitor and a martyr to his supreme authority in the household (3.5.155). For Capulet, Juliet's disobedience is linked with transgressive sexuality. Her refusal to be his gift to Paris is 'self-willed harlotry' (4.2.14) and she a 'baggage' (3.5.160). Her attitude towards the 'holy father' Friar Lawrence again shows how she has moved beyond the role of 'pensive daughter' as a subject who is determined to take her life into her own hands (4.1.37–9). The solution he offers, of course, demands just such active resolution on her part.

Juliet's return to the household in the role of submissive daughter creates a fantasy of family harmony which heightens our awareness of the proximity of 'well-seeming forms' and tragedy. The spectacle of Juliet prostrating herself on her knees before Capulet may seem hypocritical given her earlier independence, but there is painful sincerity in her wish to please her father. The scenario which Friar Lawrence sets up allows her to retreat back into the safety of the household, to obliterate, for a fleeting moment, the new feelings and circumstances that have swept her away. She can be the ideal daughter, the gift who will be 'ruled', a fantastic role she could never fulfil. As she kneels to Capulet and he joyfully raises her to her feet, the bond between daughter and father is temporarily resurrected in all its poignant fragility, something Shakespeare explores again in Lear's reconciliation and fantasy of imprisonment with Cordelia (Folio 5.3.8–23).

Juliet's liminal position between her old household and her new husband dramatizes, in extreme form, the crisis of marriage for women and speaks particularly to female spectators married or about to be married. Cleaving to one's husband meant allying oneself to his family. For women, the need for good relations between in-laws must have been felt especially strongly, which perhaps helps to explain Lucy Audley and Maria's endeavours to bring peace out of their family feud by appealing to Joan Thynne. Maria sent a lock of hair with her 'greatest affection' and 'well wishings', the first of many desperate attempts to win her mother-in-law's favour (p. 21). In 1603 she wrote 'all my desire is that you should not wrong me so much as to hold the sincerity of my affection suspected'. She points out that Joan's suspicion allies her with the prejudice of men like Mr Daunte, 'who I found was well pleased to see that you yourself being a woman did doubt the secrecy of your own sex' (p. 31). Maria's entreaty to her enemy on the grounds of their common gender suggests that Juliet's character, however unconventional her behaviour, may still have appealed emotionally to women in the audience.

Arranged marriages often strengthened bonds between families, but in cases where the parents were not automatic allies the daughter's transition from one family to another could be painful. If antagonism existed between her old and new families (as, for example, over the payment of a dowry), the bride could find herself torn apart by conflicting loyalties. As Blanche says in Shakespeare's *King John*, 'Which is the side that I must go withal? . . . They whirl asunder and dismember me' (3.1.253–6).[28] In *Romeo and Juliet*, Juliet's confusion after the murder of Tybalt heightens the emotional acrobatics experienced by a newly married wife:

NURSE: Will you speak ill of him that killed your cousin?
JULIET: Shall I speak ill of him that is my husband? . . .

    . . .

My husband lives, that Tybalt would have slain;
And Tybalt's dead that would have slain my husband.
All this is comfort. Wherefore weep I then?

(3.2.96)

Juliet's answer, that Romeo's banishment is the cause of her grief, is only partially true. Her following lines show guilt at cutting herself off from her family, and metaphorically killing them as far as her loyalties are concerned. In Juliet's confused mind, Tybalt's death should be accompanied by news of the deaths of '"Thy father" or "thy mother", nay, or both' (3.2.119). Her horror at Romeo's banishment is that she now has no family, and no identity, for 'to speak that word / Is father, mother, Tybalt, Romeo, Juliet, / All slain, all dead' (3.2.122). The letters of Maria Thynne suggest that Juliet's sense of emotional isolation, though extreme, is not untypical. In spite of her strength of character, Maria obviously felt insecure in her new home. She wrote, somewhat regretfully, to her absent 'Thomken', 'my sisters will be in London at their pleasures . . . do but haste home and make much of thy Mall' (p. 33).

Juliet realizes 'my dismal scene I needs must act alone' (4.3.19), yet even as she tries to assert her independence by taking the sleeping draft, her family surround her. In her vision of the Capulet tomb, she imagines herself 'madly playing with my forefathers' joints' and driven to dash out her 'desp'rate brains' when Tybalt's ghost returns to haunt her with her betrayal of the family (4.3.48–53). Juliet's nightmare that her own forefathers' bodies will suffocate, batter her or drive her mad gives a frighteningly vivid picture of the oppressive nature of paternal authority. Because the Capulet tomb is an imaginative space in this scene, women in the audience may have found it easy to translate the emotional crisis it depicts to their own experiences. The claustrophobia of Juliet's family heritage is brilliantly dramatized through the reactions to her supposed death and her final enclosure within the tomb. When her body is discovered, it is cocooned by the grief of the household. Capulet's extreme reaction is to identify with his daughter and claim that death has taken hold of him too. He tells Paris

> Death is my son-in-law, death is my heir
> My daughter he hath wedded. I will die
> And leave him all. Life, living, all is death's.
>   (4.4.65)

Death, like Romeo, is an invasive bridegroom who has stolen Capulet's gift. On one level the speech seems coldly materialistic with its concern for legacy, but Capulet's resignation to death reveals the depth of his love for Juliet. He cannot see a life beyond the stolen marriage where he has no control over her departure. Ironically, though, the bridegroom death has apparently stopped Juliet from leaving her father's house. Death rudely interrupts the ceremony in which Capulet would have to give her away and allows him to repossess her on her wedding morning. In a subversive alternative to the marriage bed, Capulet claims 'with my child my joys are buried' and usurps Romeo's position as chief mourner (4.4.91). The sinister relationship between death and desire, amplified by the Elizabethan pun on death for orgasm, characterizes the conflicting endogamous and exogamous energies generated by betrothal.

The incarceration of the living Juliet in the Capulet tomb translates her enclosure in the family into ghastly physical terms. The family's appetite, its outlawed desire for and its longing to control daughters, is imaged in Romeo's description of the tomb as a mouth 'gorged with the dearest morsel of the earth' (5.3.46). Juliet has been swallowed up by the passions of the Capulet family: their hate for the Montagues and the semi-incestuous reluctance to let her move outside except, in the last resort, as a paternal gift. Romeo's determination to cram himself into that 'detestable maw' (5.3.45) forces recognition of exogamous desire and inter-family love down the Capulet forefathers' throats. As the Prince says, 'all are punished' (5.3.294); Romeo dies as well as Juliet but his martyrdom at the hands of the patriarchal family is less intense than hers. The last lines of the play remind us that it is her tragedy: 'For never was a story of more woe / Than this of Juliet and her Romeo' (5.3.308).

Romeo and Juliet presents Juliet's passionate determination sympathetically, even though her agency is tragically limited. Most moralistic writings on domestic government viewed filial disobedience much less tolerantly. In *Of Domesticall Duties* (1622), for example, William Gouge commented that because 'an undutifull childe is commonly a verie lewd person many other waies', it is not surprising that 'they who in the

141

beginning shake off the yoake of government, should run headlong into all riot, loosenesse, and licentiousnesse: thus then sinne being added unto sinne, it must needs bring mischiefe upon mischiefe'.[29] The tragic plot of *Othello* (1604) relies on just such a belief that a daughter's disobedience is the starting point for further transgressive desire. Desdemona's father warns Othello 'Look to her, Moor, if thou hast eyes to see. / She has deceived her father, and may thee' (1.3.292). Othello pledges 'my life upon her faith' (1.3.294), but an underlying insecurity about Desdemona's independence of will undoubtedly contributes to the ease with which he believes Iago's lies. Even Desdemona herself claims some responsibility for her tragedy when Emilia asks her who murdered her and she replies 'Nobody, I myself' (5.2.133). Desdemona is innocent except for her initial 'crime' of abandoning her role as a betrothal gift in favour of her passion for Othello. In *The Changeling* (1622), however, the disobedient daughter takes a much more active part in her own destruction. In the same year as William Gouge's *Of Domesticall Duties* was published, Middleton and Rowley dramatize the pattern of disasters he outlines, showing how Beatrice-Joanna's actions launch her into 'riot, loosenesse, and licentiousnesse' down a helter-skelter of 'mischiefe upon mischiefe'.

At the opening of the play, Vermandero is proud of his choice of son-in-law in Alonzo de Piracquo. Beatrice-Joanna's preference of Alsemero inevitably causes a conflict of wills between father and daughter:

VERMANDERO:	I would not change him for a son-in-law
	For any he in Spain, the proudest he,
	And we have great ones, that you know.
ALSEMERO:	He's much
	Bound to you, sir.
VERMANDERO:	He shall be bound to me,
	As fast as this tie can hold him; I'll want
	My will else.
BEATRICE: [*aside*]	I shall want mine if you do it.
	(1.1.215)[30]

Strong male bonds are forged as Vermandero confides his plans to Alsemero, man to man. Alonzo is the constant goal, 'I would not change him', while Beatrice-Joanna is merely an object of exchange, 'this', the tie that will bind him to Vermandero. She does not openly dissent but sets up an alternative form of confidence with the audience, who witness her resolve to exercise her own will, making choice of Alsemero. The fact that she does not love Alonzo is immediately apparent to his brother, who appreciates the danger posed by Beatrice-Joanna's desire. Since her heart is 'leap'd into another's bosom' (2.1.132), containing her in a loveless marriage will only lead to torment for Alonzo (to say nothing of Beatrice), especially since he will never be certain of having children of his own because his wife will always be imagining another in his place (2.1.128–40). Tomazo de Piracquo's fears about the effects of enforced marriage draw on opinions expressed in quasi-medical textbooks. Sadler's *The Sicke Womans Private Looking-Glasse* (1636) argued that 'when parents enforce their daughters to have husbands contrary to their liking, therein marrying their bodies but not their hearts, and where there is a want of love, there for the most part is no conception; as appears in women which are deflowered against their will'.[31] Here parental will in betrothal is tantamount to promoting rape. Tomazo's opposition to a match that would presumably bring social advantages for him as well as his brother makes his opinions about arranged marriage seem objective and probably carries weight with the audience.

Nevertheless, as Beatrice-Joanna recognizes, her independent choice of partner would certainly not elicit automatic approval from spectators. She tells Alsemero 'the present times are not so sure of our side / As those hereafter may be' (2.2.49). Perhaps her experience will change audience opinion, she implies. Spectators are invited to participate in the debate by judging the actions of the father and disobedient daughter. Beatrice-Joanna is caught in the cross-fire of parental commands and transgressive passion. Even when she smuggles Alsemero into her chamber and delights 'I have within mine eye all my desires' (2.2.8), she is still bound to her father, wishing that Piracquo didn't exist or that there were 'no such tie as the command of parents' (2.2.19–20). Because she cannot escape from the physical and ideological framework of her father's household, she strives to fulfil her desires covertly within its boundaries. Vermandero's castle is 'spacious and impregnable', yet confining (3.1.4). Its passages are 'somewhat narrow' (3.1.6), and as passions become dangerously introverted tragedy explodes.

Beatrice-Joanna's first step is to bring the object of her desires into the castle. She asks her father to invite Alsemero inside its walls since he is 'much desirous' (1.1.159) to see it, and it becomes a metaphor for her own body. The castle is female; Alsemero must see 'her best entertainment' (1.1.201), Vermandero insists, having ascertained the young man's suitability by reference to his parentage (a curious parallel to betrothal negotiations). 'Within are secrets' (1.1.166), he confides, and Alsemero learns those secrets, conducted via a 'private way' (2.2.55) to Beatrice-Joanna's chamber. The 'best entertainment' he receives there is not, of course, what Vermandero intended. The invitation was to the public rooms, ideally to his daughter's wedding feast. Beatrice-Joanna uses it to pursue a private underground courtship in opposition to her father's wishes. She rejoices that Alsemero has 'the liberty of the house' (3.4.12),

143

and the audience are privy to the secret passages through which her desires are conducted.

Beatrice-Joanna's fall into filial disobedience seems to lead directly to ungoverned passion, which 'mounts then like arithmetic', as De Flores notes (2.2.62). The murder of Alonzo turns her desire from a secret but exogamous direction to a more perversely introverted one. Instead of allowing Alsemero to challenge the unwanted fiancé to a duel in the open air, she employs De Flores to murder him in the castle. Alonzo is lulled by the anticipation of, one day, being master of the household and its 'rich variety' of munitions (3.1.9), so he is shocked to find himself attacked from the inside. Beatrice-Joanna's reliance on De Flores embeds her even more firmly in the household which forbids her freedom. In her autobiography, Lady Grace Mildmay cautions against servants who would 'seek to know all that their master knoweth and observe and watch all that he doth and harken diligently unto every word he speaketh'. Such men are dangerous since they 'will ponder thereupon to make what use they can, as it best pleaseth them, being furnished thereby to take what part they will with or against their master as may make most fit for their own advantage'.[32] De Flores operates in just this way, observing Beatrice-Joanna and using his knowledge to manipulate her. Servants whose primary allegiance and previous service was to the husband's family often posed a greater threat to mistresses. For example, Lady Elizabeth Willoughby complained that Sir Francis's servants refused to obey her orders and even took up arms against her. Their plots against Lady Willoughby, including insinuations that she was having an affair with a neighbour, certainly deepened the animosity between husband and wife.[33] Lady Hoby and Lady Mildmay had similar unpleasant experiences. Lady Hoby says she suffered a 'domesticall injurie', in the form of an accusatory letter from the servant John Wass, and Lady Mildmay complains 'also in mine own house amongst my servants and family I have found much disturbance by their unfaithful and unthankful dealings wherein they have rendered me evil for good'.[34] Female spectators who felt trapped and exposed under the conspiratorial surveillance of servants would have fully appreciated Beatrice-Joanna's dilemma.

Beatrice-Joanna's plan to escape the lustful gaze of her father's servant by turning him into a criminal backfires disastrously. De Flores insists that the 'deed' (or murder) eliminates any difference between them, so Beatrice-Joanna is unable to pay for his services with anything else but her body. As she accepts his love, her desire moves deeper into the household and becomes more complex, entwined in a 'labyrinth' rather than simply flowing along the secret passages of her love for Alsemero. As Scott Wilson has shown, the labyrinth is highly ambiguous: it seems to be open, and yet is always closed. As such it provides an ideal trope for Beatrice-Joanna's situation in *The Changeling*, where she seems to have the freedom to pursue her own will, yet ends up imprisoned in Alsemero's closet. Like the labyrinth, the play offers a 'fantasy of escape in the form of a trap, in which escape itself is a trap. There is no escape but in the thrill and pleasure of losing oneself and one's way'.[35] The maze of giddy desire seems to take Beatrice-Joanna outside the subjection of her father's house, but in following its twists and turns she loses autonomy, becoming 'the deed's creature' (2.2.137), De Flores's creature and Alsemero's creature all at the same time.

When Alsemero discovers the compact of murder and passion between his wife and De Flores, Beatrice-Joanna and the house are brought together again in images of destruction. She warns him 'you have ruin'd / What you can ne'er repair again' (5.3.34), to which he vows

> I'll all demolish, and seek out truth within you,
> If there be any left; let your sweet tongue
> Prevent your heart's rifling; there I'll ransack
> And tear out my suspicion.
>
> (5.3.36)

Beatrice's submission, 'You may, sir, / 'Tis an easy passage' (5.3.39), shows her loss of self-possession. She has no power to resist any man's entry to her body. In spite of Alsemero's threats to pillage and destroy the household, its structure remains ominously intact at the end of the play. When he locks the couple in his closet to rehearse their scene of lust, violence and destructive passion are physically imprisoned in the house, as De Flores and Beatrice-Joanna cry out in a gruesome combination of erotic ecstasy and pain. Vermandero is horrified to find enemies within, declaring 'a host of enemies enter'd my citadel / Could not amaze like this' (5.3.147). Beatrice-Joanna defines herself as his bad blood which should be purged and cast away into the gutter, implying that Vermandero is, albeit unwittingly, the source of the tragedy by marrying her against her will. As William Gouge pointed out, 'many mischiefes ordinarily fall out upon such mariages, as utter dislike betwixt husband and wife ... wishing, yea practising one anothers death. To all these mischiefes doe parents, the cause thereof, make themselves accessary'.[36] When Vermandero points out that they are all in hell, Alsemero quickly intervenes to make a precise distinction between governors and transgressors: 'justice hath so right / The guilty hit, that innocence is quit / By proclamation and may joy again' (5.3.185). The conclusion of the play is sinister as the patriarchal structure triumphantly reasserts itself. Alsemero renews his bond with his father Vermandero, having excised the troublesome woman whose will disrupted the smooth exchange of property at the beginning of the play. The audience are invited to participate in the renewal of the family with their applause, but exactly where their approval lies is uncertain:

> Your only smiles have power to cause re-live
> The dead again, or in their rooms to give
> Brother a new brother, father a child;
> If these appear, all griefs are reconciled.
>
> (5.3.224)

The audience's opinions can replace the imperfect characters with ideal brothers and daughters, according to the prescriptions of domestic conduct books (fathers and sons are presumably already perfect since Alsemero is speaking here). More disturbingly, the audience also have the power to give life to figures like Beatrice-Joanna, the threatening embodiment of transgressive female will. For some women in the audience, the revival of a dangerous Beatrice-Joanna might have seemed more attractive than the role of wifely submission left on stage in Isabella.

The subplot of *The Changeling* shows how the house could be just as much a prison for wives as it was for daughters since Isabella is literally locked into her husband's house. The doors are fettered against her, and she is kept 'in a cage' (3.3.2–3) at Alibius's command. Isabella's only form of escape is to enter the semi-public apartments where Alibius's mad patients are simultaneously kennelled and on display. Her position is as desperate as theirs, in that here she is the object of the lustful gazes of Antonio, Franciscus and Lollio. She is trapped by the ridiculous professions of courtly love made by the supposed madmen and subject to the surveillance of Lollio, who vows, like De Flores, to 'put in for one' if she transgresses (3.3.245). Isabella considers adultery when she first talks to Antonio, but her disguise as a madwoman 'in the lower labyrinth' (4.3.102) signals the folly, the futility, of a woman trying to pursue her own desires in such a phallocentric environment, something that Beatrice discovers to her cost. Since there is nothing beyond the household but the same, Isabella remains locked up in the arms and will of Alibius (3.3.248), paraded abroad only occasionally in the company of his mad patients; like them, an object to be gazed upon or controlled by the 'commanding pizzles' (4.3.62) of her masters.

Far from being a paradise for married women, the household could be a physical or metaphorical prison, as the case of Lady Elizabeth Willoughby of Wollaton Hall amply demonstrates. In the 1570s Elizabeth was placed under a form of house arrest by her husband, Sir Francis, as a result of marital discord. When her dowry failed to materialize relations between

Elizabeth and her husband deteriorated rapidly. She would not play the role of good housewife, refusing to subject herself to her husband's authority and determining to travel away from home when she wished. Sir Francis wrote to her on one of her visits to Buxton, wishing that 'with the recovery of her health she may also put on a tractable mind, and let her self-will give place to reason'.[37] When Elizabeth returned home, however, she refused to be ruled by Sir Francis, excusing her unconventional behaviour cleverly by telling him that she owed her primary loyalty to the Queen and that he might command something against 'Her Majestie's proceedings'. As a result of her frequent insubordination, Sir Francis restricted Elizabeth to certain rooms, denied her the mistress's usual managerial role, and forbade her any part in the care of the children. Elizabeth vowed she would leave and 'goe to an inn and send for some of her friends to her'. When permission was denied, 'she fell into a most violent passion, threatening to make away with herself, and being denied a knife would have struck her scissors into her belly if she had not been prevented. Then she said she would never eat or drink more, but wth ye same knife she was next to eat wth would kill herself'. By 1582 Elizabeth had left, but recognizing that she had no future outside the household, was obliged to beg her husband to receive her once again, promising that she would 'performe all good duties that do become a loving and obedient wife'. She also recognized the dangers of returning, telling Sir Francis that she had heard 'yow would kepe me shorter than ere I was kept, that yow lock and pynn me up in a chamber, and that I should not go so much as into the garden to take the ayre, without yor leave and lycense'.[38]

Elizabeth Willoughby's unhappy experience of the household as a prison where her self-will would not be tolerated but from which she could not, finally, escape, is by no means untypical. Nor is it specific to her class, since law court presentments show that women of the lower orders felt equally trapped in their husbands' households.[39] As John Dove's 1610 sermon *Of Divorcement* pointed out, 'a servant hath more liberty in the bondage of his service than a woman in the freedom of her wedlock' since 'he may change masters, she may not change husbands, while her furst husband liveth'.[40] Aspects of Elizabeth's history – her attempts to assert self-government within the household, her futile attempt to leave it, the performance of deference she was obliged to adopt, and her determination to mutilate or kill herself – are all found in tragedies that deal with marriage. The anonymous *Arden of Faversham* (1591) takes up many of these ideas in its depiction of a middle-class household.[41]

As master and mistress, Arden and Alice are naturally at the centre of the play but it has no fixed emotional centre because the text constantly shifts audience sympathies across a range of perspectives. Arden, the point around which all the plots revolve, is not fully developed psychologically. His role as governor of the little commonwealth makes him curiously aloof in emotional terms. In contrast, Alice's feelings are of primary importance to her character. She is the heart of the household, though this does not mean that she evokes the unwavering sympathy of the audience. Alice not only challenges her husband's authority but murders him. As Frances Dolan has pointed out, legal and literary discussions of the murderous wife 'interrogated the contradictory, disturbing nature of wifely subjectivity in its most extreme and uncontainable form', using exceptional examples of violent women to exaggerate the threat posed by female agency.[42] A murderess could not be commended in a public arena like the playhouse, however much her defiance of convention may have won the secret admiration of some spectators. *Arden of Faversham* therefore uses a subtle strategy to accommodate these contradictory public and private attitudes. It manipulates women's responses to condemn Alice as an active agent in her husband's murder but to sympathize with her as a victim of the family structure. Reactions to Alice remain ambiguous today, suggesting the enduring power of the family as a trope for oppressive patriarchal influences. In cases of domestic violence, of course, the family remains a literal battleground.

Alice is actively involved in plotting the murder and finally stabs Arden 'for hind'ring Mosby's love and mine' (14.238). Audience disapproval of her physical violence is solicited by the reactions of other characters. Even the hardened villain Black Will is shocked by her longing to kill Arden (14.140), and the community's fear of Alice is glimpsed in Michael's determination to poison her with ratsbane (14.296). In the preparations for the murder, the presentation of Alice is calculated to elicit more diverse responses. She is still an active agent who plots using Michael and then Greene, but the participation of other members of the community tempers condemnation of Alice. First, their grievances against Arden undermine his nobility, casting him as a greedy capitalist adventurer, a social upstart rather than a good neighbour. The short scene dramatizing Dick Reede's complaints is particularly damaging to Arden's character (13.12–53). Second, the number of people wishing to help with the murder suggests that the community are the perpetrators of the crime. Alice is a vehicle through which the vengeance of such dispossessed people can be channelled. In their role as a temporary community in the theatre, Renaissance spectators may have sympathized collectively with the Faversham murderers who are chastising acts of unneighbourliness, even though their sympathies as individual householders might have been drawn to Arden. While Alice is condemned for leading the plot, then, the play indirectly recruits sympathy for her cause.

Alice's integrity, or lack of it, is equally contradictory, making it difficult to criticize or applaud her actions unequivocally. There is power in her determination to stand up for love, so spectators may be inclined to agree with the painter, Clarke, who tells Alice 'you show a noble mind / That rather than you'll live with him you hate / You'll venture life and death with him you love' (1.268). Clarke's vow that he would do as much for Susan constructs Alice's love for Mosby as something with which ordinary members of the community (and, by implication, the audience), can identify and respect. In contrast to Alice's daring honesty, though, we also see her as an articulate dissembler in pretending love for Arden. Having just attempted to poison him with a bowl of broth, she performs the role of disappointed housewife to perfection when he refuses to eat the food, and tells him 'never woman loved her husband better / Than I do thee' (1.392). One could argue that Alice is obliged to play the role of dutiful wife to ensure reconciliation with Arden, just as Lady Willoughby was forced to tell her husband she would 'study to conforme all good duties that do become a loving and obedient wife towards her husband', so he would take her back into the household.[43] Alice's performance is one of emotions rather than mere duty, though, and she seems to revel in the power she has over Arden. Her unwillingness to let him go from her arms (seen again in Scene 10) is 'cunningly performed', and her gleeful celebration of her skill with Mosby: 'did you mark me then how I brake off?', seems especially callous (1.418–19).

Alice plays a dangerous game by claiming that marriage vows are meaningless since 'Oaths are words, and words is wind, / And wind is mutable' (1.436). This puts all pledges of love, including those made by Mosby and Alice herself, under question, especially in the context of the stage where all declarations are performances. Mosby obviously mistrusts Alice and sets out to test her in the opening scene. Her objection, 'What needs thou try me whom thou never found false' (1.211), is deeply ironic in the light of her treatment of Arden. For the audience, her acting skills make it difficult to trust her at key moments like her repentance after reading her prayerbook (8.43–79). When she tells Greene that Arden has brutally mistreated her with 'hard words, and blows', infidelity and conspiracy against her life, this sounds more like a displacement of her own activities (1.492–505). Greene's surprise suggests the improbability of such a story (1.508), but he does not openly discredit it because it adds extra legitimacy to his actions. Greene exploits Alice's position as a victim of domestic violence, whether fictional or not, to construct himself as a good neighbour protecting a vulnerable woman as well as his own interests in the land.

In plotting to escape from her role as Arden's wife, Alice comes tantalizingly close to a sense of independent identity. She tells Mosby

'What hath he to do with thee, my love, / Or govern me that am to rule myself' (11.32). Her claim to self-government is partly realized as she takes over the house, first by secretly locking Mosby in her closet to plan the murder (1.191), and finally by placing the murderers in the counting house, replacing them and the gold with Arden's body. The ferryman who compares the mist to 'a curst wife in a little house, that never leaves her husband till she have driven him out at doors with a wet pair of eyes' (13.11), highlights Alice's usurpation of Arden's property. In spite of her claims to be mistress of herself, though, Alice cannot be truly independent. She replaces Arden with Mosby, who, as master of her heart, 'well may be the master of the house' (1.640). After Arden is murdered Alice declares 'I'll have my will', but this is to fill the vacant seat with a new master, Mosby (14.286–7). Throughout the play, Alice subjects herself to him and declares herself utterly reliant on his love:

> If thou cry war there is no peace for me.
> I will do penance for offending thee
> And burn this prayerbook, where I here use
> The holy word which had converted me.
> See, Mosby, I will tear away the leaves
> And all the leaves, and in this golden cover
> Shall thy sweet phrases and thy letters dwell,
> And thereon will I chiefly meditate
> And hold no other sect but such devotion.
>
> (8.114)

Alice seems radical in breaking away from her husband, daring to tear up the prayerbook that recommends wifely repentance, chastity, obedience and silence. Ultimately, though, she seeks to reinscribe herself within that pattern by replacing Arden with Mosby as her new, divinely appointed lord. By claiming 'if thou cry war there is no peace for me', she subscribes to the conventional idea of the godly wife as a mirror and reflection of her husband.

Alice's dependence on Mosby is her tragedy because his affection is much more uncertain. He is a 'mean artificer' (8.77), a craftsman and deceiver whose declarations of love, like hers to Arden, are 'but wind'. His soliloquy in Scene 8 shows that his primary motivations for the murder are social and financial. Alice's fear that he 'loves me not but for my wealth' (8.108) is justified when he accuses her of ruining his business prospects and compares her to a counterfeit coin (8.101–2). When their quarrel is patched up, Alice invites Mosby to kiss her in order to 'seal up this new-made match' (8.150), but there is no indication in the text, whose stage directions are remarkably full, that he ever does this. Mosby's failure to commit himself emotionally to Alice is motivated partly by fear and dislike of what she has become: a wilful agent in her own destiny. Frances Dolan draws attention to the similarities between Alice's case and that of Ann Welles, whose murder of her husband was publicized in the pamphlet *The Trueth of the Most Wicked and Secret Murthering of John Brewen, Goldsmith* (1592). Like Alice, Anne plots with her lover only to be rejected by him, because he fears 'thou would'st marry me to the end thou mightest poyson me'.[44] In *Arden of Faversham* Mosby finds it impossible to reconcile the agency of the murderess with the submissive role of wife. He suspects that, having dared to 'supplant Arden' for his sake, Alice may well 'extirpen me to plant another' (8.40–3). Alice's vow that she will not be governed 'that am to rule myself' (10.84) is particularly alarming to Mosby, as the architectural image in his following speech shows:

Why, what's love without true constancy?
Like to a pillar built of many stones,
Yet neither with good mortar well compact,
Nor cement to fasten with every blast of wind,
And being touched, falls straight into the earth
And buries all his haughty pride in dust.

(10.90)

This speech is purportedly about constancy, but Mosby's description of the building without mortar or cement betrays his underlying fear of Alice's will as an element in his own house. Without proper wifely submission, the pillar of husbandly authority and the whole hierarchical structure of the family will crumble. Mosby's ambitions for such an authoritative position ally him far more closely with Arden than with Alice and, ultimately, her tragedy is caused by a perverse bonding between these two men.

Arden and Mosby are alike in their ambitions to be masters of grand estates. Both seek to garner territory and position, even though Arden strives to distance himself from 'so base a groom' as the craftsman (1.305). Their closeness, and the exclusion of Alice, is evidenced in the opening scene when Mosby promises Arden he will no longer solicit Alice's attentions, a vow he will not break, even when Alice tells him that oaths are nothing more than wind. The bond between the two men is strengthened during the stabbing plot that Alice devises (12.62–70). Her initiative must increase Mosby's fears about her as a future wife, especially since he gets injured instead of Arden in the event (13.87). Franklin regards Arden's subsequent concern for Mosby as madness. Actually, Arden's claim that Alice is 'a mediator twixt us two' (13.134) spells out the truth. The murder scene presents Alice as a mediator between one paternal governor and the next. She claims 'I shall no more be closed in Arden's arms' but 'Mosby's arms / Shall compass me' (14.123–5). The locked doors of the house represent physically how the men around her conspire to deny agency to Alice and reduce her to a subservient, domestic role. Mosby taunts Alice 'I'll see your husband in despite of you' (14.212), and Alice must serve supper while the two men sit down together at the tables to play. This scene of male companionship and friendly rivalry is a cover for the murder, but it enacts the truth of fellowship in transactions of power. The money they gamble for prefigures the discovery that Mosby has taken Arden's purse and belt, symbols of his position as householder. Alice is trapped in the household between a husband she does not love and a master who does not love her.

The denial of female agency in the family is pointed up by the total effacement of Alice in the play's epilogue. Delivered by Franklin, Arden's loyal friend, it reaffirms homosocial bonds, focusing on Arden's body and addressing only the gentlemen in the audience. Like Alice, female specta- tors, their desires, feelings and will, are written out of the play's conclusion. Such a deliberate policy of exclusion opens the door for covert identification with Alice, where unspoken sympathy for her powerless position balances public condemnation of her actions. Women watching the play in the 1590s, and on stages now, may not only sympathize but empathize with Alice, reading the Arden household as a symbol that leads them out of the playhouse and back to their own domestic situations.

Elizabeth Cary's *The Tragedy of Mariam* (1604/6) dramatizes the wife's imprisonment in the family even more explicitly. Psychologically complex characters, male and female, are presented in conflicts that demonstrate the dangers of male tyranny and the difficulty for women to preserve their integrity in such an arena. The tension between conformity and individual will is built into the very structure of the play. The characters strive to enact their wills, while their words and deeds are contained by the Choruses that follow each Act and enclose the action within a framework of moralistic prescriptions, especially on the behaviour of women. In the opening scene, Mariam describes her marriage to Herod as a form of imprisonment, admitting 'oft have I wished that I from him was free' (1.16).[45] Herod's jealousy has barred her from liberty (1.1.25) and by ordering his servants to kill her in the event of his own death, he determines to make her sentence perpetual. Because Sohemus does not carry out the command, news of Herod's death allows Mariam to escape and speak 'with public voice' about her marriage (1.1.1). She recalls her love for Herod 'when virgin freedom left me unrestrained' (1.1.72); it is her bondage in marriage as much as the deaths of her family which has transformed that love into hate.

The Chorus criticizes Mariam's discontent, imputing it to an unstable and dangerously insatiable appetite, a 'vast imagination' that will 'guide her to she knows not what' (Chorus 1.25–34). News that Herod is still alive proves that Mariam's will is far from directionless. She grieves 'must I to my prison once again' (3.3.33) and determines not to live with 'him I so profoundly hate!' (3.3.20). As was the case with Elizabeth Willoughby, failure to conform herself to her husband's will leads to literal imprisonment. Given Mariam's earlier descriptions of her marriage, her speech from the prison in Act 4, Scene 8 may have had particularly sinister resonances if performed or read in a private household. Elizabeth Cary certainly had connections with the Countess of Pembroke's Wilton circle, in which so-called closet dramas were produced as domestic entertainments.[46] The household represented a safe space in which English women had opportunities to perform, but it simultaneously marked their exclusion from the public, professional theatre until 1660. Confined to the household, Cary may exploit its special dynamics by self-consciously staging a prison scene there. The actor reading or performing Mariam's lines from the prison is speaking in the home, the very space which immured the desires, wills and ambitions of so many women, including Cary herself.

Doris's entry to this scene of the play is highly significant since it shows her inability to live outside the domestic sphere even if that means returning to a prison. Her quest is to return home as Herod's wife, the 'companion to his private life' (2.3.20). Her first lines complain that Mariam has usurped her place as mistress of the buildings of Judea, but it is soon clear that she is not interested in political power, only regaining her place at Herod's side. Like Elizabeth Willoughby, she realizes that she has no place outside her husband's household. Standing opposite Mariam, she is just as much trapped, another victim of Herod's will. While Mariam has been imprisoned and cannot escape, Doris has been thrown out and cannot get back into the prison she loves. Blinded by her commitment to the wifely role, she directs her accusations at Mariam rather than at Herod, who has wrought the misery of both by divorcing Doris to possess his new love.

The character of Salome offers an alternative response to the problems of imprisonment and divorce experienced by Mariam and Doris. Like Mariam, she is trapped in marriage to a man she no longer loves and openly criticizes the double standard on divorce:

Why should such privilege to men be given?
Or given to them, why barred from women then?
Are men than we in greater grace with Heaven?
Or cannot women hate as well as men?
I'll be the custom-breaker and begin
To show my sex the way to freedom's door.

(1.4.45)

Salome's proto-feminist claims give the character a subversive energy which is undoubtedly dramatically attractive. Her quest to open the door of the house to freedom is enabled by Herod's absence, which allows Salome to copy her brother's actions and pursue her desires for Silleus through divorce. This is undoubtedly a more sympathetic option than murdering Constabarus, as she had arranged the execution of her previous husband under Herod's rule. The way to freedom's door is barred by the return of the patriarchal ruler, though. She tells Silleus 'my brother's sudden coming now / Will give my foot no room to walk at large' (3.2.84), and she is restricted to a violent, destructive course of action.

Salome and Mariam share the same liminal position between old and new families. Mariam's opening soliloquy shows how her loyalties are divided between Herod and her brother and grandfather whom he murdered. Like Juliet, she finds that 'one object yields both grief and joy' (1.1.10). Nostalgic love for Herod jostles violently in her memory with idealized pictures of her angelic brother Aristobolus and the 'worthy grandsire', Hircanus (1.1.31–46). Alexandra's entrance tips the balance in favour of the blood relations, as Mariam strives to conceal her grief at Herod's death and is then persuaded of his tyranny. Alexandra is a powerful matriarchal figure who replaces Herod as governor in the 'reversed state' which news of his death creates (1.2.126). Her later betrayal of Mariam to curry Herod's favour is a shocking reminder of the cost of success for women in a patriarchal environment (5.1.33–44). In Herod's absence, Alexandra can claim her own right to rule great affairs as a member of the royal house of David (1.2.127), and her pride in that family exerts a strong influence over Mariam.

With Herod's return, Cary shows that prioritizing one's blood kin above one's husband leads to tragedy for Mariam. Her refusal to rejoice is an act of personal integrity, asserting her own will rather than mirroring Herod's desires. The conventional wifely role constructed wives as mirrors of their husbands. Dod and Cleaver's *A godly form of household government* (1598), for example, pointed out that as the looking-glass, howsoever fair and beautifully adorned, is nothing worth if it show that countenance sad which is pleasant; or the same pleasant that is sad: so the woman deserveth no commendation that, (as it were) contrarying her husband when he is merry, showeth herself sad, or in sadness uttereth her mirth. For as men should obey the laws of their cities, so women the manners of their husbands.[47]

Mariam openly defies this role in her choice of 'dusky habits' of mourning to greet the joyous Herod. When he questions her costume, she tells him 'My lord, I suit my garments to my mind / And there no cheerful colours do I find' (4.3.5). By suiting her own mind, she refuses to construct herself as an extension of her husband, asserting an identity independent, even contrary, to his. Cary creates a rebellious wife utterly unlike Alice Arden, who deceives her husband to model herself on a new lord. In contrast, Mariam places utmost importance on being true to herself, an integrity which Cary also seemed to value since the inscription she carved on her daughter's wedding ring read 'Be and Seem'.[48] Mariam will not perform the role required of her by Herod even though she knows she could 'enchain him with a smile' (3.3.45); self-realization is all. She values the internal private world of her conscience and feelings at the expense of public appearances.

Ironically, Herod completely misinterprets Mariam's failure to perform as evidence of deception, inspired by her adulterous affection for Sohemus. His over-possessive love turns virtue into pitch, as he accuses Mariam of being a 'painted devil' (4.4.17) and believes 'hell itself lies hid / Beneath thy heavenly show' (4.4.45). Herod is shaken by the insubordination of his family and servants, executing offenders in a desperate attempt to get his household back into order. Plagued by the paranoia peculiar to a petty dictator, he is a volatile mixture of insecurity and power. William Gouge compared such husbands to gunpowder 'which not only taketh fire, but also breaketh out into a violent flame' at the least provocation. Therefore, 'as gunpowder is dangerous to be kept in a house', marriage to such a man was likely to prove explosive, as it does for Mariam.[49] The unstable Herod extends Sohemus's betrayal to Mariam, believing her to be guilty of adultery, petty treason and regicide when the 'poisoned' drink is served. The arch manipulator behind these metamorphoses is, of course, Salome, whose own skilful performances spell out success in contrast to the tragedy of Mariam's failure.

Unlike Mariam, Salome exploits her liminal position between old and new families to set one against the other for her own advantage. She exploits her influence in Herod's family as a means to escape from her husband's. Just as she turns gender roles upside down in the play, she also reverses the usual outward tendency of daughters and seeks to preserve the endogamous bonds of siblings rather than promoting exogamous bonds with other families. Her intense dislike of Mariam and her criticism of Pheroras's marriage (3.1.1–28) betrays her fear of outsiders who will now claim her brothers' primary affections. Herod's return puts Pheroras and Salome into roles typical of domestic tragedy: Pheroras's stolen marriage with Graphina transgresses patriarchal control of marriage negotiations and Salome's desire for divorce is turned into petty treason as she seeks Constabarus's death. Salome is able to further both these projects by binding her younger brother into her conspiracy to manipulate the elder. Herod's love for his sister becomes strikingly obvious in a slip of the tongue where he mistakes her for Mariam (4.2.42). Salome exploits his childlike need for reassurance and affection in order to turn his loyalty away from Mariam and his disordered household back to his siblings and the family of his birth.

Salome's active will, reversing household order so that 'all the world be topsy-turved quite' (1.6.50), makes her a disturbing figure. In line with the conventions of her day, Cary presents Salome as a villain, yet the play does not allow the male characters or the power structures they represent to go uncriticized. Women's inability to escape the prison of patriarchy is shown in the difference between male and female same-sex relationships. While Alexandra, Mariam, Salome and Doris are shown attacking each other, scenes between Constabarus, Silleus and Baba's sons give evidence of strong bonds between men. It is against such primary loyalties that the women have to struggle to find a place. Constabarus tells the sons of Baba that 'with friends there is not such a word as debt / Where amitie is tied with bond of truth' (2.2.14). He idealizes their love as a retreat from the treacheries of heterosexual relationships to an all-male 'Golden Age' (2.2.16–17). However noble such sentiments appear, they rely on the exclusion and denigration of women. In a second scene between the band of brothers, Constabarus has a totally misogynist tirade (4.6.32–72). He has previously been quite a sympathetic character and his bitterness about Salome is understandable, but his generalized attack on women in the audience seems wholly unreasonable. Constabarus's passionate promotion of trust between men is here presented as the product of an unbalanced mind.

Even more so than Constabarus, Herod is mentally disturbed. The Argument refers to his madness and the last two acts give ample illustration of it as he murders his subjects in complete disregard of his duties as protector of the family and the state. Cary introduces an element of black comedy into the tragedy when Herod imagines that there might be some 'strange ways of cure' to reattach Mariam's body to her head and make her breathe again after she has been executed (5.1.92). Mariam is elevated to the status of a martyr or saint and Herod seems demonically possessed, like the murderous husband in *A Yorkshire Tragedy*. In *The Tragedy of Mariam*, though, it is not so easy to separate the mad characters from the power structures they represent. By duplicating Herod's loss of self-control in Constabarus, Cary suggests that institutions which rely on a paranoid exclusion and abuse of women are radically unbalanced. In such an environment female self-assertion and self-integrity is impossible to sustain. Only characters like Salome and Alexandra who are willing to work within a patriarchal script and manipulate it for their own ends can succeed.

To preserve the household from paternal tyranny like Herod's, conduct books prescribed strict moral government. Lady Mildmay's description of the family, quoted at the opening of the chapter, recommended obedience, fear, love and duty to God for an ideal home, which 'may be called the house of God'. Religious principles were the foundation of the domestic hierarchy, and in the family that failed to follow such spiritual duties 'there is nothing to be looked for but confusion'.[50] Thomas Heywood's *A Woman Killed With Kindness* (1603) attacks the moral underpinning of the patriarchal household by showing that strict adherence to spiritual guidelines, as well as deviance from them, can cause domestic tragedy. Rather than blaming individuals, the play invites audiences to consider the devastating effects of trying to live up to the ideal models of domestic behaviour, and shows that women are the main casualties of such endeavours. The servant characters are vital in guiding audience responses to the main plot. They constitute a micro-community within the house and form a bridge between the action and the larger gathering of spectators. The audience watch events in Frankford's house from the outside, like neighbours, but are drawn into its affairs through their enclosure within the playhouse, just as the servants are involved in the future of the house although they are not primary players. Far from providing a lower-class contrast to maintain the 'position and dignity of the tragic characters', the servants are the practical upholders of household order, standards which their so-called betters signally fail to live up to.[51]

In the first part of the play, the servants' critical attention focuses on the behaviour of Anne and Wendoll, culminating in the scene where Frankford thrusts the lovers out of the 'polluted bed-chamber' and into the public arena of the hall and stage (13.14). At this crucial point, the maid's 'angel hand' stops Frankford from murdering Wendoll, as though alerting the audience to the ease with which moral outrage can collapse into domestic tyranny (13.69). Wendoll escapes easily enough, but Anne is exposed to the scrutiny of the audience and the servants, as later she will die under the gaze of her neighbours:

Enter Sisly, Spiggot, all the Servingmen and Jenkin, as newly come out of bed
ALL: O mistress, mistress, what have you done, mistress?
NICK: 'Sblood, what a caterwauling keep you here.
JENKIN: O Lord, mistress, how comes this to pass? ...
ANNE: See what guilt is: here stand I in this place,
          Ashamed to look my servants in the face.

(13.146)

Unlike Frankford, who retires to his study to consider Anne's fate, she has no such privacy in the house. In her one soliloquy, she advises women in the audience not to follow her path, for fear they should lose their husbands and children (13.133–45). This takes the form of a public confession in which she openly admits her guilt, but simultaneously and more subversively, she constructs herself as a martyr to the model of wifely purity. Her appeal to married female spectators to 'make me your instance' (13.144) seeks identification with them through suffering: 'racked, strappadoed, put to any torment' (13.137).

In contrast to the physical violence against wives in *The Tragedy of Mariam* and *Othello*, this play presents a woman crushed by psychological torture. To punish Anne, Frankford deprives her of her identity as a wife and mother. Whether this is indeed 'kindness' is questionable; Anne certainly doesn't need to be taught how to repent. Alongside its critique of the lovers' immoral actions, the play shows that Frankford's very proper adherence to the moral principles on which household government was built is destructive. From a sense of moral duty that is painful to him as well as her, Frankford condemns Anne to a state of non-being outside his house and plunges his family into tragedy. His careful removal of all objects associated with her marks both her erasure and her status as an object. By pushing her out, along with her clothes, furniture and her lute (a striking symbol of her status as an instrument to be played upon), he believes he can annihilate her. This proves to be the case. Once she receives the lute, Anne appeals to her servants to 'gird me about' (16.30) as though she will fall to pieces without their support. She has no future outside the role of wife and because she cannot reconcile the difference between what she is and that part she is expected to play, she resolves on a form of suicide which marks her status as outsider. She can no longer eat at her husband's table or as a guest in her neighbours' households, so she vows not to eat at all. Her situation is shared by other female victims of domestic tragedies, real and dramatic. Elizabeth Willoughby's vow that she would 'never eat or drink more, but wth ye same knife she was next to eat wth would kill herself' was based on the same failure to match up to the model of wifely perfection. Anne's sense of loss is poignant when she tells Nick she dare not address either husband or children since 'I am disclaimed in both' (16.86). Even the

158

loyal servant is moved to tears by her distressed state, marking a turn in audience sympathy which challenges the strict morality of his master. It is the servants who lead the way in pitying Anne, teaching Frankford and the other gentlefolk to temper their rigid moralistic judgements with humane kindness. The play suggests that only by such a balance can proper household order be maintained.

A Woman Killed With Kindness also directs criticism at Frankford for playing the part of generous host too well with regard to Wendoll, even to the exclusion of his own wife. Wendoll tells the audience

> ... He cannot eat without me,
> Nor laugh without me; I am to his body
> As necessary as his digestion,
> And equally to make him whole or sick.
> And shall I wrong this man? Base man! Ingrate!
> Hast thou the power straight with thy gory hands
> To rip thy image from his bleeding heart?
> To scratch thy name from out the holy book
> Of his remembrance, and to wound his name
> That holds thy name so dear, or rend his heart
> To whom thy heart was joined and knit together?
> (6.40)

This speech, with its imagery of joined hearts, holy vows and companionate life, would be far more appropriate in the mouth of Anne than of Wendoll. As Frankford's wife, it is she who ought to be part of his body, her image that should be lodged in his heart, her name that should be in the holy book of his remembrance. Wendoll appropriates the ideal picture of marital bonding to describe a relationship between men, showing how he has usurped Anne's position in the household. The delicate balance between homosocial/heterosexual desire in the erotic and economic triangle between the protagonists is played out in the card game. Although Frankford seems to be excluded, in fact his considerable gifts to Wendoll bind the two men together, with Anne the final object of exchange. By inviting Wendoll into the house and asking him to 'be a present Frankford in his absence' (6.78), Frankford is to some extent responsible for the tragedy himself.

The play's critique of a social structure that reduces women to goods for exchange is elaborated through its subplot, where Sir Charles Mountford uses his sister Susan to pay his debts. Like the Husband in *A Yorkshire Tragedy*, Charles feels oppressed by his sense of duty to his ancestors and will not sell the family home to repay Shafton. The Mountfords are caught in a cruelly commercial world where kinship ties have been superseded by competitive individualism. When Susan visits her relatives, their new philosophy is neatly summarized in her cousin Tydy's reproof: 'Call me not cousin; each man for himself' (9.34). Sir Charles's mistaken belief that they have secured his release produces a deeply ironic tribute to them as 'faithful kinsmen' who are 'the mirrors of the age' (10.36–42). This is exactly what they are. The Mountford plot shows the dangers of sacrificing traditional social structures in a world of emergent capitalism. Without an active network of kinship bonds and neighbourly cooperation, women and children, the most vulnerable in society, will inevitably suffer as Susan does.

Competition between men also characterizes the old feudal system of gifts and debts, however, and women fare little better under this. Sir Francis Acton's gift of five hundred pounds is another act of over-generosity like Frankford's to Wendoll, with woman again the final sacrifice in this system of gentlemanly exchange. Sir Charles cannot bear the stranger's charity and tells Susan 'under his good deeds I stooping go' (14.4). She is the 'one rich gift' (10.124) he has left to repay the debt, since to sell his house would be to prostitute 'a virgin title never yet deflowered' (7.23). Family honour is, it seems, more important than a sister's honour or happiness. Here, as in the main plot, Heywood is not criticizing individuals so much as a system of social order. Sir Charles and Susan are both presented sympathetically as victims, but Susan is the one who is sacrificed to ease the burden on her brother. In an overt display of male traffic in women, the play presents her 'tricked' or dressed 'like a bride' (14.1) and handed over as 'a pawn' (14.106) to Sir Francis, who now feels indebted to Sir Charles and so promises to marry Susan. To assume that this is a happy resolution totally ignores the fact that Susan is forced, as she says, to 'learn to love where I till now did hate' (14.148). As Anne Frankford is pushed out of the household into non-existence, Susan enters a marriage that holds no promise of the fulfilment of her desires. As mistress of Acton's household she will certainly hold a higher status position than before, but her 'preferment' may in fact be an equally damaging form of starvation. As so many plays from the period show, inclusion in and exclusion from the household could both result in tragedy for women. The system of gift-giving between men allowed little space for daughters or wives to manoeuvre in household politics. Plays sensitive to the situations of women like Juliet, Mariam or Alice Arden, whose desires and ambitions ran counter to conventional domestic structures, could make audiences vividly aware of tragedies close to home.

Notes

1 Linda Pollock (ed.), *With Faith and Physick: The Life of A Tudor Gentlewoman, Lady Grace Mildmay 1552–1620* (Collins and Brown, London, 1993), p. 47.
2 Ibid., pp. 85–6.
3 See Frances E. Dolan, *Dangerous Familiars: Representations of Domestic Crime in England 1550–1700* (Cornell University Press, Ithaca, NY, and London, 1994), pp. 21–4.
4 See Lena Cowen Orlin, *Private Matters and Public Culture in Post-Reformation England* (Cornell University Press, Ithaca, NY, and London, 1994), p. 17.
5 Thomas Heywood, *A Woman Killed With Kindness*, ed. Brian Scobie, New Mermaids (A & C Black, London, 1985).
6 Sir Edward Coke, *Reports of Sir Edward Coke* (London, 1658), Pp. 3.
7 Anon, *A Yorkshire Tragedy*, ed. A. C. Cawley and Barry Gaines, Revels Plays (Manchester University Press, Manchester, 1986). References are to scene and line numbers.
8 George Wilkins, *The Miseries of Enforced Marriage*, ed. Arthur Brown, Malone Society Reprints (Oxford University Press, Oxford, 1964).
9 Dolan, *Dangerous Familiars*, pp. 102–6.
10 William Gouge, *Of Domesticall Duties* (London, 1622), The English Experience (Walter Johnson Inc., Theatrum Orbis Terrarum, Amsterdam, 1976), p. 391.
11 *The Diary of Lady Margaret Hoby 1599–1605*, ed. Dorothy M. Meads (London, George Routledge and Sons, 1930).
12 Kate Aughterson (ed.), *Renaissance Woman: Constructions of Femininity in England, A Sourcebook* (Routledge, London and New York, 1995), pp. 31–2.
13 *The Diary of Lady Margaret Hoby*, ed. Meads, p. 101.
14 Ibid., p. 97.
15 Orlin, *Private Matters and Public Culture*, p. 187.
16 Gaston Bachelard, *The Poetics of Space: The Classic Look at How We Experience Intimate Spaces* (1958), trans. Maria Jolas (Beacon Press, Boston, 1994), pp. 14, 53.
17 Mark Girouard, *The Making of the English Country House* (Thames and Hudson, London, 1975), p. 57.
18 Susan Dwyer Amussen, '"Being Stirred to Much Unquietness": Violence and Domestic Violence in Early Modern England', *Journal of Women's History* 6 (1994), 70–89.
19 Andrew Gurr argues that Shakespeare's company promoted love above parental authority in plays like *Romeo and Juliet* (1595–7) and *The Miseries of Enforced Marriage* (1607), while the Henslowe companies presented pieces with an apparently more conservative outlook on domestic relations. See Andrew Gurr, *Playgoing in Shakespeare's London* (Cambridge University Press, Cambridge, 1987), pp. 149–50.
20 See Keith Wrightson, *English Society 1580–1680* (Unwin Hyman, London,

1982), p. 74, and Frank Whigham, *Seizures of the Will in Early Modern English Drama* (Cambridge University Press, Cambridge, 1996), pp. 122–3.

21 Lynda E. Boose, 'The Father's House and the Daughter in It: The Structures of Western Culture's Daughter–Father Relationship', in Lynda E. Boose and Betty S. Flowers (eds), *Daughters and Fathers* (Johns Hopkins University Press, Baltimore, 1989), p. 32.

22 See Eve Kosofsky Sedgwick, *Between Men: English Literature and Male Homosocial Desire*, Gender and Culture (Columbia University Press, New York, 1985, reprinted 1992).

23 Andrew Marvell, *The Complete Poems*, ed. Elizabeth Story Dunno, Penguin English Poets (Penguin, Harmondsworth, 1976), p. 51.

24 *Romeo + Juliet*, dir. Baz Luhrmann (Bazmark, Twentieth Century-Fox, 1997).

25 Alison Wall, 'The Feud and Shakespeare's *Romeo and Juliet*: A Reconsideration', *Sydney Studies in English* 5 (1979–80), 84–95.

26 Alison D. Wall, *Two Elizabethan Women: The Correspondence of Joan and Maria Thynne 1575–1611*, Wiltshire Record Society, vol. 38 (Devises, 1983), p. 9. Subsequent references are to page numbers in this edition.

27 Cited in Ann Jennalie Cook, *Making a Match: Courtship in Shakespeare and His Society* (Princeton, Princeton University Press, 1991), p. 85.

28 See also Octavia's situation in *Antony and Cleopatra* (3.3.12–20).

29 Gouge, *Of Domesticall Duties*, p. 146.

30 Thomas Middleton and Willian Rowley, *The Changeling*, ed. N. W. Bawcutt, Revels Plays (Manchester University Press, Manchester, 1977).

31 John Sadler, *The Sicke Womans Private Looking-Glasse* (London, 1636), The English Experience, no. 891 (Amsterdam, Theatrum Orbis Terrarum, 1977), p. 108.

32 Pollock (ed.), *With Faith and Physick*, p. 45.

33 Alice T. Friedman, *House and Household in Elizabethan England: Wollaton Hall and the Willoughby Family* (University of Chicago Press, Chicago and London, 1989), pp. 59, 62.

34 *The Diary of Lady Margaret Hoby*, ed. Meads, p. 185; Pollock (ed.), *With Faith and Physick*, p. 86.

35 Scott Wilson, 'Love and the Labyrinth: Sir Philip Sidney and the Extraordinary Forms of Desire', *Assays* 7 (1992), 43–69; p. 64.

36 Gouge, *Of Domesticall Duties*, p. 565.

37 Friedman, *House and Household*, pp. 54–5.

38 Ibid., pp. 62–3.

39 See Amussen, '"Being Stirred to Much Unquietness"'.

40 John Dove, *Of Divorcement* (London, 1610), D7v.

41 Anon, *The Tragedy of Master Arden of Faversham*, ed. Martin White, New Mermaids (A & C Black, London, 1990).

42 See Dolan, *Dangerous Familiars*, p. 27. Dolan's fine analysis of the play, to which my own is indebted, considers it in the context of other representations of domestic violence.

43 Friedman, *House and Household*, p. 63.
44 Cited in Dolan, *Dangerous Familiars*, p. 47.
45 Elizabeth Cary, *The Tragedy of Mariam, The Fair Queen of Jewry*, ed. Stephanie J. Wright, Renaissance Texts and Studies (Keele University Press, Keele, 1996).
46 See Stephanie Wright's critical introduction, ibid., p. 20.
47 Aughterson (ed.), *Renaissance Woman*, p. 81.
48 See Barbara Kiefer Lewalski, *Writing Women in Jacobean England* (Harvard University Press, Cambridge, MA, 1993), p. 184.
49 Gouge, *Of Domesticall Duties*, p. 395.
50 Pollock (ed.), *With Faith and Physick*, p. 47.
51 Henry Hitch Adams, *English Domestic or Homiletic Tragedy*, Columbia University Studies in English and Comparative Literature, no. 159 (Benjamin Blom, New York, 1971), p. 158.

CHAPTER 5

Queens and Subjects

The Renaissance idea of history is male. In her *History of the Life, Reign and Death of Edward II* (1627), Elizabeth Cary said that in Edward's death, Queen Isabella tasted 'what it was but to be quoted in the Margent of such a Story'.[1] The view that women should appear only in the margins of history rather than at its centre derived from two starting points: first, that women were not born to command, since all daughters of Eve should be subject to their husbands; and second, that history is concerned with matters of state: the lives of governors and national politics rather than the everyday existence of the population. Feminist theory challenges both these points, contesting the idea that women are unsuitable for office and resisting the masculine definition of history based on military and political events. Instead of this monolithic model, feminist historians outline a range of competing histories, including the study of the domestic sphere, sexuality, reproduction and female consciousness.[2] Although previous chapters have demonstrated that many other histories were being played out in the theatres of Renaissance England, this chapter focuses on women's relationship to the traditional model and its representation in plays about British monarchs and government. My readings follow two cognate feminist methodologies. Taking a historicist approach, I analyse the plays in relation to the actualities of queenship as experienced by exceptional figures like Elizabeth I, Mary Queen of Scots and Henrietta Maria. In addition, I will argue that the plays' explorations of authority and exclusion broaden out beyond the royal context to address the situations of female subjects in the audience, women who inevitably found it difficult to insert themselves into history.

In his notorious treatise *The First Blast of the Trumpet against the Monstrous Regiment of Women* (1558), John Knox declared that 'to promote a woman to bear rule, superiority, dominion or empire above any realm, nation, or city is repugnant to nature, contumely to God, a thing most contrarious to his revealed will and approved ordinance, and finally it is the subversion of good order, and all equity and justice'.[3] Nevertheless, both England and Scotland had female monarchs. Knox's *First Blast of the Trumpet* was aimed at the rule of Mary Tudor and just after its publication, Elizabeth became queen of England, ruling for forty-five years until her death in 1603. In later sixteenth-century Britain the main players on the political stage were female. Catholic plots to depose Elizabeth centred round Mary Queen of Scots and, later, Lady Arbella Stuart (1575–1615), who claimed the throne via her great-grandmother Mary Tudor (sister to Henry VIII). Uncertainty about the succession up until just before Elizabeth's death prolonged Lady Arbella's hopes for power and conception of herself as a commanding royal figure.

The intervention of such women into the masculine province of history had disturbing consequences for the individuals and the institutions of power they moved into. The conflict between a queen's gendered subject position as the weaker vessel and the high-status role of commander created both personal and ideological difficulties as she struggled to define an identity in a traditionally masculine role. To succeed in that role and maintain the reins of government meant performing the patriarchal ideology that went with it. The queen regnant was therefore an isolated example of female empowerment rather than the figurehead of a feminist revolution; the status of women overall did not necessarily improve as a result of her rule.

Nevertheless, the figure of the queen seemed to be a potent icon for other women in Renaissance England. Knox's *First Blast of the Trumpet* was '*to awake women degenerate*', suggesting that queenship was a rallying point for women of all classes who might resist patriarchal dominance. The cases of Mary Baynton and Anne Burnell show that even commoners from the lower end of the social scale dreamed of queenship as a way of finding a voice and a public role. By claiming to be the daughters of Henry VIII and Philip II of Spain, Mary and Anne achieved a short-lived power way beyond that usually assigned their sex or class.[4] The death of Elizabeth marked the end of an era. The rule of James I (1603–25) and then Charles I (1625–49) reasserted the traditional pattern of male government, but the spectre of female authority which Elizabeth's reign symbolized lingered in the cultural memory, especially in the minds of women, it seems. In 1630, Diana Primrose offered to 'all noble ladies and gentle-women' her poem, *A Chaine of Pearl or A Memoriall of the peerles Graces and Heroick Vertues of Queene Elizabeth of Glorious Memory*, celebrating Elizabeth as an 'English Goddesse, Empresse of our Sex' whose 'Name still raignes in all our hearts'. By continuing the cult of Elizabeth, female readers can become like her and 'crowne your selves with never-fading fame', the poem proclaims.[5] Iron-ically, Elizabeth's iconic power seemed to increase in her absence, perhaps as a reaction to the inadequacies of the Stuart kings who replaced her. As men reclaimed the throne, Elizabeth ascended to mythical status, an inspiration for her sex in a climate where women were largely dis-empowered and relegated to the margins of history.

How do these arguments about queenship relate to history plays on the Renaissance stage? Few women in the audience had the opportunity to wield power like Elizabeth or Mary Stuart, so the majority of female spectators would have little direct interest in the making of political history or its dramatization, although the topical issue of gender and authority may well have given them special points of access to the plays, as this chapter will go on to explore. The exclusion of women from history-making is registered in the plays, where female characters normally play only subordinate parts. In Shakespeare's *Richard II*, for example, Queen Isabella can only encourage or grieve for her husband. She has no story of her own, and when Richard falls from power, he forecasts that her future will be as *his* chronicler: 'Tell thou the lamentable tale of me, / And send the hearers weeping to their beds' (5.1.44). Although in Greene's *James The Fourth* (1590) Princess Dorothea has a more substantial role, she still defines herself in relation to a male God and a royal father and husband when she becomes Queen of Scots:

> Thanks to the King of Kings for my dignity;
> Thanks to my father, that provides so carefully;
> Thanks to my lord and husband for this honour;
> And thanks to all that love their king and me.
>
> (1.1.32)[6]

She endures the wrongs inflicted by her unfaithful husband as a Patient Griselda, even forgiving his plot to murder her. Her 'wondrous constancy' (5.6.72) looks forward to the character of Katherine Gordon in Ford's later play *Perkin Warbeck* (1634), a woman whose history is also tied to those of her father, the King, and her husband. Katherine remains faithful to Warbeck even in his downfall, a 'pattern / For every virtuous wife' (5.3.93).[7]

Female characters who do try to intervene as history-makers may be presented with some sympathy, but they are generally condemned by others in line with Knox's view that women's rule is unnatural. Queen Margaret, the ruthless commander of the Lancastrian army in Shakespeare's *Henry VI, Part 3*, is called a 'tiger's heart wrapped in a woman's hide!' for her cruelty, an opinion that everyone on stage seems silently to share

(1.4.138). Similarly, Lady Macbeth appears unnatural in wishing to become a dominant queen, unsexing herself to instigate regicide. She appeals to the immortal spirits to turn her milk to gall, but later admits that she could not murder Duncan because he resembled her father. She retains an ingrained loyalty to the patriarchal family model even while she drives Macbeth to overturn it. Lady Macbeth cannot transcend the limits of the domestic sphere; the transformation of her household to a site of violence destroys its mistress. She loses her position as hostess of the feast when Banquo's ghost disrupts the festivities, and later her place as Macbeth's wife: 'The Thane of Fife had a wife. Where is she now?' (5.1.36). The conflict between her desire for power and her confinement within patriarchal ideology finally proves self-destructive. She cannot step outside the so-called woman's place to enter the world of history, in which Banquo's male descendants stretch out to the crack of doom.

The construction of history as an introverted all-male enterprise is taken to an extreme in Marlowe's *Edward II* (1592).[8] The play explores power shifts in a triangular relationship between dominant and oppressed groups where gender, class and sexual preference are all determining factors. Even if 'homosexuality' was not fully constituted as a distinct category of sexual orientation in Renaissance England, sodomy was a punishable crime and Marlowe's play highlights homophobic persecution in Edward's death. The governing peers and churchmen, including the Mortimers, emerge as the dominant group in *Edward II* and it is easy to assume that the two minority groups, homosexuals and women, occupy equivalent positions under this oppressive patriarchal and heterosexual hegemony. The women cannot be identified with the King and his low-born lovers, however. Marlowe plays on differences to dramatize a much more complex interaction, in which women are the victims of each exclusively male group. To explore ways in which female spectators might have read a performance of *Edward II*, I will compare Marlowe's play with a female-authored version of the story: *The History of the Life, Reign and Death of Edward II*, by Elizabeth Cary, Viscountess Falkland. Although these two accounts were written more than thirty-five years apart, they are brought together by the circumstances of history.[9]

In 1627, when Cary probably composed her *Life*, the royal situation depicted in Marlowe's play was being re-enacted on the wider stage of Stuart England. King Charles I continued to promote his father James's former favourite (and lover), the Duke of Buckingham, to the relative exclusion of his peers and his French queen, Henrietta Maria. Like Gaveston, the Duke of Buckingham enjoyed a meteoric rise to power from a minor gentry family to effective ruler of the realm, much to the annoyance of Charles's peers. The history of Edward II provided a parallel for those wishing to offer veiled criticism of the monarchy and, amongst other accounts, Marlowe's play was revived and republished.[10] Elizabeth Cary's *Life, Reign and Death of Edward II* may have been influenced by Marlowe's text, and although it is written in prose, it includes verse passages as though designed for reading or performing aloud. In the preface to the manuscript Cary says 'I wright to please the truthe, not humour others. And in that sense you may partake my labors', indicating that she is willing to tell uncomfortable truths to those at court.[11] Her closeness to Queen Henrietta Maria makes her presentation of Queen Isabella particularly pertinent to the contemporary political situation.

In Marlowe's *Edward II*, Isabella first defends Edward against the threats of the barons and even helps to repeal Gaveston, suggesting solidarity with the oppressed king and his minion. The three are caught in a triangular relationship of sameness and difference in which Isabella is bound to come off worst, since she cannot change Edward's sexual preferences and Gaveston will always usurp her place in his affections. News of Gaveston's banishment crystallizes the irreconcileability of passions between the three, as Edward bids her 'fawn not on me French strumpet' and she replies 'On whom but on my husband should I fawn?' (1.4.145–6). Who is the French strumpet and who is the legitimate lover of Edward is neatly problematized in this exchange, as Isabella challenges her rival: 'Villain, 'tis thou that robb'st me of my lord', and he turns her words back on her: 'Madam, 'tis you that rob me of my lord' (1.4.160–1). In soliloquy, the Queen's sense of loss becomes obvious. Although she begins with classical allusions which suggest both tragic grandeur and a controlled response to the situation, the mention of Jove, his minion Ganymede and the wretched Juno then precipitates a collapse in which her personal anger and pain breaks through:

> Like frantic Juno will I fill the earth
> With ghastly murmur of my sighs and cries,
> For never doted Jove on Ganymede
> So much as he on cursed Gaveston;
> But that will more exasperate his wrath;
> I must entreat him, I must speak him fair,
> And be a means to call home Gaveston;
> And yet he'll ever dote on Gaveston,
> And so am I forever miserable.
>
> (1.4.78)

The Queen's complete sense of hopelessness in a world of male exclusivity speaks not only to her personal situation but to a more general sense of marginalization and dispossession felt by women in the audience. She cannot cry her pain to the world; her sufferings have to be muted in a 'ghastly murmur' so as not to disturb the powerful god-like authority which tortures her. What is worse, to participate at all, she must ventriloquize against herself. She can do nothing but to plead for Gaveston's return, and Edward delightedly offers to hang a golden tongue about her neck for her success. The irony of this symbol is apparent: the only voice Isabella can use is to speak the King's desires, which are diametrically opposed to her own. The 'second marriage' that Edward celebrates with her while Gaveston is absent (1.4.334) is only a mockery.

Elizabeth Cary's *Edward II* makes much of the Queen's sense of injury, arguing that it was because she was not rightly valued that she caused Edward's ruin.[12] The Queen is completely excluded from a relationship where Edward and Gaveston's hearts 'seemed to beat with one and the self-same motion' (p. 86) like 'long-divided lovers' (p. 99). In Charles's court Henrietta Maria's position was likewise usurped by Buckingham, or at least so the French members of her household encouraged her to believe, arguing that he was the cause of her estrangement from Charles. Rumours that Charles 'was known to have committed all manner of lewdness with his confidant, the duke' abounded, and whether or not the relationship involved sex, Buckingham certainly dominated the king's emotions, making it impossible for him to develop deep feelings for his wife until after the favourite's assassination in 1628.[13] It was Buckingham, whom Charles used to refer to as his 'Sweet heart', who accompanied the king to the podium in the coronation ceremony. Henrietta Maria was notable by her absence.[14] Elizabeth Cary's closeness to Henrietta Maria must have made her keenly aware of the Queen's unhappiness in her marriage and may have influenced the emphasis on Isabella's suffering in her *Edward II*. Even Isabella's turn to Mortimer is presented sympathetically: 'She saw the king a stranger to her bed and revelling in the wanton embraces of his stolen pleasures, without a glance at her deserving beauty. This contempt had begot a like change in her, though in a more modest nature' (p. 166).

Isabella is not the only woman to fall victim to the dominant claims of homoerotic desire in Marlowe's *Edward II*. The tragedy of the royal marriage is echoed in that arranged between Gaveston and Edward's niece, the daughter and heir to the Earl of Gloucester. These scenes show how homoerotic desire and homosocial bonding sit cheek by jowl. The young woman is shown eagerly preparing for marriage, reading Gaveston's letter with the poignant optimism that it 'shows the entire love of my lord' (2.1.63). Her innocence contrasts with the knowledge of Spencer and Baldock, insiders to a world of homosocial preferment. Her promise to Spencer that his past service will be rewarded is doubly sad, in that the

169

betrothal between her and Gaveston is eclipsed by a preferment scene where Gaveston pleads for the promotion of Spencer and Baldock and does not speak a word to his bride. The niece attempts to defend Isabella, asking Edward to 'speak more kindly to the queen' (2.2.227), a moment which allies the two women as victims excluded by relationships between men.

In spite of the barons' quarrels with Edward, a sense of male solidarity easily overrides differences in sexual orientation, as is shown in Mortimer Senior's claim that 'the mightiest kings have had their minions' and his list of heroic examples:

> Great Alexander loved Hephaestion,
> The conquering Hercules for Hylas wept,
> And for Patroclus stern Achilles drooped:
> And not kings only, but the wisest men:
> The Romish Tully loved Octavius,
> Grave Socrates, wild Alcibiades . . .
>
> (1.4.390)

These allusions to figures from classical tradition contextualize Edward's sexual inclinations in the world of ideal, passionate male friendship. Boundary lines between Edward and his peers are easily dissolved in a culture where psychosexual preferences are still indeterminate. It is not Edward's violation of sexual 'norms' that incenses the nobles and churchmen but his violation of class codes and his redistribution of power in the realm. The lords object to Edward's promotion of a commoner to positions of authority as Lord High Chamberlain, Chief Secretary of State, Earl of Cornwall and, notably, King and Lord of Man (1.1.153–5). In Jacobean England, Buckingham's rise to power was greeted with equal hostility. A contemporary observer noted, with the same bitterness as the lords in *Edward II*, that 'he jumped higher than any Englishman did in so short a time from private gentleman to dukedom'.[15] Elizabeth Cary's political allegory includes several generalized comments on the dangers of royal favouritism, extrapolations from the narrative that were surely intended as criticisms of Charles's behaviour. The generalized advice she gives Charles and Buckingham is politically sensible as well as sensitive to the position of the Queen. She warns 'let the favourite taste the king's bounty, not devour it' and 'let him participate his love but not enchant it' and lastly, 'let it be with moderation, and not with rapine' (p. 207). Her imagery of love, appetite and sexual violation combines the personal and political, allowing her to express the grievances of Henrietta Maria as part of the wider interests of the country.[16]

After Gaveston's execution, the primary goal of the nobles is to reform

Edward's government, not his sexual behaviour. In Marlowe's play, they ask him to cast off Spencer, his new base-born minion, and substitute the 'virtue and nobility' that can only be offered by 'old servitors' such as themselves (3.2.161–9). Like the peers who see Spencer as a 'putrefying branch' (3.2.162), one of Charles I's subjects lamented:

Just God! I humbly pray
That thou wilt take that slime away
That keeps my Sovereign's eyes from viewing
The things that will be our undoing.[17]

In *Edward II*, such solicitude for the political health of the realm on the part of the nobles does very little to help Queen Isabella, whose problems are rooted precisely in the personal world to which the lords appear indifferent. When they confront Edward with a list of his misdemeanours, neglect of the Queen is only introduced after a long list of governmental matters involving foreign affairs, territory, civil unrest and neglect of poverty. Isabella has value as the 'sole sister to Valois', the French king who may object to her treatment (2.2.161–73). Mortimer uses her to promote his own ambitions, setting himself up in chivalric terms as her defender but having little regard for her wishes.

Unable to win back her place at Edward's side, even by repealing Gaveston, the Queen shifts her allegiance from the oppressed male group to the dominant one and aligns herself with the barons as defenders of class boundaries and good government. The savagery of her reorientation is well conveyed in Derek Jarman's film of *Edward II*, which adapts the play to the struggle over gay rights provoked by British legislation on homosexuality. Jarman depicts the barons as a governmental House of Thatcherite politicians, both male and female, reminding us that, far from identifying with the problems experienced by other oppressed groups, women can adopt a persecutory role from positions of power under patriarchy. The Queen's transformation from hunted to hunter is shown in stark terms as she takes up a gun and aims at her target, a dead stag, with chilling accuracy.[18] Jarman uses the arrest of the Queen by her son, who warns her 'think not to find me slack or pitiful' (5.5.82), as a starting point to rewrite the end of Marlowe's tragedy as the triumph of gay rights over female tyranny. The incompatibility of homosexual liberation and female ambition figures in both Marlowe's play and Cary's account, where Isabella moves into a persecutory role, though each author explores women's suitability for government from contrasting perspectives.

Cary's Isabella skilfully takes command of her own affairs and the rebellion when her pleas as victim elicit no help from the French king. Cary approvingly comments 'thus women's wit sometimes can cozen statesmen' (p. 186), as the Queen outmanoeuvres Spencer. Her ability to govern is never in doubt but her vengeful triumph over her rival is shown in decidedly unsympathetic terms: 'a kind of insulting tyranny, far short of the belief of her former virtue and goodness' (p. 202). Once in power, she is seized with uncontrolled ambition and is motivated by 'revenge, despite and private rancour' (p. 202). Cary's criticism is not of female authority *per se* but of the abuse of power, possibly a warning to Henrietta Maria not to tyrannize over Buckingham if he should fall from favour. In contrast, Marlowe depicts Isabella's change of allegiance as an inevitable, gradual drift in which the Queen remains a victim of the powerful men around her. Even if we see her secret conversation with Mortimer as a careful piece of manipulation to plot Gaveston's murder (1.4.225–52), she can never wield power openly. The rebels say they are rallying behind her cause so that she 'may repossess / Her dignities and honours' (4.4.24), yet Mortimer is unwilling to let her speak as commander of the rebel forces. The Queen gives the most considered speech on the political situation, lamenting the need to set countrymen against one another in 'civil broils' but justifying the rebellion as a result of the King's neglect of his paternal duty to the kingdom (4.4.1–14). The emotional balance of the speech is delicate; it is too politically sensitive for Mortimer's ambitions and he cuts her off, denying her any role beyond that of a figurehead. Mortimer tells her 'be ruled by me and we will rule the realm' (5.2.5); she has no future as a queen regnant. Edward cannot see Isabella as a ruler either; he automatically assumes it is Mortimer who has taken his place (5.1.37).

Isabella's part in the murder of Edward is most unsympathetic in Marlowe's play. It is she who first suggests that Edward should be killed, giving her sanction for his death as long as she does not have to arrange it. Denied her traditional role as a wife and consort, and then denied an active place in the government, the only course of action left open to her is that of personal revenge on the homosocial system by destroying the King who stands at its head. The tragedy of Edward's death is a petty act committed by a queen who is disenfranchised. Since Isabella abuses the little authority she has, and dare not even be honest with Edward (5.2.68), the portrait hardly increases confidence in women's abilities to rule. Indeed, Sara Munson Deats has argued that Isabella's devious callousness is already hinted at in the first part of the play, when she is implicitly involved in the plot secretly to murder Gaveston.[19] In contrast to Marlowe's play, tragedy in Cary's history is caused by the Queen's surrender of power. This Isabella passionately denies her consent to Mortimer's suggestion that Edward must die, and Mortimer, shocked by her refusal, criticizes her until she breaks down and relents. It is the Queen's submission, 'I am a woman; / Fitter to hear and take advice, than give it' (p. 222), which leads to the final tragedy. While Marlowe's Isabella acts viciously from a position of disempowerment, Cary's, who has shown her skills in governing affairs, subsequently feels guilty about submitting herself to male authority. She tastes 'with a bitter time of repentance, what it was but to be quoted in the margins of such a story' (p. 223).

In 1627 Queen Henrietta Maria was relegated to the margins of royal history-making, but when Marlowe's play was first performed women occupied a very central position, more akin to that of Edward than Isabella. For Elizabethan audiences, whose monarch was female, the play's concern with Edward's royal identity, authority and will could be read in relation to gender politics. While the play presents women and gay men as two different and often conflicting groups, in broader terms, the 'otherness' of sodomy unsettles definitions of gender and sexual identity, so making an identification between Elizabeth and Edward possible. Simon Shepherd has argued that, in Marlowe's work, sodomy repeats the power relationships of patriarchy in order critically to expose these, since (in his opinion) men who are subject to the gaze of other men are effeminized.[20] According to this view, both Edward and Gaveston occupy female subject positions since the usual status boundaries marking class and sex are dissolved in gazes of mutual passion. Edward may be King, but he is subject to his love for Gaveston, who vows to 'draw the pliant king which way I please' (1.1.52). Sodomy and effeminization are directly linked in French iconography of the period, as Stephen Orgel has shown. Contempt for the personal behaviour and royal policies of Henri III, King of France (1574–89), was expressed through satirical portraits depicting him as a harpy with breasts or a royal hermaphrodite with a woman's hairstyle and a noticeable absence of codpiece on his breeches or beard on his face.[21] In these images, Henry's attachment to his *mignons* transforms the king to a cross-dressed woman who, by reason of her sex, has no 'natural' (biological) right to rule.

Thus, although sodomy appears to exclude women, it simultaneously deconstructs the very biological differences on which gender is founded. As Jonathan Goldberg points out, sodomy 'allows for ways of conceiving sexual relations and gender construction that cannot be reduced to the normative structures of male/female relations'.[22] Categories of sexual difference and the accepted behaviour that accompanies them are undone, and into the vacuum created, the possibility of female dominance finds a place. The instability and hybridity of gender constructions that Marlowe's play exposes was highly pertinent in 1590s England. Queen Elizabeth recognized the anomalous position she occupied, most famously in her Tilbury speech when she purportedly told her people 'I have the body of a weak and feeble woman, but I have the heart and stomach of a king'.[23] In the case of a queen, the difference between the monarch's two bodies, the fallible natural one and perfect body politic of the ruler, was even more extreme since one was female and the other traditionally masculine. As a member of the second sex, a queen was paradoxically both a ruler and a subject. Only by remaining independent of rival male authority, in the form of a husband, could she maintain her 'masculine' position of power. When Elizabeth's final round of marriage negotiations broke down, Sir James Melville understood her policy of refusal since 'gin ye were married, ye would be but Queen of England, and now ye are King and Queen baith. I know your spirit. Ye cannot suffer a commander'.[24] Playing the hermaphrodite, trying to balance the biological and social identity she had been given with the huge patriarchal tradition she was supposed to uphold, inevitably proved precarious for Elizabeth I and her cousin Mary Stuart. The androgynous image of the queen pointed up the performative nature of monarchy, so undermining royal authority. At the same time, and perhaps even more disturbingly, it exposed the performative nature of gender itself; highlighting the arbitrary relations between sex, power and identity.

In the light of this cultural environment, one way of reading the performance of monarchy in Marlowe's *Edward II* may have been in relation to Elizabeth. In the absence of hard evidence, we cannot know whether this happened, but it would certainly provide an alternative point of entry to the masculine world of the history play for female spectators. Edward's difficulty in assuming absolute authority in the opening scene dramatizes that of any woman trying to assert herself in the masculine world of public affairs. After his accession Edward is in uneasy conflict with his peers, reprimanding them, 'beseems it thee to contradict thy king?' (1.1.91), and exclaiming 'Am I a king and must be overruled?' (1.1.134). Similarly, Elizabeth regarded her first Parliament's suggestion that she should marry as an opportunity to remind them of their proper duties, remarking that it would be 'unfitting and altogether unmete for yow to require them that may commande, or those to appoynte whose partes are to desire, or such to bynd and lymite whose duties are to obaye, or to take upon yow to drawe my love to your lykinges or to frame my will to your fantasies'.[25] For both monarchs, the pursuit of desire is an act of will, an assertion of royal authority. Edward's identity as king does not exist in opposition to his love of Gaveston, as Claude Summers suggests, but is intrinsically linked to it.[26] He determines 'I'll have my will and these two Mortimers / That cross me thus shall know I am displeased' (1.1.77). Gaveston assumes an importance beyond his status as a love object; displaying him in court becomes Edward's means of broadcasting his ability to rule. He insists 'The headstrong barons shall not limit me; / He that I list to favour shall be great' (2.2.261). Elizabeth's public display of intimacy with her favourite, Robert Dudley, worked in a similar way. In response to criticism that her behaviour was spreading rumours, Elizabeth declared 'if she had ever had the will or had found pleasure in such a dishonourable life, from which God preserve her, she did not know of anyone who could forbid her'.[27] Her insistence on seeing any prospective marriage partner, in order to ascertain whether they pleased her, continued the public display of wilful desire. If the original audiences did read an allegory of their own monarch's behaviour as one layer of meaning in *Edward II*, then the dreadful punishment of Edward's desire, itself commanded by a wilful queen, seems to comment darkly on the consequences of ungoverned female autonomy.

Throughout the reign of Elizabeth, women's right to exercise authority remained a matter of debate. As late as 1584, Thomas Smith could declare 'we do reject women, as those whom nature hath made to keepe home and to nourish their familie and children, and not to medle with matters abroad, nor to bear office'. In exceptional circumstances, absolute rule by 'the sexe not accustomed (otherwise) to intermedle with publicke affiares' could be mitigated by the understanding that 'such personages never do lacke the counsell of such grave and discreete men as be able to supplie all other defaultes'.[28] Even defences of queenship remained deeply conservative, such as Lord Henry Howard's 'A dutifull defence of the lawfull regiment of woemen' presented to Elizabeth in 1590. Howard claimed that if women 'have as great interest as men in that which is enacted for a common good why do we shut them out of counsel or deprive them of all means by which they may most aptly further us', a seemingly enlightened point of view. He went on to argue, though, that while women's spiritual equality with men gave them the right to rule when exceptional circumstances placed them in positions of power, their physical inferiority always justified the traditional bias towards male government.[29] There was always a hint of illegitimacy surrounding a female governor, something of a contradiction in itself to Renaissance ears. However secure her succession, a queen was always a second best actor of the royal role, not a natural owner of the crown and sceptre. Her blood link to a royal father may have given her the heart and stomach of a king, but, as a woman, she was usurping a man's position.

Thomas Heywood pinpoints this in his 'Play of Queene Elizabeth', *If You Know Not Me, You Know Nobody* (1605–6). In Part One, when Mary Tudor ascends the throne, she says 'By gods assistance and the power of heaven / We are instated in our brothers throane' (l. 48), as though it still belongs to him, not her.[30] A new king is swiftly introduced through her marriage to Philip of Spain. It is the King, not the Queen, who is subsequently shown signing and authorizing state documents (l. 1141), and although Shandoyse believes no one 'dares gaine-say the Queene' (l. 548), Howard and Sussex challenge her authority over the imprisonment of Elizabeth and solicit Philip's help. After the King's return to Spain, Mary seems unable to rule alone. She faints, is reported 'craysy very ill' (l. 1393) and shortly dies. In his presentation of Princess Elizabeth, Heywood also seems to be deliberately exposing the 'body of a weak and feeble woman', even though the play sets out to celebrate her. Elizabeth first appears in her sick bed, ready to faint and afraid that her 'feeble legs' will not support her 'bodies waight' (l. 224). Her imprisonment confines her to a 'private' realm and she is depicted in idealistic feminine terms as a pious young woman longing to exchange her estate with a milkmaid (l. 1189), and then serenely giving alms to the poor (ll. 840–61). Even at the end of the play, when Elizabeth becomes ruler, the coronation scene demonstrates her dependence on men by balancing each image of her royal power with one of male government. When Sussex gives her the crown, she returns his staff of office, saying 'Whil'st we this Crowne so long your place enioy' (l. 1522); when Howard offers her the 'imperiall Sceptre' (l. 1523), she hands it back and creates him Lord Admiral (ll. 5123–4).

In Part Two of *If You Know Not Me, You Know Nobody* (1606), Elizabeth, as queen regnant, is ironically pushed to the sidelines of the play until the end. Here, she sounds a commanding tone in the Tilbury scenes, where she declares 'A mayden Queene will be your general' (l. 2639), but throughout the play her power is iconic. The expanded 1633 version of the ending highlights this. In spite of her appearance in armour and her claim 'Your Queene hath now put on a Masculine Spirit' (l. 2697), she recognizes, with frustration, that she cannot escape her body and join in the sea battle:

> O had God made us manlike like our mind
> Weed not be heere fenc'd in a murre of armes,
> But ha' bin present at these sea alarmes.
>
> (l. 1747)

Trapped in a woman's body, she is 'fenc'd in' in the protection of her male troops. She may be able to speak with foreign ambassadors in Spanish, Latin, French, Greek, Dutch or Italian, since she is 'a rare Linguist' (l. 1445), but on the battlefield she becomes a symbolic rather than a material presence. This is reinforced by her part in the main business of the play: the building of the Royal Exchange. Gresham plans to hang the Exchange with pictures of the 'English Kings' (l. 1387) from '*Brute* unto our Queene Elizabeth' (l. 1491). Her decorative role is supplemented only by the ceremonial function of opening the Royal Exchange, a duty not unlike that performed by her namesake, Elizabeth II, today. In spite of idealizing

Elizabeth, then, Heywood's plays constantly reinforce the insecurity surrounding queenship.

Earlier history plays, staged when Elizabeth was still on the throne, deal more obliquely with the role of queen and the problematic relationship between the queen's two bodies. A case in point is Greene's *Scottish History of James The Fourth* (1590). In spite of its title, this play's representation of the English princess, Dorothea, comments pointedly on the difficulties faced by Elizabeth, especially in relation to Scottish monarchy in the threat of Mary Queen of Scots. As noted above, Dorothea defines herself in relation to male relatives and God (1.1.32–5), thus advertising the 'proper' role for a queen: a consort to be matched to her country's advantage. The problems facing a woman obliged to take a more active part in history are shown in Dorothea's trials. She tellingly remarks that 'to be great and happy – these are twain' (3.3.78), as though commenting on the personal cost of power for queens like Elizabeth and Mary. The idea that royal status brings female autonomy is immediately dismissed when Dorothea describes herself as 'poor unhappy queen / Born to endure what fortune can contain' (3.3.68). Her inability to wield power becomes obvious in a scene resonant with allegorical implications. She is obliged to cross-dress and take up a sword, as though trying to disguise the weak and feeble body of a woman with the trappings of masculine authority. Dorothea is uncomfortable in the costume, as no doubt Elizabeth and Mary were in having to reconfigure themselves as 'Princes'. She asks her servant 'What should I wear a sword? To what intent?', and his reply points to the superficial nature of her power:

Madam, for show; it is an ornament.
If any wrong you, draw; a shining blade
Withdraws a coward thief that would invade.
(3.3.109)

The queen is not a true warrior, 'not a man, yet like a manly show' (4.4.10), and when a Frenchman does come to kill her, the symbols of power are useless. Left alone to confront her enemy, she is badly wounded and has to be rescued by her dwarf and a loyal knight, hardly a great exhibition of invincible majesty. Like the Tilbury scenes in Heywood's play, Dorothea's cross-dressing exposes a lack behind the queen's authority as Prince, something which Elizabeth and her subjects were well aware of.

Mary Stuart's position as a powerless queen is also dramatized in the play through the characters of Ida and James IV. The virtuous Ida, a paragon of female domesticity, claims that she has no desire for a crown or a place in the court (1.1.102–3), and prefers to sew in the privacy of her home with her mother (2.1). This was exactly the image Mary promoted of herself while under guard in various houses in England. She preoccupied her time with elaborate embroideries, rich with an emblematic significance which showed that this typically feminine activity was far from an innocent pastime. Indeed, the emblem of her Oxburgh hanging, depicting a gardening scene with a pruning knife and mottoes, was produced in the Duke of Norfolk's trial as evidence of his plotting to depose Elizabeth and put Mary on the throne. In *James The Fourth*, Ida's embroidery also involves some sinister elements. Having compared herself to the divine creator, she tells her mother 'I with my needle, if I please, may blot / The fairest rose within my cambric plot' (2.1.25). In spite of her supposed innocence, she is, as Sir Bartram points out, a threat to Dorothea:

> This is the blemish of your English bride.
> Who sails by her are sure of wind at will;
> Her face is dangerous, her sight is ill.
>
> (1.3.41)

Such lines could apply equally well to the recently executed Mary Stuart, who had stood at the centre of Catholic plots to depose Elizabeth: the Northern rebellion in 1569, the Ridolfi plot of 1571–2, the Throckmorton plot of 1583 and, finally, Babington's plot of 1587, which led to Mary's execution. In all these, Mary was the figurehead for the religious and political ambitions of the male plotters. In *James The Fourth*, Ida is likewise a focus for the ambitions of men – the parasite Atekin and the French captain who is hired to murder Dorothea – just as foreign agents planned to dispose of Elizabeth and make way for a reconversion of England, through Mary.

In the character of James IV, the play presents another aspect of Mary's position as powerless queen. The characterization of a weak king susceptible to flatterers has been read as a commentary on the rumours about James VI's behaviour circulating in London in 1590. James IV's obsession with Ida relates more closely to Mary Stuart's situation, though. Like the dramatic character, Mary had lost the support of her nobles because of her obsessive love for Bothwell and her implication in the murder of her husband, Darnley. James IV's love for Ida leads to complete irresponsibility as far as politics is concerned:

> for Ida will I hazard life
> Venture my kingdom, country and my crown
> Such fire hath love to burn a kingdom down.
>
> (1.1.170)

Mary had no better sense of duty to her kingdom when her feelings for Bothwell were concerned. In one of her sonnets, used as evidence against her to make her step down from the throne, she surrendered everything, including her country, to Bothwell:

> Entre ses mains et en son plein pouvoir
> Je mets mon fils, mon honneur et ma vie,
> Mon pays, mes sujets, mon âme assujettie ...
> [Into his hands and wholly in his power
> I place my son, my honour and my all,
> My country, my subjects, my surrendered soul ...][31]

The weaknesses of James IV, so closely connected to the political incompetence of Mary, look forward to Shakespeare's *Richard II*, which also resonates with the insecurities surrounding queenship.

Queen Elizabeth famously declared 'I am Richard II. Know ye not that?'. When the Earl of Essex mounted an ill-fated coup in 1601, some of his followers paid Shakespeare's company to perform a play of Richard II (probably Shakespeare's) in order to rally support for their cause. Elizabeth's sensitivity to the likeness between her and the deposed king meant that Act 4, Scene 1 of *Richard II* was never printed during the Queen's lifetime.[32] Elizabeth's self-confessed identification with Richard II went back much further than Essex's rebellion, though. In the 1580s her courtiers made joking references to themselves as 'King Richard the Second's men' and although none of her nobles tried to usurp her position, there were many disturbing counter-claims to the throne, especially since she had no heir.[33] Mary Queen of Scots, the most dangerous rival, had been executed only seven years before the play was probably written. Elizabeth was never deposed, of course, but Mary had been, so she too could have claimed 'I am Richard II'. Indeed, Richard's political ineptitude finds more parallels with Mary's mismanagement of her kingdom than with Elizabeth's exemplary tight government of hers.

The way in which the play was used by Essex's followers highlights the fact that Elizabethan spectators did not read *Richard II* as a museum piece about a medieval past but as a commentary on a disquieting Elizabethan present where a woman sat on the throne, recently challenged by another woman. Phyllis Rackin has shown how the play uses different temporal perspectives to shift the audience from their position as nostalgic spectators (the usual passive role assigned to women on the margins) to active participants, implicated in the rewriting and reading of history in terms of their own political situations and recent events.[34] Elizabeth I and Mary Stuart, whose absolute claims to the crown were always compromised because of their sex, provide the starting point for my analysis of *Richard II*. Alongside this gendered reading of monarchy and political struggle, I will suggest that the tragedy also dramatizes the personal, emotional histories of Renaissance women subjected to male authority. My discussion focuses on three main areas that relate to gender: the insubstantial nature of right, name and language as the bases of power; the illegitimacy of snatching authority; and, finally, the problem of structuring an identity when deposed or excluded from positions of command.

Unlike any subsequent monarch in Shakespeare's histories, or indeed in England, Richard II has an indisputable right to the throne. His God-given authority and belief in that divine appointment is widely shared by his subjects. It is the foundation on which the play rests and then throws into question. Because Richard's hereditary right is unimpeachable, his performance of monarchy is not associated with a hollow claim as it is in Shakespeare's other history plays (even in the case of Henry V, a master of theatrical manipulation). Unlike subsequent kings, Richard has not assumed the role; he has been born into it and moulded by it. Shakespeare builds on the fact that the real Richard II became king as a child to create a character who has no identity outside his royal one. King Richard's performance of monarchy is therefore sincere and, as such, its effect in the play is even more subversive than dramatizations of usurped monarchy, since it demonstrates the hollowness of right itself.

This was an aspect of monarchy of which Elizabethan audiences were all too conscious. The split between nominal right and material force in the play relates directly to the position of a queen. A queen's right to rule was in her name, her connection back to a paternal ancestor (Henry VIII and James V in the cases of Elizabeth Tudor and Mary Stuart). However elaborate a queen's use of rhetoric and symbolism, nothing could replace the automatic male authority to command. Richard II is similarly disempowered in material terms and relies on words to defend himself. Since divine power is invisible, its only manifestation is through language and symbol, which Richard is able to invoke with great authority in his conviction that God will send angels to defend him and that nothing can wash away the power he has received in being anointed at his coronation (3.2.50–8). His name is also a source of great strength. When his military support evaporates in the face of Bolingbroke's superior numbers, he confidently rouses himself with reminders of his royal identity:

Is not the King's name forty thousand names?
Arm, arm, my name! A puny subject strikes
At thy great glory.

(3.2.79)

180

Richard's authority is therefore rhetorically constructed, as was that of Elizabeth and Mary. It is his command of English that allows him to hold on to the command of England for as long as he does. This is a particularly feminine form of government, as Mowbray points out when he rejects Richard's attempts at peace-making:

> 'Tis not the trial of a woman's war
> The bitter clamour of two eager tongues
> Can arbitrate this cause betwixt us both.
> (1.1.45)

In Act 1, Richard controls the use of language. Having allowed free speech to Mowbray and Bolingbroke, he silences them both by banishing them to foreign territories, off stage, and forbidding them to communicate with each other while abroad. Mowbray complains to Richard that, by depriving him of his native English, 'within my mouth you have engaoled my tongue', and sentenced him to 'speechless death' (1.3.154–67). Richard's magnanimous gesture in shortening Bolingbroke's banishment by four years also allows him to display his mastery. 'Such is the breath of kings' (1.3.208), exclaims Bolingbroke, who recognizes that Richard has monopolized the discourse of power. He too is silenced, and ominously 'hoards [his] words', saying he has 'too few' to say farewell (1.3.242–6).

Because King Richard is accustomed to exclusive control of a specifically English rhetoric, Gaunt's appropriation of that powerful language in Act 2, Scene 1 infuriates him. Unlike Bolingbroke, who will return silently in arms, the Duke of Lancaster becomes a rival poet to Richard. Gaunt's word games on his own name, and his metaphors of sickness and health in the body politic, challenge Richard's authority to speak as the voice of 'this blessed plot, this earth, this realm, this England' (2.1.50). It is a conflict over language use as much as ideas. Richard's anger at being upstaged by a better speaker than himself is clear in his threat to execute Gaunt for 'this tongue that runs so roundly in thy head' (2.1.123). The scene reveals Richard's fundamental insecurity; the fact that his power relies exclusively on language rather than political skill. Only when Gaunt's death renders his tongue 'a stringless instrument' (2.1.150) can King Richard take centre stage again. On his return from Ireland, Richard deploys royal symbols in skilfully composed speeches that elevate him in splendid isolation from the material realities of his situation.

The poetics of monarchy that upholds Richard in the first part of the play was also fundamental to Elizabeth and Mary. To support their position as queens regnant in a world of male government, both cultivated a specialized poetics of queenship.[35] Each had the ability to communicate in

181

several languages and used speeches and writing to define themselves in empowering ways. Like the poet King in the play, both were well known for writing verse. In fact, Mary had Pierre de Ronsard, the famous French Renaissance poet, as her literary mentor.[36] In *The Teares of the Muses* (1591), Spenser openly recognized the political importance of poetry to 'Kesars' and 'Kings' and praised Elizabeth as a 'Most Peereless Prince, most peereles Poetresse'.[37] It is her skill in poetry that sustains her identity as a 'Prince', a governor. In 1598, Frances Meres also complimented Elizabeth as 'an excellent poet herself'.[38] Such images of the Queen invite identifications with the poet King of *Richard II*.

Like Elizabeth, Richard makes use of a metaphorical maternity to describe his relationship with the 'dear earth' of his kingdom, greeting the land 'As a long-parted mother with her child / Plays fondly with her tears, and smiles in meeting' (3.2.8). Richard's adoption of this feminine image parallels Elizabeth's rejection of real motherhood, with the physical and political dangers it held, in favour of a stylized political maternity. Elizabeth simultaneously re-created herself as 'a good mother of my Countrye' and as a 'Prince' who would not allow herself to be confined by her ability to produce children.[39] In another striking use of poetic symbolism, Richard responds to the military threat posed by Bolingbroke by styling himself as a heavenly sun who will reappear and shame the rebels into submission:

> when from under this terrestrial ball
> He fires the proud tops of the eastern pines,
> And darts his light through every guilty hole,
> Then murders, treasons, and detested sins,
> The cloak of night being plucked from off their backs,
> Stand bare and naked, trembling of themselves.
> So when this thief, this traitor Bolingbroke,
> Who all this while hath revelled in the night
> Whilst we were wand'ring with the Antipodes,
> Shall see us rising in our throne, the east,
> His treasons will sit blushing in his face,
> Not able to endure the sight of day,
> But, self-affrighted, tremble at his sin.
>
> (3.2.37)

To cover his lack of military strength, Richard employs an image of omnipresent blazing power, a royal sun which can look everywhere but cannot be looked at. The exact strength of the King is inscrutable to the trembling foe who is dazzled by the poetically crafted appearance of majesty. Elizabeth I used a very similar rhetorical strategy in the face of Catholic plots to put Mary back on the throne. When Mary fled to England in 1568 she sent Elizabeth letters and a sonnet, appealing to her as a fellow queen, a 'chère sœur' [dear sister], and asking for protection in the safe harbour of her country.[40] Elizabeth responded with another sonnet, 'The Doubt of Future Foes', (c. 1570),[41] revealing and simultaneously disguising the extent of her knowledge about Mary's plots:

> The doubt of future foes exiles my present joy,
> And wit me warns to shun such snares as threaten mine annoy;
> For falsehood now doth flow, and subjects' faith doth ebb,
> Which should not be if reason ruled or wisdom weaved the web.
> But clouds of joys untried do cloak aspiring minds,
> Which turn to rain of late repent by changed course of winds.
> The top of hope supposed the root upreared shall be,
> And fruitless all their grafted guile, as shortly ye shall see.
> The dazzled eyes with pride, which great ambition blinds,
> Shall be unsealed by worthy wights whose foresight falsehood finds.
> The daughter of debate that discord aye doth sow
> Shall reap no gain where former rule still peace hath taught to know.
> No foreign banished wight shall anchor in this port;
> Our realm brooks not seditious sects, let them elsewhere resort.
> My rusty sword through rest shall first his edge employ
> To poll their tops that seek such change or gape for future joy.[42]

The 'foreign banished wight' and 'daughter of debate' is Mary. Elizabeth warns her that although her display of majesty and ambition has dazzled the eyes of her supporters (and blinded Mary herself to the immorality of her actions), Elizabeth is able to see through all their 'grafted guile', just like Richard's omnipresent sun whose apparent absence in the Antipodes only defers the disclosure of his knowledge and the downfall of his enemies. Elizabeth offers Mary an example of her power to humiliate offenders, alluding to the defeat of the 1569 rebellion in her image of clouds turning into showers of belatedly repentant tears (ll. 5–6). Like Richard's royal sun, Elizabeth is able to dart her 'light through every guilty hole' (2.3.39), and warns Mary that she already knows of future plots and will undo these before they come to fruition. Rather than displaying her force immediately, Elizabeth, like Richard, uses a literary image of that force, invoking the masculine metaphor of her rusty sword that will be drawn to execute offenders. The image of hidden omnipresent power and deferred execution was prophetic, in that Elizabeth kept Mary under house imprisonment for nineteen years before signing her death warrant. The sonnet demonstrates

Elizabeth's power, but simultaneously, her reliance on imagery to create the masculine strength needed to wield it. Her authority depended on a fictional androgynous identity, no less fantastic than Richard's idea that angels will fight on his side.

In the figure of the poet King, whose strategies matched those of their own monarch, women spectators could see both the attractions and dangers of entering the male world of public speech and affairs. Richard's ability to sustain his position through language and right alone, without the masculine force usually needed to substantiate it, suggests the possibility that power is a construct of performance, available to both men and women. When he confronts Bolingbroke's forces at Flint Castle, Richard's power is purely theatrical. His crown, robe and commanding eye combine with his superior stage position on the walls to create 'so fair a show' of 'controlling majesty' that he is still able to assert his royal will (3.3.69–70). He demands that Northumberland should kneel in 'aweful duty' (3.3.75) and then warns him of the consequences of rebellion with an image that feminizes both monarch and realm, with reminders of the Virgin Queen:

> Ten thousand bloody crowns of mothers' sons
> Shall ill become the flower of England's face,
> Change the complexion of her maid-pale peace
> To scarlet indignation, and bedew
> Her pastures' grass with faithful English blood.
>
> (3.3.95)

Behind the idea that authority is theatrically constructed lies the disturbing thought that gender is no more 'natural', that it too is performative. If this is so, female spectators can play commanding roles just as well as their male counterparts. Their so-called inferiority is no more natural than the patriarchal discourses which create that widely accepted 'truth'. The dramatization of power in *Richard II* hints at such possibilities.

The obvious lack of substance behind Richard's splendid display simultaneously cautions spectators of the essential fragility of any unorthodox claims to rule, even those of their own Queen. It is not surprising that the key turning point in the play is Richard's self-surrender rather than a battle between armies. The crisis of language, identity and power that it stages was central to the authority of a queen regnant. Richard's crucial mistake is his failure to sustain the rhetoric of command – something which Elizabeth never did, but which cost Mary her throne. Richard invites the nobles to take over by subjecting himself to Bolingbroke and publicly staging his own abdication:

What must the King do now? Must he submit?
The King shall do it. Must he be deposed?
The King shall be contented. Must he lose
The name of King? A God's name let it go.
                    (3.3.142)

This sounds like Mary's verbal surrender of herself, her son and her country to Bothwell (quoted above), in which she forgot her royal identity and rewrote herself as a female subject. It was not so much the sexual slander surrounding Mary's relationship with Bothwell or even her alleged complicity in Darnley's murder that caused her downfall, but her failure to sustain the image of powerful monarchy that justified her position as a queen regnant. Her willingness to adopt the subservient position of a wife gave her male Parliament the chance to step in and demand a restoration of patriarchal government.

Richard II's essential impotence is feminized by the presence of the grieving women who shadow him and, like him, have only words at their disposal. When the Duchess of Gloucester fails to persuade York to help her, she can apply only to a higher patriarch, God, 'the widow's champion and defence' (1.2.43). Personally, she can do nothing to avenge her husband's murder but resign herself to a house filled with sorrows. The Queen too has only words and tears to express her outrage at Richard's downfall. Throughout the play, she prefigures or reflects Richard's own position like a mirror image, an embodiment of the feminine that is marginalized yet always hauntingly present.[43] Although she has only few lines, her symbolic role as Richard's female alter-ego forges important links between Richard and Elizabeth, between the medieval past and the political world of the 1590s, and highlights a feminist angle on the operations of power. In the garden scene (3.4), gender is an essential element of the political allegory of government for Elizabethan spectators since it illustrates the split between feminine and masculine roles which their own monarch had to manage. The Queen has to stand aside to watch the men tend the garden, symbol of government, just as Elizabeth had to marginalize her female identity in order to govern as Prince. Elizabeth uses the garden topoi herself in 'The Doubt of Future Foes', while in a garden scene in Part Two of Heywood's *If You Know Not Me, You Know Nobody*, Elizabeth moralizes, 'In such a Garden may a Soveraigne, / Be taught her loving subjects to maintaine' (1.2325), as though alluding back to the lessons taught by the gardeners in *Richard II*.

Opposite the insubstantial pageant of monarchy that Richard creates through language stands the brute force of Bolingbroke. On first appearances, this is an exclusively masculine world. There are no female characters amongst the rebels; Northumberland, Willoughby and Ross find their joys in the speech and company of Bolingbroke, whose 'presence makes us rich' (2.3.63). They share a common belief in primogeniture, the passing of titles and land from father to son and, on those terms, win the Duke of York to their side. In Scrope's description of Bolingbroke's army, however, the rebels take on a curiously feminized quality. Scrope reports to Richard that

> Whitebeards have armed their thin and hairless scalps
> Against thy majesty. Boys with women's voices
> Strive to speak big, and clap their female joints
> In stiff unwieldy arms against thy crown.
> The very beadsmen learn to bend their bows
> Of double-fatal yew against thy state.
> Yea, distaff-women manage rusty bills
> Against thy seat.
>
> (3.2.108)

The references to 'women's voices', 'female joints' and 'distaff-women' [spinners] who take up arms all combine to present a forceful message of how inappropriate it is for women to enter into battle on the political scene. The speech highlights the illegitimacy of female claims to wield power, and in the rebels, women are offered a picture of the temptation to snatch what is not theirs by right, to move into roles which, according to conventional Renaissance thinking, they are not fit to play. Bolingbroke's appetite for power, expressed from a position of lack, must have had a powerful appeal to women in the audience:

> O, who can hold a fire in his hand
> By thinking on the frosty Caucasus,
> Or cloy the hungry edge of appetite
> By bare imagination of a feast,
> Or wallow naked in December snow
> By thinking on fantastic summer's heat?
>
> (1.3.257)

Bolingbroke describes the situation of ambitious women in the audience, whose relationship to power was, for the most part, confined to the realms of fantasy and imagination. His hungry desire tunes into theirs, and offers them the opportunity to identify with his successful ascent to government of the realm as a projection of their own dreams of power. However,

Bolingbroke's claim to the throne is always a usurpation, and the female ambition it represents is always outlawed, unnatural. The monstrosity of the unruly woman who takes it upon herself to command recalls John Knox's view that 'to promote a woman to bear rule, superiority, dominion or empire above any realm, nation, or city is repugnant to nature ... the subversion of good order, and all equity and justice'.[44]

Both Mary and Elizabeth are associated with this grotesque ambition. The Papal Bull of 1570 denounced Elizabeth as 'usurping (monster-like) the place of the chiefe Sovereigne of the Church' and the State.[45] The English Parliament, fearful of Mary's ambitions for the English crown, described her as 'the monstrous and huge dragon'.[46] As early as 1568 she had told the Spanish ambassador, 'I shall be Queen of England in three months',[47] and after her death, Lady Arbella Stuart's ambitions to succeed Elizabeth put another woman centre stage. Like Bolingbroke, Lady Arbella Stuart had been disinherited (by Elizabeth and James) and hoped to succeed to the English throne. When she was brought to court in 1591–2, Elizabeth had, according to Arbella, 'by triall pronounce[d] me an Eglett of hir owne kind as worthy even yet' to 'carry hir Thunderbolt'.[48] In the eyes of Elizabeth's counsellors, Arbella's resolution soared at just as high a pitch as Bolingbroke's: the crown itself. In 1592 and 1597 Catholic plots to abduct her, marry her to a Catholic and depose Elizabeth were discovered. While Arbella managed to remain darkly obscure, like Bolingbroke, about the true motives behind her plots to marry advantageously, in a 1603 letter she drew many sympathetic parallels between herself and the Earl of Essex, who supported her claim and whom Elizabeth had recently executed for his attempted coup. Arbella wrote that she was determined to 'shape my cote according to my cloth' in a way becoming to the 'native property of that bloud I comm of or an infective virtu of the Earle of Essex'.[49] All these details suggest that, even after Mary Stuart's execution, the figure of the usurping woman still hovered as a dangerous presence on the Elizabethan skyline.

In *Richard II* the monstrosity of female appetite for power finds another voice in John of Gaunt's speech, which appropriates Elizabeth's symbol of the pelican as a supremely nurturing figure and turns this back on Richard as an image of cannibalistic prey:

> That blood already, like the pelican,
> Hast thou tapped out and drunkenly caroused.
> My brother Gloucester ...
> May be a precedent and witness good
> That thou respect'st not spilling Edward's blood.
> (2.1.127)

Gaunt's reminder that Richard was indirectly responsible for the murder of his kinsman takes on an extra frisson for Elizabethan audiences because the pelican was a central part of Elizabeth's own political imagery. Like Richard, Elizabeth had 'drunkenly caroused' the blood of her kinswoman, Mary Stuart, only seven years before, and like Gloucester's murder and later Richard's, Mary's execution had been clouded with mystery.[50] Having told Parliament that she wouldn't execute Mary because it would be scandalous that a 'maiden queen could be content to spill the blood even of her own kinswoman', Elizabeth had eventually been persuaded to sign the death warrant.[51] Immediately after signing, however, she had apparently proposed to have Mary secretly assassinated so as to avoid having to use the warrant. Elizabeth's attempt to conceal her part in the execution bears close resemblance to Bolingbroke's behaviour with Exton, who reports the King's repeated invitation to murder Richard in his hints to '"rid me of this living fear"' (5.4.2). When Exton does carry out the murder, Bolingbroke's reaction puts into words Elizabeth's attitude to the execution of Mary: 'They love not poison that do poison need' (5.6.38). Elizabeth's fear of executing her cousin was not just related to personal feelings, though doubtless these played a major part. To be seen taking up the sword, or even the pen, herself brought her far too close to the image of the bloodthirsty pelican, the unnatural woman whose capacity to nurture had been reversed into destructive power. For women watching the play, then, Bolingbroke's guilt about usurping the throne could be read in specifically gendered terms, dramatizing their own guilty feelings about wishing to usurp men's rightful places as commanders of the polis or, in its more domestic form, the household.

In the deposition scene (Act 4, Scene 1), two images of abused authority confront each other face to face: Richard representing an incapacity to govern properly, and Bolingbroke the illegitimate usurpation of another's power. Like reflections in a mirror, each sees in the other an absence within himself. Read as feminized figures, they represent the Scylla and Charybdis between which women were trapped in relation to the exercise of authority, offering female spectators a stylized image of their own situations. To assert themselves as commanders or insert themselves into history-making, like Bolingbroke, was an inversion of order. They would never have Richard's automatic right. On the other hand, even if they were placed in positions of command by a quirk of fate, the weaknesses of Richard II could all too readily be levelled against them because of their sex. They would never have Bolingbroke's strength. In the deposition scene of *Richard II*, the weak monarch and the usurper face each other on opposite sides of the crown, as the cousins Mary and Elizabeth had to during the long years of Mary's imprisonment. Richard tells Bolingbroke:

> Here, cousin, seize the crown.
> Here, cousin. On this side my hand, on that side thine.
> Now is this golden crown like a deep well
> That owes two buckets filling one another,
> The emptier ever dancing in the air,
> The other down, unseen, and full of water.
> That bucket down and full of tears am I,
> Drinking my griefs, whilst you mount up on high.
>
> (4.1.172)

The visual image on stage and the literary image of the buckets highlights a critical truth: the mirroring of opposites exposes sameness. Richard's situation reveals to Bolingbroke his own weak position on the throne and the likelihood of deposition by his nobles. This was something Elizabeth recognized too. She criticized the Scottish Parliament for putting pressure on Mary to abdicate, saying 'They have no warrant nor authority by the law of God or man to be as superiors, judges or vindicators over their prince and sovereign, howsoever they do gather or conceive matters of disorder against her'.[52] Elizabeth saw in Mary's fate what could so easily happen to her if she allowed her male counsellors to challenge her right to govern as a 'Prince' on the grounds of 'matters of disorder against her', a specifically gendered failure to manage her affairs.

Richard's loss of the crown plunges him into an even more fundamental loss of identity and his quest to find a self outside the public realm dramatizes the experience of female spectators who had to reconcile themselves with their own powerlessness, defining themselves in terms of subjection and lack. The nature of the self in Renaissance England is a thorny issue. New historicist and cultural materialist critics such as Greenblatt, Dollimore and Belsey have argued that, for Shakespeare's contemporaries, the self was constituted by outside forces (social, linguistic and cultural) rather than existing as a unified inner core of identity.[53] According to this view, Renaissance audiences could not see themselves or characters on stage in terms of inner consciousness, only in terms of relations with the world that defined them. Thus, in one of the most challenging examples of this school of thought, Francis Barker declares that 'at the centre of Hamlet, in the interior of his mystery, there is, in short, nothing'.[54] *Richard II* explores the same sense of nothingness, as the protagonist journeys to the vacuum at the centre of his being. The journey has particular significance for female spectators. Since, in principle, Renaissance women were denied a public or social role except as negative reflections of their husbands or fathers, they lacked the foundation of an identity and were automatically 'nothing'. In Richard's attempts to find a role outside power and his slow recognition of self as absence, Renaissance women could watch their own struggles to constitute themselves as subjects.

In the deposition scene Richard tells Bolingbroke

> I have no name, no title,
> No, not the name was given me at the font,
> But 'tis usurped.
>
> (4.1.245)

'Richard' does not have an existence independent of 'King'. This was exactly the situation Mary Stuart was in, having inherited the Scottish crown when she was only a week old. After her deposition, she lamented 'Je ne suis plus ce que je fus [What I was I no more remain]' and travels the same path as Richard in search of an alternative identity.[55] Placing her writings alongside Richard's speeches opens up specifically feminine ways of reading the tragedy.

Personal tragedy is imminent from early on in the play and Richard is aware that his identity as king is fragile. The news of Bolingbroke's invasion leads him to consider the sovereignty of death in the courts of kings:

> there the antic sits,
> Scoffing his state and grinning at his pomp,
> Allowing him a breath, a little scene,
> To monarchize, be feared, and kill with looks,
> Infusing him with self and vain conceit,
> As if this flesh which walls about our life
> Were brass impregnable; and humoured thus,
> Comes at the last, and with a little pin
> Bores through his castle wall; and farewell, king.
>
> (3.2.158)

This is a peculiarly feminine way of thinking about power. Richard's recourse to narrative, to 'tell sad stories of the death of kings' (3.2.152) and his meditations on transience are similar to those of Mary. After the death of her husband Francis II, she wrote 'J'entre en discours, non frivole ou léger, / Considérant du monde l'inconstance [I enter discourse, not on shallow ground, / Considering the world's inconstancy]'. Like Richard, Mary recognized the insignificance of all material achievements, in which 'Les plus grands rois, monarques, empereurs, / De leurs états et vies ne sont surs [The surest monarch, emperor or king / Is not sure of rank, nor life, nor anything]', and where wealth and status swiftly fall into loss (pp. 68–9). For a woman, the achievement of material wealth or power was a matter of chance anyway due to the death or absence of male relations. Mary's sensitivity to the instability of rank was probably due to her awareness that she herself would only be allowed 'a little scene, / To monarchize' before another male ruler would properly succeed her.

Women listening to Richard II's speech are therefore already attuned to the idea of transience since their ownership of a building or estate, or place in office, was only a temporary position, an accident of fate rather than a natural possession of authority. Richard gives expression to their awareness when he tells his Queen

> Learn, good soul,
> To think our former state a happy dream,
> From which awaked, the truth of what we are
> Shows us but this.
>
> (5.1.17)

Allying himself with both the Queen and the women in the audience, he warns that possession of authority is 'swift as a shadow, short as any dream' (*A Midsummer Night's Dream*, 1.1.144), soon to be swallowed up by the restoration of male command. Mary had seen this in her own lifetime when she was forced to abdicate in favour of her son, and Elizabeth would soon surrender her crown to the same king, James. Her feminization of the Tudor throne would shortly be eclipsed with the establishment of a rigidly patriarchal Stuart monarchy. Richard's farewell to his 'good sometimes Queen' (5.1.37) reminds the audience that female government is only temporary and in the unkinging of Richard, *Richard II* stages the immanent appropriation of queenly power as part of its tragedy. Female authority retreats to the realms of fantasy as Richard strives to be both father and mother to a little world of subjects in the prison house of his still-breeding thoughts (5.5.1–10). His crazy dreams of being 'kinged again' look forward to the fantastic imagination of Margaret Cavendish, who introduced her utopian vision of female rule with the words 'though I cannot be *Henry* the Fifth or *Charles* the Second, yet I endeavour to be *Margaret* the *First* . . . since Fortune and Fates would give me none, I have made a world of my own: for which no body, I hope, will blame me, since it is in every one's power to do the like'.[56] For women watching *Richard II* in the 1590s, Richard's identity as a 'mockery king of snow' (4.1.250), dissolving in front of the masculine force of Bolingbroke, played out the bitter truth about their own futile attempts to insert themselves into history. In the public world or the household, the powerful sun of patriarchal discourse always cast them as shadows or pale reflections because of their sex.

The fragmentation of Richard II's identity is represented in visual terms when he looks into the mirror in Act 4, Scene 1. As in Lacan's mirror stage, he perceives an image of himself as a united whole but simultaneously fails to recognize or identify with it completely. Although he sees 'the face / That like the sun did make beholders wink' and was able to command ten thousand men, that image of masculine authority is alien to him (4.1.273). In the same way that Elizabeth and Mary could never actually unite the monarch's two bodies, so Richard experiences a discontinuity between the idealized image of monarchy created by texts such as *A Mirror for Magistrates* (1559), and his physical and emotional reality. By smashing the mirror he physicalizes the fissures in his identity:

> A brittle glory shineth in this face.
> As brittle as the glory is the face,
> > [*He shatters the glass*]
> For there it is, cracked in an hundred shivers.
>
> (4.1.277)

In this supremely theatrical gesture, Richard shatters himself into a hundred reflections of Bolingbroke's bright sun. Bolingbroke points up Richard's secondary role as an actor or imitation by telling him 'The shadow of your sorrow hath destroyed / The shadow of your face' (4.1.282). Richard's identity as a shadow or reflection places him in the position usually occupied by woman. He must constitute himself in relation to a male 'original' by shifting from role to role. As Luce Irigaray comments in *Speculum of the Other Woman*, 'woman's improper access to representation, her entry into a specular and speculative economy' makes it impossible for her to formulate her own desires so all she can do is to play the parts scripted for her as 'other' by her patriarchal environment.[57] Once deprived of his original role as king, Richard performs a similar masquerade, moving restlessly between subject positions, none of which satisfy him: 'Thus play I in one person many people / And none contented' (5.5.31).

Neither Richard nor Mary Stuart are willing to fade gently into 'nothing'. In fact, their attempts to substitute other roles for the one they have lost reveals their horror at being relegated to the customary feminine position of lack. Even before he has lost the crown, Richard creates a new role for himself as martyr, offering to swap his jewels for a set of beads and his sceptre for a palmer's staff (3.3.146–53). He expands on this, likening himself to Christ and his nobles to Judases or 'Pilates' who 'have delivered me to my sour cross' (4.1.230–1), when he is deposed. Mary's response to betrayal by her false friends is every bit as extravagant. In a poem written in her Book of Hours, late in her imprisonment, she imagines them casting lots for her clothes as she dies, as the soldiers did with Jesus (John 19.23–4).[58] The role of sacrifice was one immediately available to many women, of course, and in Richard's self-conscious manipulation of that role, female spectators are offered a way of turning subordination into affirmation, by theatricalizing their subjection instead of internalizing it.

In Act 5, Richard moves closer to recognizing the self as lack or 'nothing', the negative associated throughout western culture with women. The experience of absence at the heart of selfhood was shared by Renaissance women spectators from whatever class. Richard's Queen (significantly unnamed in the play as if to highlight her emblematic quality) already knows it by Act 2, Scene 2 of the play.[59] She embodies an 'unborn sorrow' begot of 'nothing', which she describes using images of pregnancy (2.2.10–13). News of Bolingbroke's invasion makes her declare that he is her 'sorrow's dismal heir' (2.2.64), but it is Richard, not Bolingbroke, who inherits both her grief and her preoccupation with nothingness. By Act 5, he is unable to escape the lack in himself and, as though to emphasize the relevance of his experience for female spectators, the play marks this moment with a scene in which the identities of Richard and the Queen merge. As Scott McMillin has argued, they are brought together as one indivisible being through reminders of their marriage and their shared grief, even as they are physically divided from each other.[60] The Queen reproves Richard for 'kissing the rod' that demands his subjection (5.1.31–4), but in this feminine position he is able to share her insights into selfhood as absence.

Richard is driven off the public stage and confined to a private world behind walls, a feminine space. In Deborah Warner's production of *Richard II*, Fiona Shaw is seen in the prison through a lattice of shadows falling across her face and body like bars, successfully suggesting both the literal imprisonment of figures like Mary Queen of Scots and Lady Arbella Stuart, and the metaphorical confinement of all women within the domestic sphere.[61] In the prison, Richard casts off his roles to confront himself as absence:

> But whate'er I be,
> Nor I, nor any man that but man is,
> With nothing shall be pleased till he be eased
> With being nothing.
>
> (5.5.38)

Women, already 'nothing', could readily identify with this position.

Indeed, Mary Stuart recognized the same truth in her last poem, written from her prison at Fotheringhay Castle where she was executed:

Que suis-je hélas? Et de quoi sert ma vie?
Je ne suis fors qu' un corps privé de cœur,
Une ombre vaine, un objet de malheur
Qui n' a plus rien que de mourir en vie.
[Alas what am I? What use has my life?
I am but a body whose heart's torn away,
A vain shadow, an object of misery
Who has nothing left but death-in-life.]

(pp. 108–9)

Both Richard and Mary's words are dominated by a death-drive, a consciousness of the radical instability of the subject which can only be resolved by its dissolution into nothing. As Jonathan Dollimore has demonstrated, such an idea seems to belong more properly to modern psychoanalysis in Freud's *Beyond the Pleasure Principle* or Lacan's idea of the 'Real', but it was shared by Renaissance writers such as William Drummond, who pointed out that the 'discording humours' in an individual were *'inward cause of a necessarie dissolution'*.[62] The wish to eliminate the self, to annihilate the public persona in all its myriad forms, seems destructive, yet out of that dissolution emerge glimpses of an inwardness or consciousness that does not depend on others. It emerges through the speech or writing of the self, necessarily problematic given the instability and duplicity of language, but alive with possibility. As Mary's motto so tellingly put it, 'en ma fin est mon commencement [In my end is my beginning]' (p. 84). When Richard smashes the mirror and his public identity into shivers, he simultaneously gropes towards a new identity through a grief which 'lies all within', beneath the vain shadows of his outward appearances. 'There lies the substance', claims Richard, with a simple certainty that far outweighs the strength of all his earlier rhetorical flourishes (4.1.289).

Richard's sense of self-annihilation and rebirth is also apparent in Elizabeth's 'The Mirror or Glass of the Sinful Soul', a translation of Queen Marguerite of Navarre's *Le Miroir de l'âme pécheresse*. Elizabeth wrote the translation as a girl, presenting it to Queen Catherine Parr in 1545 and allowing John Bale to publish it in 1548, but as Queen, she authorized new editions in 1568, 1580 and 1590.[63] The poem's relevance to the ageing Queen is apparent in its images of public withdrawal, self-annihilation and death. Elizabeth translates 'as for me, I am dead, for death is nothing else to me but the coming out of a prison. Death is life unto me, for through death,

I am alive'.[64] Elizabeth's words, 'I am Richard II. Know ye not that', could have referred to Richard's personal situation as much as his political one.

The shift from a public to an inward sense of self is explored further in Richard's meditations on time in the prison. He contrasts his former power with his current subjection, in the thought that 'I wasted time and now doth time waste me' (5.5.49). Rather than a king, a maker of history, he is now time's subject, a 'numb'ring clock' or passive instrument of this male historical chronometer (5.5.50). The sense of waste is internalized as he imagines 'My thoughts are minutes, and with sighs they jar / Their watches on unto mine eyes' (5.5.51). Grief, like the sorrow of the Duchess of Gloucester and the Queen, is the only outward contribution he can now make 'So sighs, and tears, and groans / Show minutes, hours, and times' (5.5.57). Mary Stuart experienced the same sense of subjection to history in her long imprisonment, and expressed it, like Richard, in poetic form. In verses pencilled, appropriately, in the margins of her Book of Hours, her life becomes a clock to number the hours and days:

Les heures je guide et le jour
Par l'ordre de ma carrière,
Quittant mon triste séjour
Pour ici croître ma lumière.
[I guide the hours and guide the day
Because my course is true and right
And thus I quit my own sad stay
That here I may increase my light.]
(pp. 88–9)

In these prison writings, Shakespeare's Richard II and Mary Stuart both give expression to the sense of waste and frustration experienced by so many women who were excluded from public affairs. Significantly, Mary left her Book of Hours to Lady Arbella Stuart, whose own confinement in Hardwick Hall relegated her too to the status of 'num'bring clock'.[65] As with the dissolution into nothing, however, enforced passivity leads to an alternative form of selfhood. Through the bitterness, Mary recognizes that 'ici croître ma lumière [here I may increase my light]' and Richard too enjoys an increasing light of self-discovery. He admits that previously he 'had not an ear to hear my true time broke' (5.5.48), but his loss of social identity allows him to recover a sense of his 'true time', a heart beat and consciousness beyond public performance.

As Richard Hillman remarks, such self-discovery is both religious and personal. Conscience and consciousness are linked;[66] Richard and Mary use speech or writing to formulate spiritual identities out of 'nothing', again

195

difficult since duplicitous words 'do set the faith itself / Against the faith', as Richard recognizes (5.5.13). Richard considers his situation in terms of scriptural encouragements about the ease of winning salvation, and the biblical proverb of the camel and the eye of the needle. Mary's writing becomes more religious as she retires from public identity as a queen and thinks of herself as subject to God's judgement and mercy, wishing him to drive out all worldly thoughts of 'l'amour et la rancœur [love and hate]' and 'vain émoi [vain desire]' from her heart (pp. 98–101). The deposed Richard II and Mary Stuart reconfigure their identities in relation to a divine 'Other', a powerful (male) God or origin. This route to self-definition, via the inner space of religious meditation, was an alternative readily available to women who were excluded from the public world of history-making and exhorted to devote themselves to prayer in the household. It was not necessarily a liberating process, however, since it inevitably reproduced negative self-images, even for powerful women. In the *Glass of the Sinful Soul* Elizabeth defined herself as sister, wife and daughter to an all-powerful 'Father, brother, son, husband' (p. 133):

> For I, casting mine eyes on high, I see in Thee goodness so unknown, grace and love so uncomprehensible, that my sight is left invisible ... there is no comparison between us both; for Thou art my God, and I am of Thy work. Thou art my creator, and I am Thy creature. Now, to speak short, I cannot define what it is of Thee, for I know myself to be the least thing that can be compared unto Thee. (p. 132)

Nevertheless, in the inner world of conscience, sexual difference, like social identity, is irrelevant. Men and women are equal in the eyes of God; both are nothing, and from that 'nothing' both are equally able to achieve bliss. In the light, or shadow, of a patriarchal godhead, spiritual mediation therefore offered women a form of subjectivity as men's equals which utterly deconstructs gendered ideas of worldly power. Mary's last poem ended with the lines 'ici bas, étant assez punie, / J'aie ma part en la joie infinie [being punished in a world like this / I have my portion in eternal bliss]' (pp. 108–9). In spite of being excluded from authority because of her sex on earth, she will have an equal right to her portion or place in God's eyes. Richard too ends with a powerful reassertion of the self, condemning Exton for shedding the King's blood and confident that his soul will ascend to majesty:

> Mount, mount, my soul; thy seat is up on high,
> Whilst my gross flesh sinks downward, here to die.
>
> (5.5.111)

Richard's dying words encapsulate the difficulties facing any woman who occupied a position of power. In order to mount up on high in the world of politics, Elizabeth Tudor and Mary Stuart necessarily had to leave their 'gross' and downward-looking female bodies, an obviously impossible task while on earth. For each, the spiritual context was a way to validate their female identities. The sovereign self that emerges as Richard's soul, however, was available to all women, not just to queens. His certainty that his soul will mount on high advertises discovery of an inner sense of self, a subjectivity that is not subject to male authority, in the private, especially female world of spiritual meditation. By exploring personal tragedy along-side state politics, then, *Richard II* interrogates the foundations of history. While women found it very difficult, if not impossible, to thrust them-selves into 'official' histories, plays on the Renaissance stage could represent history in ways which problematized the relationship between gender and authority and opened doors to worlds elsewhere.

Notes

1 Elizabeth Cary, *The History of the Life, Reign and Death of Edward II*, Written by E. F. in the year 1627 (London, 1680), p. 155.

2 See, for example, Gerda Lerner's *The Majority Finds Its Past: Placing Women in History* (Oxford University Press, Oxford, 1979), extract in Maggie Humm (ed.), *Feminisms: A Reader* (Harvester Wheatsheaf, New York, 1992), pp. 325–30.

3 Kate Aughterson (ed.), *Renaissance Woman: Constructions of Femininity in England, A Sourcebook* (Routledge, London and New York, 1995), p. 138.

4 Carole Levin, 'Mary Baynton and Anne Burnell: Madness and Rhetoric in Two Tudor Family Romances', in Carole Levin and Patricia L. Sullivan (eds), *Political Rhetoric, Power and Renaissance Women* (State University of New York Press, Albany, 1995), pp. 173–88.

5 Diana Primrose, *A Chaine of Pearl or A Memoriall of the peerles Graces and Heroick Vertues of Queene Elizabeth of Glorious Memory* (London, 1630), pp. A2–A3v. Extracts in Germaine Greer, Jeslyn Medoff, Melinda Sansone and Susan Hastings (eds), *Kissing the Rod: An Anthology of Seventeenth-century Women's Verse* (Virago, London, 1988), pp. 83–9.

6 Robert Greene, *The Scottish History of James The Fourth*, ed. Norman Sanders, Revels Plays (Methuen, London, 1970).

7 John Ford, *Perkin Warbeck*, ed. Donald K. Anderson, Jr, Regents Renaissance Drama Series (Edward Arnold, London, 1966).

8 Christopher Marlowe, *Edward The Second*, ed. W. Moelwyn Merchant, New Mermaids (A & C Black, London, 1967).

9 *The Historie of the Life, Raigne and Death of King Edward II* exists in two printed versions, both printed in 1680: a folio written by E. F. in February 1627, and an octavo, which claims it is by Henry Cary, Viscount Falkland (Elizabeth's

husband), since it was found among his papers. D. R. Woolf's view that the 1680s texts are a bogus work, written in the Exclusion Crisis of 1680, has been undermined by the discovery of a manuscript version (North Hants Record Office MS Finch-Hatton 1). The existence of the manuscript, which connects the folio and octavo versions, strengthens the case of Elizabeth Cary's authorship considerably. Elizabeth signed herself E. F. (Elizabeth Falkland) on letters. I am grateful to Dr Stephanie Hodgson-Wright of Sunderland University for this information. For an interesting comparison of queer and feminist politics in these texts see Dympna Callaghan, 'The Terms of Gender: "Gay" and "Feminist" Edward II', in Valerie Traub, M. Lindsay Kaplan and Dympna Callaghan (eds), *Feminist Readings of Early Modern Culture: Emerging Subjects* (Cambridge University Press, Cambridge, 1996), pp. 275–301.

10 Marlowe, *Edward The Second*, ed. Moelwyn Merchant, p. xiii.
11 'The Author's Preface to the Reader', MS Finch-Hatton 1 (North Hants Record Office).
12 All quotations are from the text in Diane Purkiss (ed.), *Renaissance Women: The Plays of Elizabeth Cary, The Poems of Aemelia Lanyer* (William Pickering, London, 1994), pp. 79–237; p. 100. Subsequent references are to page numbers in this edition.
13 F. W. Fairholt (ed.), *Poems and Songs Relating to Charles Villiers* (1850), cited in Charles Carlton, *Charles I: The Personal Monarch* (Routledge and Kegan Paul, London, 1983), p. 382, n. 58, and p. 108.
14 Carlton, *Charles I*, pp. 77–9.
15 Ibid., p. 23.
16 Cary was close friends with the Buckingham family, so her unflattering picture of the court favourite may seem odd at first. However, in 1626 Buckingham and his sister had betrayed Cary's confidence about her secret conversion to Catholicism. This caused a breakdown in Cary's marriage which left her virtually destitute, so her bitterness is easy to understand.
17 Attributed to Alexander Gill, Calendar of State Papers (Domestic), 1628–9, p. 240, cited in Carlton, *Charles I*, p. 96.
18 Derek Jarman, *Queer Edward II* (British Film Institute, London, 1991), p. 78.
19 Sara Munson Deats, 'Marlowe's Fearful Symmetry in *Edward II*', in Kenneth Friedenreich, Roma Gill and Constance B. Kuriyama (eds), *'A Poet and a Filthy Play-Maker': New Essays on Christopher Marlowe* (AMS Press, New York, 1988), pp. 241–62; pp. 249–51.
20 Simon Shepherd, *Marlowe and the Politics of Elizabethan Theatre* (St Martin's Press, New York, 1986), pp. 199–205.
21 Stephen Orgel, 'Gendering the Crown', in Margreta de Grazia, Maureen Quilligan and Peter Stallybrass (eds), *Subject and Object in Renaissance Culture* (Cambridge University Press, Cambridge, 1996), pp. 133–65.
22 Jonathan Goldberg, *Sodometries: Renaissance Texts, Modern Sexualities* (Stanford University Press, Stanford, 1992), p. 129.
23 Christopher Hibbert, *The Virgin Queen: The Personal History of Elizabeth I* (Viking Penguin, London, 1990), p. 221.

24 Ibid., p. 199.
25 *Proceedings in the Parliaments of Elizabeth I: Vol. I 1558–1581*, ed. T. E. Hartley (Leicester University Press, Leicester, 1981), p. 45.
26 Claude J. Summers, 'Sex, Politics and Self-Realization in *Edward II*', in Friedenreich, Gill and Kuriyama (eds), '*A Poet and a Filthy Play-Maker*', pp. 221–40.
27 Cited in Ilona Bell, 'Elizabeth I – Always Her Own Free Woman', in Levin and Sullivan (eds), *Political Rhetoric, Power and Renaissance Women*, pp. 57–84; p. 66.
28 Thomas Smith, *De Republica Anglorum* (1584), ed. Mary Dewar (Cambridge University Press, Cambridge, 1982), pp. 64–5.
29 Lord Henry Howard, 'A dutifull defence of the lawfull regiment of woemen' (1590), BL Lansdowne MS. 813, 140v. For a full discussion of Howard's text, see Dennis Moore, 'Dutifully Defending Elizabeth: Lord Henry Howard and the Question of Queenship', in Levin and Sullivan (eds), *Political Rhetoric, Power and Renaissance Women*, pp. 113–38, and Amanda Shephard, *Gender and Authority in Sixteenth Century England*, Keele University Press (Ryburn Publishing, Keele, 1994).
30 Thomas Heywood, *If You Know Not Me, You Know Nobody*, Part One and Part Two, ed. Madeleine Doran (Malone Society, Oxford, 1935).
31 *Bittersweet Within My Heart: The Love Poems of Mary, Queen of Scots*, trans. and ed. Robin Bell (Chronicle Books, San Francisco, 1992), pp. 44–5. On Mary's poetry see Sarah M. Dunnigan, 'Scottish Women Writers 1560–c.1650', in Douglas Gifford and Dorothy McMillan (eds), *A History of Scottish Women's Writing* (Edinburgh University Press, Edinburgh, 1997), pp. 15–43; pp. 17–26.
32 See Richard Dutton, *Mastering the Revels: The Regulation and Censorship of English Renaissance Drama* (Macmillan, London, 1991), pp. 117–27, and Cyndia Susan Clegg, '"By choise and invitation of al the realme": *Richard II* and Elizabethan Press Censorship', *Shakespeare Quarterly* 48 (1997), 432–48.
33 John Dover Wilson, 'Introduction to *Richard II*' (1939), in Jeanne T. Newlin (ed.), *Richard II: Critical Essays* (Garland Publishing, New York and London, 1984), pp. 5–22; pp. 14–15.
34 Phyllis Rackin, *Stages of History: Shakespeare's English Chronicles* (Routledge, London, 1991), pp. 117–20.
35 See Jennifer Summit, '"The Arte of a Ladies Penne": Elizabeth I and the Poetics of Queenship', *English Literary Renaissance* 26 (1996), 395–422.
36 See *Bittersweet Within My Heart*, trans. and ed. Bell, p. 12.
37 Edmund Spenser, *Poetical Works*, ed. J. C. Smith and E. de Selincourt (Oxford University Press, Oxford, 1970), p. 486.
38 Cited in Summit, '"The Arte of a Ladies Penne"', p. 398.
39 On Elizabeth's use of maternal imagery, see Christine Coch, '"Mother of my Countreye": Elizabeth I and Tudor Constructions of Motherhood', *English Literary Renaissance* 26 (1996), 423–50.
40 *Bittersweet Within My Heart*, trans. and ed. Bell, p. 62.

41 Summit, '"The Arte of a Ladies Penne"', p. 402, dates the poem 'at around 1570' based on evidence from the surviving manuscript copies.

42 Text from Betty S. Travitsky (ed.), *The Paradise of Women: Writings by Englishwomen of the Renaissance*, Morningside edition (Columbia University Press, New York, 1989), pp. 93–4.

43 Jeanie Grant Moore argues that Isabel's role alerts audiences to alternative ways of reading the play, although she does not discuss Elizabeth's oblique representation in the tragedy. See 'Queen of Sorrow, King of Grief: Reflections and Perspectives in *Richard II*', in Dorothea Kehler and Susan Baker (eds), *In Another Country: Feminist Perspectives on Renaissance Drama* (Scarecrow Press, Metuchen and London, 1991), pp. 19–35; p. 21.

44 Aughterson (ed.), *Renaissance Woman*, p. 138.

45 Cited in Lily B. Campbell, *Shakespeare's Histories: Mirrors of Elizabethan Policy* (Huntington Library, San Marino, 1978), p. 153.

46 J. E. Neale, *Queen Elizabeth I* (Penguin, Harmondsworth, 1960), p. 206.

47 Hibbert, *The Virgin Queen*, p. 173.

48 Sara Jayne Steen (ed.), *The Letters of Lady Arbella Stuart* (Oxford University Press, Oxford, 1994), p. 162.

49 Ibid., p. 166.

50 Lily B. Campbell notes that these lines would have recalled Mary Stuart's execution but sees the conflict between the two cousins played out in Shakespeare's *King John* rather than *Richard II*; Campbell, *Shakespeare's Histories*, pp. 136–65.

51 Hibbert, *The Virgin Queen*, p. 210.

52 Neale, *Queen Elizabeth I*, p. 164.

53 See, for example, Catherine Belsey, *The Subject of Tragedy* (Routledge, London, 1985), Jonathan Dollimore, *Radical Tragedy* (Routledge, London, 1989) and Stephen Greenblatt, *Learning To Curse: Essays in Early Modern Culture* (Routledge, London, 1990).

54 Francis Barker, 'Hamlet's Unfulfilled Interiority', in Richard Wilson and Richard Dutton (eds), *New Historicism and Renaissance Drama* (Longman, Harlow, 1992), pp. 157–66; pp. 163–4.

55 *Bittersweet Within My Heart*, trans. and ed. Bell, pp. 11, 90–1. Subsequent references to poems are to page numbers in this edition.

56 Margaret Cavendish, *A Description of a New World, Called The Blazing World* (1666), in *The Blazing World and Other Writings*, ed. Kate Lilley (Penguin, London, 1994), p. 124.

57 Luce Irigaray, *Speculum of the Other Woman*, trans. Gillian C. Gill (Cornell University Press, Ithaca, NY, 1985), p. 124.

58 *Bittersweet Within My Heart*, trans. and ed. Bell, pp. 90–1.

59 Scott McMillin, 'Shakespeare's *Richard II*: Eyes of Sorrow, Eyes of Desire', *Shakespeare Quarterly* 35 (1984), 40–52; p. 42.

60 Ibid., p. 50.

61 *Richard II*, dir. Deborah Warner, Royal National Theatre, 1995, filmed for television (An Illuminations Production for NVC Arts, 1997).

62 Jonathan Dollimore, 'Desire is Death', in de Grazia, Quilligan and Stallybrass (eds), *Subject and Object in Renaissance Culture*, pp. 369–86; pp. 373–4.

63 *A Godly Medytacyon of the Christen Sowle… and aptely translated into Englysh by the ryght vertuouse lady Elyzabeth doughter to our late soverayne Kynge Henry the viii* (Wesel, 1548). Another edition with editions by J. Cancellor, n.d. but entered into the Stationers' Register 1567–8. Another edition (London, 1580; reprinted London, 1590). For a discussion of the poem see Anne Lake Prescott, 'Marguerite de Navarre's *Miroir* and Tudor England', in Margaret p. Hannay (ed.), *Silent But for the Word: Tudor Women as Patrons, Translators and Writers of Religious Works* (Kent State University Press, Kent, OH, 1985), pp. 61–76.

64 Elizabeth I, *The Glass of the Sinful Soul*, in Marc Shell (ed.), *Elizabeth's Glass* (University of Nebraska Press, Lincoln, NB, and London, 1993), p. 132. Subsequent references are to page numbers in this edition.

65 Steen (ed.), *The Letters of Lady Arbella Stuart*, p. 17. For a sharp analysis of the creative process behind Mary's marginal poems in the Book of Hours see Dunnigan, 'Scottish Women Writers 1560–c.1650', pp. 25–6.

66 Richard Hillman, *Self-Speaking in Medieval and Early Modern English Drama: Subjectivity, Discourse and the Stage* (Macmillan, Basingstoke, 1997), pp. 17–30 and 108–11.

Index